JON TAIT
Midden Ratcher
Found Northumbrian Histories

First published by Bernician Books 2021

Copyright © 2021 by Jon Tait

All rights reserved. No part of this publication may be reproduced, stored or transmitted in any form or by any means, electronic, mechanical, photocopying, recording, scanning, or otherwise without written permission from the publisher. It is illegal to copy this book, post it to a website, or distribute it by any other means without permission.

Jon Tait asserts the moral right to be identified as the author of this work.

Designations used by companies to distinguish their products are often claimed as trademarks. All brand names and product names used in this book and on its cover are trade names, service marks, trademarks and registered trademarks of their respective owners. The publishers and the book are not associated with any product or vendor mentioned in this book. None of the companies referenced within the book have endorsed the book.

First edition

ISBN: 9798506501015

This book was professionally typeset on Reedsy. Find out more at reedsy.com

Contents

Foreword	v
IN THE GLOW OF THE TARRY LIGHT	1
A SHORT HISTORY OF THE ROTHBURY BREWERY	26
FIRE IN THE HILLS – ALWINTON AND ANGLO-SCOTTISH STRIFE	37
ON THE HUNT FOR ROTHBURY CASTLE	40
CARTINGTON CASTLE IN THE CIVIL WAR	48
PHYSIC LONNEN AND THE KNIGHTS HOSPITALLERS	51
WAS ROBIN HOOD FROM THE ROTHBURY FOREST?	54
THE LEGEND OF THE BUCCLEUCH SWORD	59
A DACRE! A DACRE!	65
KICKING OFF WITH THE POTTS	68
'BLACK WALTER' SELBY AND THE MITFORD GANG	72
BRAVEHEART IN CLENNELL	76
IN THE MAD MEAD HALL AT HROTHGARBURGH	80
DE NEVILLE, PENRITH CASTLE AND HOTSPUR	86
A BODY SNATCHER IN ROTHBURY?	89
JOHN LUNN - SWORD AND GUN	92
HORSLEY, HORSLEY DON'T YOU STOP	97
THE UMFRAVILLES OF HARBOTTLE	100
PERCY GIBSON AND THE TYNE EXPLOSIVES INCIDENT	103
THE BLACK STABLE DOORS OF BAMBURGH	110
SHIPWRECKED IN WARKWORTH	116
THE BRINKBURN HOARD	122
BUTCHER BILL, BOOTLEGGING AND GRAIN	126
BIG JACKIE, THE PITMEN & THE CPGB	133
THE ROTHBURY COLLIERIES	138
THE UP NORTH COMBINE	145

THE NORTHERN ASSOCIATION	153
THE LAST NORTHUMBRIAN PIRATE	158
THOMAS BURT: FROM PIT TO PARLIAMENT	161
TROUBLE AND STRIFE IN LITTLE MOSCOW	168
THE BLYTH CONTINGENT – THE N.U.W.M. HUNGER MARCH	178
FROM THE CATRAIL TO CARHAM	184
WHERE IS THE NORTHUMBRIAN SUTTON HOO?	193
THE ASSASSINATION OF DAVIE THE CARLING	197
BADGER BAITING, COCK FIGHTING AND BLOOD SPORTS	203
THE PAINTED WALLS OF COCKLAW TOWER	209
EBB'S NOOK AND THE GREAT HEATHEN ARMY	213
THE ALNWICK RIOTS	218
ROTHBURY CARNIVAL	223
FOR A PURSE OF GOLD: THE ROTHBURY RACES	234
About the Author	248
Also by Jon Tait	249

Foreword

There is something wonderfully mindful and relaxing about the practice of midden ratching; getting your head down and looking in the dirt for any human objects whiles away many an hour and shuts out some of the constant noise of modern living. Midden ratching is better known in the academic world as field walking.

The first find that I recall making was a flint scraper in a ploughed field in Rothbury. I remember watching Jimmy Jackson metal detecting in the nearby school field as a child and him handing me a little lead ship that he dug up. I found a 1776 Dutch coin in the sand while digging the foundations for a building in Belsay; just small insignificant objects that somehow find their way to you and bring a feeling of amazement that you're the first person to hold them in hundreds or even thousands of years. Possibly a bone gaming piece, perhaps a broken bit of a glass nafl-tafl set – the trick is to believe high and work your way down until you get the chance to show it to an expert, or the doubt would creep in and you'd throw everything that you picked up away.

The stories in this book are a bit like that – they've been ratched from the dirt of history, found and presented as they are. They're not spectacular museum pieces. They're practical finds, something like the broken Samian ware pottery that the moles dig up along the length of Hadrian's Wall and lie in the soft brown earth of their hills. Northumbrian stories, from Coquetdale in the main, told in a local accent while that local accent still remains, from a journalist with no newspaper to write for.

Just small social histories that give a flavour of our wonderful county.

Love letters to Northumberland.

IN THE GLOW OF THE TARRY LIGHT

As long as there have been fish in the river Coquet, there have been people keen, able and willing to pull them out. The thrill of the silver flash in fast-flowing brown peaty water has proved irresistible to the generations that have lived in the valley carved by the famous river as it meanders its way from the foothills of the Cheviots through fertile farmlands and out to the North Sea at Amble.

The 'Bull' or Sea Trout and salmon that run up the Coquet to spawn every year between September and January leap best in the first couple of months, but the blackest winter nights have long seen men engaged in the dark country art of lifting fish under the twinkle of starlight with the rush of the rapids in their ears.

The earliest Coquet poachers did little damage to the stocks of fish in the river as at the turn of the 1800s the oft-quoted old angler in *Oliver's Rambles* claimed that 'aw mind o' seen troots that thick i' the Thrum that if ye had stucken the end o' your gad into the wayter amang them, it wad almaist hae studden upreet.'

By the 1840s the most common method of poaching fish on the river Coquet was by light and leister. A Coquet salmon leister was like a trident, but with four or five prongs that were used to pin a fish to the riverbed. The prongs were around seven inches long and an inch and a half or two inches apart on a six-inch honnel. Sometimes the prongs had two barbs, or 'weekers' as they were known locally. The shank was around 5 or 6 foot long.

The lights were made by soaking canvass in tar and making them up into two bundles, or faggots, that were carried on a two-pronged fork with a long iron honnel to prevent the tar burning the wooden shank. The light could also be used as a weapon if the water bailiffs turned up.

The men poached in gangs of 10 to 12 with faces blacked up in disguise, in their roughest clothes and a woman's straw bonnet of the old coal skuttle style that both shaded their eyes from the orange glare of the tarry light and further hid their face in shadow. Leistering had long taken place on the rivers in the North East; on the 28th November 1612 one Ralph Skirfeld, a yeoman of Kibblesworth in Co. Durham, pulled 6 salmon out of the river Team with a fish spear (leaster).

Those engaged in more solitary poaching employed the gaff or cleek. A gaff is a large hook while a cleek is a large hook with a barb or weeker to be carried in the pocket and fastened to the end of a walking stick, traditionally made from hazel in the Coquet Valley. The most skillful of all used their hands to tickle fish at the riverbank.

One of the earliest Coquet poaching characters was a tinner from Rothbury named William Hedley. He was first fined £5 in January 1840 along with the labourer Joseph Howey of Haystack Hill, and the weavers John Stafford, Robert Gilroy, Thomas Faircleugh, Robert Bailney, and Thomas Rogerson, all of Acklington Park, for 'killing and having in their possession salmon fish of the river Coquet in close season.' Gilroy, Faircleugh, Bailney and Rogerson couldn't afford to pay the fine and ended up in the Alnwick House of Correction for two months.

Hedley was fined a huge £10 in January 1842 for killing fish in the Coquet as it was his second offence. The same day Duncan McIntire, a labourer, and Cowan Watson, a blacksmith, both from Rothbury, were fined £5. McIntire for killing fish, and Watson for merely attempting to.

On the Christmas Day of 1843 the Thropton joiners John Hudson and Thomas Mackie, along with a labourer called Francis Thompson from Pondicherry, were all caught in possession of salmon that they'd lifted from the river and were fined £5 each plus costs. Earlier in the December Joseph Stoker and the labourer William Hedley, both of Longhorsley – though most likely our friend the tinner from Rothbury - had been caught with 12 salmon from the river on them and were also fined £5 with 15s costs by the petty sessions at Alnwick. Stoker's fine was later upped to £7 after he failed to appear.

Hedley was fined £5 again in January 1855 for taking one fish, while his son young William, also a tinner, was part of a poaching gang who were summoned for killing salmon in the Coquet during the close season at a special sessions at the justice rooms in Alnwick in December 1847.

His co-accused were James Elliott, farmer, of Hepple Demense, John Kirkup, a labourer on the farm, Peter Williams, tinker, and the butcher George Foggon, all of Rothbury, with the labourers Lancelot Turnbull of Snitter, William Telford of High Trewhitt, James Armstrong of Trewhitt Steads, and Simon Telford of Whittle. Elliott and Kirkup (Kirsopp) were found guilty at the Northumberland Quarter Sessions but were only confined until the rising of the court, while the others were dismissed on an irregularity and no evidence being offered.

In November 1845 James Thompson of Newton-on-the-Moor received the full penalty of £10 for killing salmon in the Coquet near Warkworth, but an Act was passed in the second Quarter Sessions in Northumberland in 1848 against 'parties poaching for salmon, salmon trout and fish of the salmon kind,' so when James Douglas of Radcliffe Terrace was caught taking six salmon trout that October, he was fined £5 plus costs and if he was in default of payment to be imprisoned at the House of Correction in Morpeth for two months.

A couple of months later William Arkle and Robert Watson of Acklington Park found themselves sentenced to two months hard labour at Morpeth if they didn't pay up their £5 fines after being caught taking salmon out of the river.

The mason William Douglas of Felton actually found himself behind bars doing the two months hard labour at Morpeth in January 1849 when he couldn't pay the £5 fine imposed on himself and the joiner John Wilson, of Hepple, after they'd been caught taking just two salmon fish down near Warkworth. That December the labourers Robert Allan, Andrew Allan, Joseph Anderson, John Todd and John White, all of Framlington, faced the £5 fine or two-months hard labour at Morpeth after they were caught poaching near Weldon Bridge.

Despite complaints that the moonlight activities of the light and leister men were depleting fish levels, sportsmen were enjoying successes with the rod on the river and on the 27th of September 1845 it was reported in the *Newcastle Journal* that a Mr. Thomas Wakinshaw had caught a trout measuring 24" inches in length, 16" in circumference and weighing 6lb 8oz just below Rothbury which was reckoned to be 'by far the largest trout ever killed in the Coquet.' However, in 1867, a saddler called Mr. Mack, at Felton, took a bull trout on the fly which was described as 'one of the handsomest fish ever taken out of the Coquet.' It measured 27" in length, had a 16" girth and weighed 10lbs.

Unusually, a report in the *Tyne Mercury* in 1828 noted that a rod fisherman on the Coquet had seen a creature swimming from an island in the river towards the bank he was stood on and when he went to see what it was found it was 'a large adder' which he struck a couple of times with a stick, but it got away. The gentleman reckoned it 'swam very buoyantly and swiftly, keeping its head considerably raised above the water.' It is an incredibly rare sight, but it is a little-known fact that the adder can swim.

*

Thomas Forster, the constable at Warkworth, was a scourge to the poaching men. He was appointed under the Salmon Fisheries Act of 1861 for the river Coquet and that November seized six barrels of salmon trout (Sea Trout) at a railway station, reputed to weigh upwards of half a ton. The barrels were addressed to one Felix Morges, agent, Boulogne-Sur-Mare, France, and exposed a supposed huge illicit trade in poached fish from Northumberland to the continent.

Forster had brought up James Scott, of Felton, on a charge of unlawfully killing one salmon trout in October 1858 at the petty sessions in Alnwick. The usual £5 fine was issued, but Scott was to write himself forever into Coquet poaching folklore in January 1862 when he was drowned during a battle between poachers and the County Constabulary at Brainshaugh, about two miles downstream from Felton.

Scott was aged 29 and a respectable shoemaker, though 'strongly suspected to be a habitual fish poacher,' and was part of a gang of 12 men who were taking fish from the flooded river with a pont net when the lawmen showed up. While some of the poachers ran off into the darkness, others stood their ground and a vicious hand-to-hand fight with sticks and staves broke out.

Four were captured and taken by cart straight to Alnwick to be dealt with by the magistrates. They were pitmen from Shilbottle, named Thomas, James and William Buglass and John Bryson. Three apparently leapt into the swollen river in an attempt to get away and while two managed to get to the other bank, the unfortunate Scott was swept away in the current.

It wasn't the first time that fights had broken out by the river. Back in the December of 1850 a large number of poachers had assembled near Felton on a dark Monday night, their breath rising in plumes in the frosty air. The Keepers were on the look-out and having around the same numbers they launched an attack and a battle ensued.

Many of the poachers fled leaving their nets, sacks, and fish while two of them – the potters Duncan Angus and Thomas Douglass, both of Morpeth - were held prisoners, all bruised and beaten. They were fined £10 each and £4 costs, or spent four months imprisoned in Morpeth Gaol with hard labour, with Angus also being fined a further £5, or two-months additional imprisonment, for assaulting the keepers when in discharge of their duty. He'd obviously fought back and lumped a few of them in the riverbank scuffle.

The use of a net to catch salmon and sea trout was an ancient skill that is still used today by the haaf net fishermen on the Solway and is reputed to have brought by the Vikings. Old Tommy Redhead of Whitton was reputed to be one of the first Rothbury men to use a net for poaching around the mid-1850s in what was probably a revival of the art, because two conservators had been appointed to prevent the destruction of salmon coming up the river to spawn as far back as 1267. They were Adam Gallon and John de Kestern (Caistron) with 'any nets found to be burned.'

Joseph Anderson, Archibald Snowdon, Matthew Snowdon, Thomas Ainsley and Edward Scott of Longframlington caught six salmon trouts at Weldon Bridge on the 18th December 1851 and were fined £5 and 19s 6d costs. Archibald Snowdon and Joseph Anderson were sent down to the House of Correction at Morpeth, while the others paid.

In December 1854 John Watson and his son Robert of Acklington Foundry were charged with taking just one fish from the river. John was fined £5 with 18s costs while his son paid a hefty £8 fine with 18s costs. In January 1855 Smith Dixon of Rothbury was charged with killing one fish and when he defaulted on his fine was sentenced to two months in Morpeth. The shoemakers William Wood and John Watson of Felton were fined for a similar offence and paid, while in December 1858 George Turnbull, a labourer, and James MacDonald, a weaver, of Acklington Park, were caught taking three fish at Acklington Park and received the regular £5 fine plus costs.

While such cases led to the imposition of the Salmon Fisheries Act in 1861, it also saw a number of heated and impassioned letters appearing in the local press with the intention of stirring up resentment against the poachers, who had always been regarded in their communities as local rogues that were hurting no-one.

The letters weren't subtle and while condemning the poachers also called for the formation of an Angler's Association on the river. When meetings were held at Felton and Rothbury in February 1862, it was easy enough to work out who the articulate and long-winded writers that had signed themselves by names such as 'Anti-Otter' and 'River Angler' were.

The Reverend T. Ilderton of Felton Vicarage and the Reverend S. Day of Felton represented the Church and the landowners were represented by the likes of the chairman Thomas Riddell Esq, of Felton, the solicitor Joseph Watson of Newcastle and other gentlemen of Northumberland and Tyneside, who asked the Duke of Northumberland to consider 'the annual devaluation of his fishery' through poaching.

With miners, tinners, joiners, labourers and other workmen being the principal people being brought up on poaching charges, it was perfectly clear to see that a class distinction was being made. Gentlemen could fish the river with rods if they paid a subscription, and that fishing would be made easier if they could keep the working classes from taking those fish to feed their families and neighbours – or make a few quid selling them to the French market, even after they had spawned and were dying.

A newspaper report in the December of 1862 recorded that the small gangs of poachers on the Coquet had 'divided among themselves upward of £500' during the winter of 1861/62 and further claimed that 'salmon during the winter season is regularly to be found in the grand hotels of Paris. Although it is unwholesome, and not fit for food, our clever neighbours on the other side of the Channel are such adepts in the art of cookery, that with the aid of piquant sauces and savoury garnishing they can disguise the real character of the dish, and give a relish to that which the gourmand would loathe if served up without condiment.'

It further urged the French government to ban the importation of 'fish out of season, and often in a state of decomposition' and told the story of 'a gentleman resident in this neighbourhood' who on leaving a hotel in Boulogne, engaged in the following conversation with the landlord – "I see from your address, that you come from Northumberland?" "I do." "Do you know Felton?" said the host. "Yes, I know Felton," answered our friend; "but how is it that you are acquainted with such place?" "Ah! Monsieur," was the reply, "I receive large quantities of salmon from Felton in the winter season." 'There is doubt that this was true,' continued the reporter gamely.

How much Upper Coquetdale had played in the trade is unclear; on the 10th January 1862 Thomas Rutherford of Holystone appeared before the bench at Rothbury charged with having 13 unclean salmon trout in his possession and was handed the penalty of £3. Rutherford was identified by a local policeman and was reputed to 'pursue his usual nightly vocation of poaching in the Coquet' with 11 unidentified others, so they were well known to the local courts.

The meetings of the gentry led to a code of rules being agreed to for a club called 'The Northumberland Angling Club.' The club subscription was two guineas a year and around 20 gentlemen initially signed up as members. The landowners also formed an association 'for preserving the river Coquet from poaching' called the Coquet Salmon Fisheries Association and they agreed to allow the members of the Northumberland Angling Club 'to fish for thirty days every year, in the waters leased by them.' Of the two guineas subscribed by the members of the Northumberland Angling Club, one went to the landowners as compensation.

*

When the rod fishing opened on the Coquet in February 1863, it was boasted that the river was 'literally swarming with salmon' after the newly-formed landowners Coquet Salmon Fisheries Association had 'effectually put a stop to poaching by the strict guard which is maintained over the river.' The Northumberland Angling Society, which was comprised mainly of well-to-do Tyneside gentlemen, had been trying for ten years to secure fishing rights on the river and on the 1st August 1864 claimed that poaching had completely stopped.

However, by the 10th October, a butcher called John Robson, from Felton, and his son, were spotted by a policeman named John Armstrong throwing stones at a salmon in the river just below Felton Mill Dam. Father Robson used a rod to cast into the side of the fish after they'd chased it into shallow water and dragged it back towards the bank where his son struck the fish with a gaff and landed it. John Robson was fined £3 and his son £1 for the matter which was prosecuted on behalf of the Coquet Salmon Fisheries Association by the Morpeth solicitor Mr. Wilkinson. Poaching, while mostly a secretive night-time activity, was back on the news pages.

By December a number of poaching cases were heard at the Alnwick petty sessions, which were crowded with onlookers in the public gallery. Lawrence McKie and Fenwick Bowman were fined £1 each for using a snatch and a gaff to land fish from the Coquet. Others caught using a snatch, as the fish ran in October, included Felton men Thomas Mack, Thomas Ilderton, Thomas Steele, Anthony Hutchinson, John Hutchinson, G.L. Willis, Thomas Byers and John Robson (again), Thomas Dobson of Newcastle and the Warkworth men Thomas Embleton, Richard Brown, Robert McInnes, John Egdell and Thomas Turnbull. Thomas Ilderton did not appear, but pleaded guilty by letter. You have to wonder how he was related to the Vicar.

F. Bowman, Robert Reay, John McVicars, Richard Fowler and John Watson of Felton were charged with using gaffs. There was some debate about the use of the 'snatch' or the 'stroke haul' (which were the names of certain devices in Ireland) which consisted of 'two, three or more hooks fastened together backwards and attached to the end of a string or line and trolled rapidly among the fish' which Robson had used in his case.

It was decreed that the snatch and gaff were only to be allowed to be used as 'an auxiliary to landing a fish after it has been caught with honest angling with the hook and line.' Thomas Dixon of Brainshaugh was caught in possession of 41 unseasonable fish on the 18th of November and was charged the bumper penalty of £1 for each fish. £41 in 1864 is worth around £5,243.59 today. He couldn't pay and was sent to goal in Morpeth for three months instead.

In 1867 it was reported that 'all friends of Rothbury and honest angling' would be delighted that Superintendent Gilhespie had 'been able to verify the suspicions he had long entertained' and had caught two tailors, named Robson and Mavin, on the Coquet at four in the morning with a trout net in their possession as well as 'several parr and trout below the standard length.' Although his first name wasn't given, you have to wonder what relation the man was to the famed 'Coquet Angler' Walter Mavin.

Walter would have been 53 at the time and acted as a guide for those wealthy anglers visiting the Coquet. He was reputed to have learned Lord Armstrong how to use a rod, though he was four years his junior and Armstrong had been a keen fisherman all his life. He'd visited Rothbury often as a child and bought the land to build his Cragside estate in 1863.

By the January of the following year it was reported that the Duke of Northumberland was to 'resume all the salmon fishings belonging to him in the Northumbrian rivers' and was to 'proceed at once to take steps for their improvement.' It was reckoned that the bull-trout (sea trout) of the Coquet would probably be 'extirpated and its place supplied by the pure salmon' as 'the bull-trout is far inferior to the salmon in edible quality; and although, when in season, he affords excellent sport to the angler, yet he is so shy of taking a fly.' It was also noted that it was notorious that some of the feeders of the Coquet – the Alwin and Wreigh for example – were regularly poached and 'the policemen capture but an inconsiderable proportion of the delinquents.'

In 1872 an application was made to the Home Office from the Conservators of the river Coquet for an extension of the open season on the river from the 31st August to the 31st December 'for the extermination of bull trout, and the multiplication of true salmon in the river Coquet.' It was felt that the 'wholesale destruction of bull trout' in the river may affect bull trout frequenting other rivers. London decided to withhold the power to sell fish caught on the Coquet between 14th September and 15th February as 'nothing has conduced more to the diminution of the capture of kelts (fish that have already spawned – 'springers' are fresh fish) and unclean salmon than the measures adopted by the English and French Governments to stop their exportation to France.'

The highest powers in the land may have shown an interest, but the practice of poaching continued on the water and the Coquet Salmon Fisheries Conservancy reported in 1876 that 'there had been a good deal of poaching, principally above Rothbury,' and that '22 persons had been caught, there were 11 convictions and 7 cases had been dismissed. The fines had varied in amount from 2s. 6d. to £1 and costs.'

The men of the village continued to make their forays on the water and in 1887 the mason Mark Rutherford and the slater Thomas Detchan were charged with having unclean salmon in their possession when caught by Sergeant Bowmaker and water bailiff Henry Hornsby. They denied it mind, and said Hornsby was only bringing them to court out of spite. The joiner Thomas Hume of Snitter took an unclean salmon out of the Wreigh burn, as did the joiner Robert Farrage of Thropton. Hugh Ross, a hind, of Low Trewhitt was fined for killing a fish, while the labourer David Rogerson of Thropton was charged with using a light and gaff on the Wreigh burn after being spotted by bailiff William Ballentine. John Wallace, a labourer from the Raw, was also charged for using a light and gaff on the Coquet while the labourer John Heron of Little Tosson, and Edward Luke of the Chirnells, were both fined for having unclean salmon in their possession. Robert Wilkinson, a labourer, and George Browell Robinson, a joiner, both of Sharperton, appeared in front of Lord Armstrong at the Rothbury petty sessions charged with using a gaff near Sharperton bridge. Robinson was also accused of assaulting the Harbottle water bailiff Joseph Anderson. He had the last laugh, though, as Lord Armstrong fined Anderson himself £1 plus costs and also made a representation to the Conservancy Board 'remonstrating them for appointing persons who are incapable of discharging their duties in a proper manner.' You had to celebrate the little victories.

At the mouth of the river in October, 1896, salmon poaching was carried on to such a large extent at Warkworth locks that the bailiffs were unable to cope with the raids. Inspector Sanderson of Alnwick was sent there, and assisted in the arrest of a number of men who were convicted of salmon poaching and wilful damage to property, with heavy fines being inflicted. A standing battle also took place in a considerable depth of water between the officers and the poachers.

There were further changes on the river, however, when the Northumberland Angler's Federation negotiated taking over the water from the Duke of Northumberland from Warkworth to Felton, and from Brinkburn to Rothbury, in February 1897. They intended to 'suppress poaching and all illegal activities on the Coquet' and had appointed qualified watchers or bailiffs. It was the beginning on fishing on the river as we know it in the modern sense, with the purchase of season tickets and permits as a precursor to the fishing license.

*

But the Federation could do little to prevent men poaching fish from the river. Thomas Detchen was again fined £2 10s, John Fairgrieves £1, John Clark 15/-, and Thomas Butters, John Ballantyne, and Thomas Henderson, who gave the false name David Brown when charged, fined 10/- each by the solicitor Mr. Chas. Percy of Alnwick for the Conservancy Board in December 1905 after being caught poaching in the river Coquet.

Henry Tait, labourer, was fined 5/- including costs for using a gaff for the purpose of catching salmon at the Thrum Mill in November 1908 and the following month Edward Cummings, labourer, Rothbury, was charged with assaulting William Davidson, a water bailiff, and was also charged with using a snatch for the purpose of catching salmon in the River Coquet at Rothbury – but both charges were dismissed. The case against the Longhorsley labourer Robert Pringle, who was charged with using a gaff for the purpose of catching salmon WeldonBridge, was also dismissed.

Rothbury blacksmith Armitage Welton, of South Terrace, was another charged with unlawfully possessing a gaff for the purpose of poaching at the Thrum in Februaury 1911 and in November 1916 Robert Scott, Alfred Young Snaith, John Snaith and John Anderson were charged with using a gaff for the purposes of catching salmon in the Coquet. Water Bailiff Ferguson gave evidence against the first three and Worsley the last. Fines of 10/- were imposed.

The following year Walter Robson and Edward Cummings of Rothbury were caught catching salmon in the close season and fined £1 each, while 16-year-old John Foggon and 18-year-old William Hornsby were fined 7/6 each for using a gaff.

Following the First World War, in October 1920, engineman James Telford and farmer Robert Redhead were charged at Rothbury petty sessions with taking salmon by means of a gaff on the evidence of Bailiff Worsley and were each fined 10s.

Although the poaching cases are not so prominent in the press following that time, the practice was still on-going and at a meeting of the River Coquet Fishery Board in November 1937 it was agreed to employ temporary water bailiffs at 50s a week with agreed travelling expenses to 'protect the spawning beds of the river.' The Watch Committee heard that there had been flagrant and open snatching of fish and that a great amount of poaching went on in the higher reaches of the Coquet from cars, where people drove up and got fish off the spawning grounds. When an un-named Rothbury man was caught at the riverside at midnight with a bicycle lamp and a gaff that year, he blandly told the magistrate that he was just down 'having a look at them.' When fined 15s he commented 'Well, it's plenty,' which was said to have caused much amusement in the public enclosure of the court.

The farmer Basil Dagg, of Low Farnham, denied using a snatch in August

1937 which as described as 'a fearsome and terrible weapon' by Mr. Hugh Percy of the Coquet Fishery board. "I mean, really, it goes beyond vitriolic description. It is weighted with a heavy, solid piece of lead, a hook more like a shark hook or anchor than could be used for salmon, and that awful weapon is flung into the water and if a fish is anywhere near the fish cannot miss it," he said. Basil was poaching off Sharperton bridge with John Telford, a roadman from Thropton, who was accused of gaffing a 'beautiful fresh run 12lb fish.' They were both fined 30/- each, with £1 8s 6d costs. Wily Basil asked water bailiff George Common where he was watching them from in the court, but Percy wouldn't allow it to be known in public and said it could be written down, if desired.

In January 1938 an un-named 15-year-old Rothbury apprentice bricklayer was accused of using a gaff hook and snatch between Tosson Ford and Storey's Hole to take a 14lb fish, while the labourer William McLean of the Malting Yard was accused of aiding and abetting by the water bailiff Allison under the River Salmon and Fresh Water Fisheries Act, 1923. The boy pleaded guilty, McLean not guilty, and both were fined. John George Wilson and Robert Rogerson, both of Scrainwood, used lights and gaffs to take salmon around the same time.

Rothbury butcher John Robert Fairgrieve was charged with being in possession of a gaff at the Thrum when he had the misfortune of bumping into water bailiffs Easton, Common and Graham in January 1939. When they captured and grappled with Fairgrieve, he threw a sack away with a gaff hook in it. He was fined £2. The labourer George Patrick Farndale of Embleton Terrace was charged with being in possession of a light for the purposes of taking or killing salmon or trout at the Maglen Burn, Rothbury, and was fined 5/-and his lamp forfeited. The mason George Thomas Muckle and shepherd Henry Jackson of Kidlandlee were fined £1 each for possessing a gaff to take fish out of the Alwin up at Clennell and John Robert Davidson was also fined £1 for unlawfully using a light to take fish up the same stretch of water with water bailiff George Common spotting them all up that way. Frederick Hounam was also caught by Common and Graham using a gaff down near the Thrum Mill.

The Northumberland Anglers Federation determined to put a stop to poaching on the Coquet and water bailiff Graham, of Felton, told the local papers in the February of 1941 that: "I am convinced that if magistrates inflicted heavy fines or imprisonment, those who poach would soon realise the error of their ways. I appeal to all members of the Federation to assist us in our fight against poaching."

A month earlier Robert Wood Redhead, a farm worker from The Cottage, Snitter, had been charged with fishing with a gaff and light in the Wreigh Burn and also of obstructing a water bailiff, George Common, in the execution of his duty. John Shell of Pine Tree House, Rothbury, was charged with fishing with a gaff at the Thrum Mill and fishing in close season. He admitted both of the charges, but said he'd taken the fish to help with rations.

In the December of 1941 the 18-year-old Peter Angus, painter, was charged with using a gaff and his neighbour Samuel Nesbit Harris, joiner, both of the Woodlands, of aiding and abetting. Angus claimed he was just watching the fish run down at the Thrum Mill, which was in flood, and hadn't gaffed the 11lb fish he was accused of. There were a number of people gathered there, including a few soldiers. Angus said that Sergeant Carruthers and water bailiff Common 'had told the biggest lies. Their souls must be as black as a chimney.' They were fined £1 each.

Ronald Stewart, labourer, who was also of the Woodlands, Rothbury, was at the Thrum Mill in October 1951 when he wrapped his handkerchief around his hand and seized a fish by its tail and chucked it on the bank, but it got away back into the water. "It wasn't very successful," Stewart told the magistrates court in the village as he pleaded guilty and was fined £2 and £2 2/- costs. Stewart had tried to run away when he saw the bailiffs, but was quickly overtaken by local champion high-jumper George Davidson. "I thought I would have myself a wee bit salmon to try and build myself up a bit," said Stewart.

The farmer John Aynsley, of the Lee Farm, plead guilty to charges of using a lighter and gaff to take trout from the Forest Burn in November 1951 and was fined £4 and £2 2/- costs at Rothbury magistrates court. The gaff was ordered to be confiscated but the acetylene lamp, normally used not for night poaching, but for attending the farm stock after dark, was allowed to be retained by the owner. Mr. Charles Webb, defending, asked the bench to impose a modest penalty because of Aynsley's youth and previous good record. "His was an act of bravado. He is sorry and will not do it again."

The Rothbury barber and insurance collector John Cummings was also fined £2 and £2 2/- costs for poaching at the Thrum Mill in July 1951. Head bailiff John Thomas Percival reckoned that John had arrived with a rod and line and a gaff and had searched the pool for fish. When he found one, it was alleged that he picked up his rod and beat the water, stoned it, and waded in with his gaff to take the fish, which he then hid among some nettles. John denied the charges and asked the bench to allow him £2 costs after he'd missed half a day's work the previous month when another poaching charge against him and another man had been found not valid. Cummings claimed he'd been fishing with his rod the previous evening and had snagged his line, and was returning with the gaff to reclaim it.

One of the most famous court days at Rothbury occurred in December 1953 when 32 fishing charges were brought up in an eight-hour session – with some legendary names in Coquet poaching appearing in front of the bench. Gaffs, snares, wires, snatches, lamps and sticks were all produced in quantity as evidence, and all were confiscated, as were salmon and sea trout preserved in cold storage. The court was packed all day with the defendants, members of the public, water bailiffs, police, press and solicitors. George Tait and John Hounam, both of Rothbury, were both fined £10. Michael Aynsley of the Lee Farm, who had grabbed a fish by the gills while watching them jump at the Forest Burn, and John Douglas Sinton of West Town Head, Otterburn, were fined £8. Basil Dagg, rabbit catcher, of Holystone, Sharperton, was charged with having a gaff with intent to take salmon from the River Coquet, but said in a letter that he used the hooked stick for pulling dead rabbits out of holes. He could not stoop to the job because of his artificial leg, and he could not attend because the leg had broken down and was away for repair. He was fined £7. Archibald Bertram, of Rookland, Harbottle, was fined £5 for having a light and gaff with intent to take salmon from the River Alwin; he was chased and overtaken in the darkness by Head

Water Bailiff Percival when he saw lights flashing and the figures of three men beside the river bank. Locals who were dismissed included Francis Wood Proudlock of the Cross Keys, Thropton, James Earle of of Rye Hill, John Aysnley of Lee Farm and Henry Arkle of Holling Hill.

Mr. N. H. Thomas, clerk of the Northumberland and Tyneside Rivers Board, said: "This might, at first sight, appear to be a battle between the River Board and the poachers. It is nothing of the kind. None of these charges ace based on any bye-law of the River Board. They are criminal offences. These were offences long before river boards were thought of."

Major Rubert Milburn, the chairman of the bench, agreed and said: "I am very glad you have brought this up. I think it is very important that people in every area should realise what you say—if they realise it, that would go a long way towards stopping poaching."

Because they had been first up, and because all the bailiffs and police were still in the court, Tait and Hounam made their way straight back down to the river to recoup their fine money – by lifting more fish from the water!

*

In the far north of the county of Northumberland, The Tweed was once reputed to be the 'most poached river in England.' But as the vast bulk of the mighty water runs through the Scottish Borders, it must be regarded as a truly international case where poaching was long known as 'Burning the Water.'

In September 1755 there was a meeting of the proprietors of fisheries on the river Tweed at the house of George Redpath in Berwick in order to 'concert proper measures for applying to Parliament for an Act for preserving the Kipper Fish and Salmon Fry in the river,' while another meeting regarding the same was to be held at the house of Mrs. Wood in Kelso. Acts for the Tweed were also passed in 1771 and 1775, while in 1783 more concerns were raised over 'the killing of salmon in close time, and the destruction of the salmon fry' on the river. The proprietors of the River Tweed Association proposed that 'every fisherman or tenant found offending in any respect against the statutes should be dismissed by the Proprietor as soon as it was in his power to do so,' as they attempted to crack down on the numbers of fish being pulled from the river.

And there must have been plenty salmon in the Tweed at the time. Some fishermen were startled just above the Bridge in Berwick in 1757 when they caught a large green shark, about six-foot long, in the Tweed. They got the shark out of the water on the shore where someone reckoned that it was an East India shark that had followed the salmon upstream, and a penknife was found in its belly when they cut it open. In 1763 the Berwick fishmonger Alex Cockburn had obtained a patent for his new method of curing salmon with spices. Kippered salmon was long a traditional part of the larder in homes at Berwick and Tweedmouth.

By 1800 there were 300 men employed in the salmon fisheries on the Tweed, where the fish were said to be of 'the very best quality.' The fishing season ran from 10th January to the 10th October. In 1814 a salmon weighing 60lb 11oz, measuring 4 feet 4 inches long and a girth of 2 feet 5 inches, was caught on the Tweed. It was sold for 5 and a half guineas by the Old Shipping Company.

With such riches available in the water, it was not surprising that by 1824 it was being reported that the salmon fishing industry was in decline partly due to 'poaching, which is carried out to a great extent on the Tweed and other rivers…the salmon are destroyed when they are breeding, and when they ought to be allowed to rest.' In one of the earliest prosecutions of a poaching case on the Tweed, Robert and William Sanderson, William and Thomas Strother and William and James Bolton, all of Norham, were all fined 40 shillings each for 'trespassing on grounds adjacent to the river Tweed with intent to fish for salmon.' Alexander Fulton of Twisel was fined 20s for a similar offence. The labourers William Lewins of Donaldson's Lodge and Roger Moffat of Twisel were fined 40 shillings each for 'fishing in close time' while the labourer Robert Swan of Norham was fined 50s.

It was resolved in April 1834 by the Tweed Commissioners that they would 'put the Law in force against all persons who may be found guilty of any offences' on the river. That November the labourers Francis and Thomas Elliot, Adam Dickson, William Ruffat, Andrew Scott and James Dodds, all from Spittal, were committed to Durham goal for two months for failing to pay penalties imposed on them for poaching on the Tweed.

In the April of 1840 James Paxton, the superintendent of water bailiffs, brought a complaint about George Pringle of Scremerston for setting a 90-yard bag net within the mouth of the Tweed 'so as to prevent salmon, grilse, trout etc. from entering the river,' it being a contravention of the Tweed Fishery Act. That December it was revealed that at Tweedside, in Scotland, around 10 o'clock on a Thursday night 'a party of ten and upwards had 'burned the water' for a mile or two; made noise enough wake anything but a water bailiff, or the dead, and returned at 12 o'clock by the way they came, literally 'amidst pitch and tar, and fire and smoke.' The letter, in the Monmouthshire Merlin, also stated that 'bands of depredators, 10, 20, 30 in number set at defiance alike the law and its officers. No water bailiff or other watchman can dare do anything to oppose them; and in consequence, for every fish killed in the legal and open season of the year in the upper parts of the Tweed, there are hundreds killed in the illegal or close season.' The Gala and Tweed were 'burned by upwards of 50 persons and a party, apparently around 20 or 25 in number, called at the house of one of the persons employed to protect the water, knocked at his door and windows, exhibited their flambeaux, and thus in effect dared him to deal with them.'

By 1857 the 'unusually large number of fish of the salmon kind' spawning in the Tweed had led to a big increase in poaching activities. There had been 40 cases prosecuted earlier in the year and in the December Mr. Mitchell, the superintendent for the Tweed, was travelling to Carlisle by train when he noticed a large and suspicious box on the platform which he was told contained rabbits. It was addressed to a Mr. H. Farren at Billingsgate Market in London, and when Mitchell opened it, contained 13 salmon from 12 to 25lb in weight. Another large box destined for Billingsgate was found to contain 37 fish and three 'veteran Peebles poachers, all of whom have been several times convicted' were very much suspected of being involved in the trade. 119 people had been detected poaching in the Tweed and its tributaries by the river police in the first four months of that close season.

In February 1861 it was reported that both poaching for fish and assaults on water bailiffs on the Tweed had reached an all-time high. There had been a battle in the water between the superintendent of the bailiffs and the leader of a gang of 24 men at Ashiesteil, the windows of the house of a bailiff had been smashed while he lay in bed and in another incident, stones were thrown at the bailiffs in the street in the dark. Further down the river from the Tweed bridge at least 50 poachers were out in sight of the bailiffs with light and leister.

The labourers George Thomson, James Oliver and John Mustard, and the junior blacksmith Adam Fox, all of Kelso, were all fined for taking two salmon at Kelso Mill with a cleek and lantern in November 1895, while by the March of 1898 a writer to the Morning Post complained of the 'increasingly disgraceful lawlessness which is ruining the finest salmon river in Great Britain.' He reckoned that 'thousands of tons (of fish) were every year dispatched to the great market towns in long boxes marked 'glass, with care' by poachers. Over a thousand nets had been captured on the Tweed over the previous three years but the writer's vivid description of the gangs – 'a wild and loose population of seamen lacking berths, of deep-sea fisherman and their wives – great broad-backed women as dangerous as their mates – stiff weather-stained netters from Goswick to Norham, who can at a moment's notice form a mob careless of consequences' seemed somewhat over the top. He did, however, hit the nail on the head when he stated that: 'The worst of the evil is that public sympathy, especially that of the poor, is with the poacher.' The tight-knit rural communities of north Northumberland and the Scottish borders enjoyed cheap fish and didn't want to see the practice stopped.

'There is no other district in Great Britain so notorious for its poachers as the country watered by the Tweed and its tributaries. The Whiteadder, Blackadder, Gala, Leader, Yarrow, Teviot, Till, Jed, Kale, Bowmont and all other streams, large and small, that feed the main current are infested by men who from youth upwards have practiced every known art for killing fish; and the worst of it is that the deadliest implements are not worth more than a few pence and can be made by the village blacksmith,' grumbled another in the newspapers as they went on to paint a dark picture of 'gangs of leisterers with blacked up faces, in disguises, whose tradition was to fight with cudgels and stones if captured by the bailiffs.'

While it was generally believed that the leister wasn't used on the Tweed so much at the time as a boat would be needed in addition to the torches, the implement was still used by more solitary poachers on the Teviot. The writer also noted the use of the gaff, the cleek, and the drag hook – 'a triangle of large bait hooks weighted with lead and drawn over the spawning beds (redds).'

The drag hook had been employed for a number of years and in 1890 a Galashiels man and his sons had taken 16 large salmon by this means, as had another un-named but well-known local poacher who similarly raked or 'sniggled' the bed to take 5 on the Tweed near Thornilee, so when a newspaper report in 1910 claimed that a new method of poaching was in use on the Tweed, they were wrong. The 'new method' was to use, instead of the net, 'heavily leaded treble hooks, which are dragged through the water, especially at deep pools.' Or drag hooking.

On the reiver Teviot, the 'Denholm' or 'Hawick Worm' was the name employed for the rake hook around 1881 when a 30lb salmon was taken out of the water below Denholm bridge. 'The bailiffs are of course on the alert, but so great is the destruction of fish that some are of the opinion that the waters of the Teviot and its tributaries might as well be open as protected,' a writer in the Hawick Express explained.

There were so many salmon running in the Tweed in the February in 1904 that huge crowds gathered at the weirs, or 'caulds' across the river, all the way up to Melrose. A reporter watched two men cleek a 30lb fish and claimed that the poachers were formed into a 'club' where lads around 14-years-old were employed to track the water bailiffs all day. When one showed up, a signal went all along a line to the men who were employed in pulling the fish out. The money from the sale of poached fish – reputed to be sold in the towns and villages for 2d, 3d and 4d a pound – went into a common fund and fines were paid out from it, the remainder being divided up among the members of the club at the end of the season. That March the mason William Lamb and the labourers Michael Matthews, Duncan McQueen and William Hush were all fined £1 each at Berwick for taking salmon from the river with cleeks. McQueen said that he was hard up and took the fish, which were lying in their thousands, to eat, not to sell.

Robert Stewart, a labourer from Spittal, and Abraham Yule from Tweedmouth were charged with carrying a cleek and stick in February 1938 near Toddles Salmon Fishery. Stewart was found guilty and fined £2 while Yule was let off. "This poaching of salmon by hooks must be stopped," said Major Rae at the Norham and Islandshires petty sessions. The labourer Andrew Weatherburn of Berwick was also fined £2 by the River Tweed Commissioners for cleeking a fish. "There has been great activity in this district in the sale of diseased salmon, and diseased salmon are fish caught by the instruments in this case," said H.R. Peters for the Commissioners. "I need hardly emphasise what an exceedingly dangerous article of food it is for anyone to eat diseased fish. Those men who go out with these instruments generally know the fish are diseased but very often the party who buys the fish is not aware of this, and a diseased fish is being palmed off as being sound."

The following year three men from Peebles – the labourers Thomas Scott and James Mitchell, and the baker John Todd – were all fined for merely watching the fish in the water. Scott and Mitchell did have previous poaching convictions, however. Herbert Cleghorn of Peebles was fined for 'attempts by cleek and line' and the Innerleithen men Henry Curry and James Blake were also fined for the same offence.

*

The river Aln flows through Alnwick and runs out to the sea at Alnmouth. In 1849 William Taylor and William Rochester were fined £2 and £1 respectively for attempting to take salmon trout from the Aln while in November 1865 William Robinson was charged under the Salmon Poaching Act after using a gaff for the purpose of catching salmon near Denwick Bridge. Henry Schofield was charged with aiding and abetting him. Robinson was fined £3 and Schofield, who was described as 'an old offender,' £5.

in January 1868 Mr Snowball, on behalf of the Duke, was endeavouring to take and destroy the bull trout in the river Aln and make the river, if possible, into a salmon river from the 1st January the following year.

He must have enjoyed some degree of success as in 1899 the stonebreaker Thomas Carr and the labourers John William Kelly and Michael Naevin, all of Alnwick, were charged with using a gaff for killing salmon at the River Aln. Edward Culley, a water bailiff under the River Aln Angling Association, had spotted all three of the men using the gaff in the river and, although they never caught a fish, all three were fined 10s and 8s 6d costs. The following year, Carr – who was now working as a quarryman – along with the stonebreaker George Lawson, labourer John Lundy and cartman John Black, from Alnwick, were more successful with the gaff and took two fish out of the water before being spotted by Police Inspector Sanderson. Carr said the fish were not salmon, but bull trout, and it was the first time he had taken a salmon in his life. It was pointed out that he'd been convicted for it the year before. Black had also been up for poaching before, in 1898. Lawson was fined 10s and costs and the others each £2 and costs. The labourer Thomas Rennison of Alnwick was fined 20/- plus costs for using a gaff to kill salmon at the Denwick Cauld on the Aln in December 1901, while miller Edward Dover of the town was charged with killing a salmon in the close season at Denwick Mill in 1902 after he'd reached down and pulled it out of the water when the mill wheel stopped.

Labourer Alexander Howard, of Alnwick, was fined £20 with £2 2/- costs for using a gaff to take trout and salmon from the river Aln in November 1952. Howard took two 3lb sea trout and a 5lb salmon from the flooded water and had hidden them in nearby nettles. Head Bailiff John Percival said the fish was a salmon proceeding to the spawning ground. "I have never seen a salmon spawn in the Aln, but I have no doubt that they do," he said.

A little further down the county, as far back as 1363 Robert de Ogle owned a fishery at Seaton Woodhorn on the river Wansbeck which was 'held of Mary de Sancto Paulo, countess of Pembroke, by service and suit of court every three weeks.' Just up the coast at Warkworth, in the time of King Henry III, Roger Fitzjohn had a mill and a fishery with a small ship called a 'cobel,' so the traditional open, flat-bottomed and high bowed Northumbrian coble boats had been in use for many hundreds of years.

The miners John Moody, Andrew Lowther, and John Dinsdale, all from the neighbourhood of Choppington were charged with poaching in the river Wansbeck at Bothal Mill in 1886. Moody and Lowther picked up £1 fines but Dinsdale was discharged after a policeman saw them going to to the river at four o'clock in the morning with lights and taking a salmon which they put in a bag.

Fines were again handed out to George and James Millican for taking five salmon out of the Wansbeck 'during 'the prohibited time' in 1895. They were on a boat near the Stakeford bridge when they were rushed by several policeman and captured. The police took their nets and they were both fined 20s and costs by the Bedlington Bench. Four years later another gang of pitmen were up at Morpeth for poaching at Sheepwash. James Dixon and Roger and Henry Emery were fined 10s and costs each after a policeman caught them with 3 three unseasonable salmon in a bag and a shackle and net.

In 1913 the drover John Wilson of Morpeth was charged with having unlawfully used EXPLOSIVES for the purpose of obtaining fish in the River Wansbeck. Wilson was only fined £5 and costs, despite numbers of dead fish being found floating in the water and PC Baty, an additional constable for the Duke of Portland, stating that 'there was an explosion and the water rising 10 or 15 feet high.'

By 1939 there were still concerns over the level of poaching on the Wansbeck and at the annual meeting of the Wansbeck Angling Association held in the Newcastle House Hotel, Morpeth, it was decided that the Association should back up prosecutions taken up by the elected bailiffs. One member said he had 'heard of men coming away from the Black Bridge area with a pail full of trout,' while a member from Ashington said that 'in the past the Association had been looked upon with amusement in some quarters, because they had not taken any action, and was time they put their foot down.' The bailiffs at that time for the Wansbeck Angling Association were G. Turnbull at Bothal, J. Green at Morpeth and P. Strong at Quarry Wood.

The biggest and mightiest Northumberland river lies around fifteen miles to the south of Morpeth and the Umfraville family, the ancient lords of Redesdale, had fisheries at Ovingham on the Tyne as far back as the 13th century. He who owns the fish and the veal owns your stomach and your labour. People have to eat.

If reports are to be believed, a monster 54-pound salmon was taken from the river Tyne on May 29th 1760. The fish stocks in the hefty river before the industrial revolution were immense and it is reckoned that 2,400 salmon were caught in June 1755 and over 2,000 again in June three years later. The eventual depletion of the Tyne fish stocks was initially attributed to a lock at Bywell and Winlaton mills which prevented the fish from getting further upriver to spawn, and obviously an increase in industry on Tyneside led to the river becoming more heavily polluted.

In October 1873 Robert Forster was fined £38 – a pound for each fish he'd taken out of the Tyne at Newcastle. His co-defendants were the fishmonger Thomas Brown and Collingwood Forster.

An unusual case in Bellingham in 1925 was reckoned to be the first time that women had been charged with salmon poaching in the Tyne. Margaret Potts and Margaret Murray, of Plashetts, were caught wading in the water where the fish were spawning with a lamp and a gaff by the bailiffs. They told the court that they had no gaff and had flashed the lamp at the bailiffs for 'a lark.' The case was thrown out of the court.

In 1870, while the authorities were attempting to rid the Coquet of bull trout, the fish started to make an appearance in the river Rede for the first time and in 1886 an amazing poaching incident took place on the river when a gang of 36 Scottish men wearing black face masks and sheets over their clothes had crossed the border to lift salmon from the water. It turned into a pitched battle when police showed up to arrest them, and then a mad dash back into Scotland to evade justice just as their reiver forebearers had done some 300 years earlier.

The men, who were armed with gaffs, leisters and torches, kept the police back by throwing stones at them but were then chased over the Carter Bar where a massive, brutal 20-minute fight took place between the gang and the officers with the poaching gear being used as weapons as well as more stones, fists, heads, knees and feet. Six were arrested and brought up on charges, though the Northumberland Magistrates at Hexham said they had no jurisdiction as the assaults had been commited in Scotland and the poaching in the Bellingham division.

John Hope, a labourer; James Elliott, farm servant; Alexander McKenzie, gardener; Charles Scott, forester; James Hall, farm labourer; and William Mitchell Hill, a roadman, all from the Camptown district, were remanded and refused bail. The other 30 got off, Scot-free.

A SHORT HISTORY OF THE ROTHBURY BREWERY

It was Robert Storer who opened the Rothbury Brewery in around 1749. He had put Pasture House Farm near Snitter up for sale or let four years earlier, and you have to wonder if that was to raise the funds to get into the liquor game. In 1756 the gentleman Storer was described as a 'merchant' and it is a possibility that the word 'spirit' is missing off the front of that occupation description.

The Storers were an old Rothbury family with an entrepreneurial bent and they owned a pit near the village, probably up by the Lee. There was a disaster there in 1753 as a Putter named Dixon jumped onto the rope at the chain-knot at the head of the shaft and plummeted 17 fathoms, was buried and quickly died. Things took a sinister turn when it was discovered that the rope had been cut to a single strand and it was reckoned that someone had tried to do in the Under Overman, as he was generally the first to ride down the mine shaft.

The Storers were a respectable lot and were among the founder members of the Rothbury Association – an early version of the local constabulary – which was formed along with the men of Netherwitton 'for the prosecution of Felony.' Their aim was to convict any robbery, theft or felony, and detecting, apprehending and convicting any person 'who shall injure or attempt the person of any member of the Association.'

Robert, Thomas, and William Storer were signatories along with the rector Edward Drummond, Walter Trevelyan, George Potts, Samuel Donkin,

George Wilson, John Smith, George Leighton, John Robson, William Donkin, Robert Detchen, George Common, Thomas Readhead, John Coull, John Aynsley, Henry Robson, John Potts, Thomas Readhead, Robert Readhead, Andrew Carmichael, Robert Forrige, Lionel Aynsley, George Storey, William Charter, Christopher Urpeth, George Rennison, Jonathon Earl, Thomas Arkle, George Graham, and James Sproat.

The Rothbury brewery was a large concern and if you ever stood on the Gallowgate Terrace at Newcastle United in the 1980s then you'll be aware of the unmistakable smell of hops that must have drifted over the village from Brewery Lane just as it used to from the Scottish & Newcastle Brewery in the Toon.

There was a disaster in the October of 1781 when a fire broke at in a brew house in the Market Place around 12 at night and burned for three hours, destroying 16 houses, most of which were thatched. No lives were lost, however, and most of the furniture of the houses were saved. By 1791 the Brewery had stables for the drays and horses, a yard that must have had straw strewn over cobbles, with a house attached. One can only imagine the big wooden vats of beers, perhaps copper pipes running into stills, the amazing aromas as men walked down wooden stairs with handrails worn smooth in leather pinnies, the bustle and noise of barrels being rolled.

But in the April of that year the brewery fell silent as it was put up for sale by auction at John Burn's Black Horse pub in Rothbury. It must have been a fairly sudden decision, because the stock of the ale, malt, barley, hops etc. could also 'be had at a fair valuation.' The brew house was 'in the occupation' of Robert Coward, and enquiries where to be directed through his relation Henry Coward, who lived at New Whitley near Shields. Whether Coward was the manager or owner is not clear; the following month Thomas Storer's daughter Peggy married a Rothbury Spirit Merchant and Brewer named Mr. Ridpath at Felton and by the December Robert Storer of Rothbury, common brewer, was declared bankrupt.

George Storey, his friend and colleague from the Rothbury Association, was a farmer up at Caistron. He employed Willie Redpath and John Robson as hinds and John Weathenson as a shepherd on his land and he became one of the principal partners in the Brewery business along with James Storey and Robert Hindhaugh. Other people seem to have invested in the brewing concern, as a Colonel Judson of Carterside was for many years a senior partner in what was now called the Messrs. Geo. Storey & Co. Rothbury Brewery.

Although it is unclear who the Brewery had been selling their beer to, in 1773 John Forster was an innkeeper of a public house in Rothbury and he conducted the sale of the late Rev. Salkeld's lands from there; Anthony Bell was the landlord of a Rothbury inn in 1783 and John Potts was a carrier and innkeeper in the village in 1788. Amos Turnbull was an innkeeper in 1789, a Mr. Hugguns kept a bar in Rothbury in 1807 and John Arkle in 1811. In 1813 a man named Bartholomew Murray, of Kendal, was gaoled at Morpeth for passing forged Scottish one guinea bank notes to a Rothbury innkeeper.

The Black Horse was gone by 1820 when the well-known directory of Rothbury pubs was issued – William Bolam having the Star Inn, Ned Riddell the Sun Inn, Robert Hall the Turk's Head, Thomas Shotton the Blue Bell, George Coulson the Black Bull, David and Rachel Maxwell the Three Half Moons, Ben Perry the Rifleman and Jane Snowdon the Golden Fleece. The Black Bull is now the Newcastle House and the Golden Fleece is now the Queen's Head. Other pubs that were once in the village included The Malt Shovel, The Fighting Cocks (now the Turk's) and The Fox and Hounds.

The fresh cold water from the well at Wellfield is reputed to have provided the main ingredient for the production of ales at the Brewery Road (now Lane) establishment and the farms of the fertile Coquet valley the hops, barley and corn required in the brewing process. By 1874 the brewery production included the prime Rothbury Ales of mild and bitter which were available in casks and bottles, so it must be assumed that mild and bitter were what they were supplying to the local pubs back then.

If anyone has made an attempt at home brewing, then they'll know the joys of rigging up a big plastic bucket in a shed and checking in delight as the fermenting bubbles rise on the top of the water. The large scale affair at the Rothbury Brewery must have been some sight as the brown head crowned in rooms of steam and heat and almost alchemical ancient arts.

Beer has been produced in Britain for thousands of years and it should be something of a source of pride for Northumbrians that 'Atrectus the brewer' was supplying the Roman legions at Vindolanda with local ales.

By the October of 1842 it appeared that the Brewery was in trouble again as all the malting, with a cottage adjoining, in the centre of Rothbury – presumably the old Malting Yard – owned by the Rothbury Brewing Company, were put up to let. The advertisement claimed that the malting was 'situated in an excellent barley district, with an abundance of water and every other requisite for carrying out an extensive business.' George Rutherford of Rothbury would show the property to anyone interested.

The brewery itself was put up for sake by auction the following month at the Swan Inn at Alnwick. It was described as an 'old and well-established business' with various out offices, the brewery being fitted out with 'every necessary convenience' and a dwelling house attached. It is unclear whether any outside buyers came forward, as two years later the partnership that owned the common brewers and spirit merchants G. Storey and Co. was dissolved. The people involved were Eleanor Storer, R, W, and H Nicholson, N. Hindhaugh, George Storey, James Storey, and Robert Hindhaugh.

The Brewery limped on and was put up for sale again in 1852 at an auction in the Three Half Moons. It was still in the possession of George Storey & Co. but they noted that 'room is no doubt left for fresh spirit and enterprise which may extend what is already a viable concern.' It was put up for sale again in 1856 by private contract.

The Rothbury Brewery Company, consisting of Spirit, Ale, Brewery and Malting Trades, had been established for 'upwards of 100 years' in the village and, interestingly, there were 'a number of public houses belonging to the company' as they sought sealed bids to James Moffatt at the Brewery office. The following year Messrs George Storey and Co. were advertising for an experienced maltster to join the firm as they looked to improve their business but the following year the Rothbury Brewery Company suffered heavy losses as pikes of hay were swept away by massive floods of the Coquet.

The boom times, however, were just around the corner. Rothbury was to get a massive boost as the formation of the Central Northumberland Railway in 1866 was seen as a huge opportunity to bring people and business to the rural market town. George Storey & Co. intended to enlarge their brewery and were rebuilding the Blue Bell, which they owned and Mrs Hindhaugh – who had certainly been involved in the company at some point – was going to rebuild the Three Half Moons as they looked to address 'increased demand for accommodation which had already set in.' The Alnwick and County branch were going to build a new bank, pure spring water from the south side of the Coquet was being piped in and the Joint Stock Hotel Company intended building a new hotel with 40 rooms near the river, which became the Railway Hotel.

When there was a bad winter the following year, the Brewery displayed their community spirit and gave the poor people of Rothbury a substantial supply of coals, but they appeared less public-minded when George Storey, the son of the original owner, went to court to get Isabella and Thomas Shotton ejected from the Blue Bell Inn. The Bell was made up of three rooms and a saddler's shop with a house, stables, outbuildings and a garden. Old George Storey had died in 1867. James Storey had died in 1853 and Robert Hindhaugh in 1850, those three being the three trustees of the Rothbury Brewery Company that had owned the pub.

The Rothbury Branch, or Wannie Line, from Morpeth through Scots Gap, Rothley, Ewesley, Fontburn and Brinkburn eventually opened up in 1870. John Hounam at the Star Inn took advantage by putting on transport from the station straight to his pub.

The popular Ephraim Temple was brought in to manage the Rothbury Brewery on the death of old Mr. Storey and he was an affable and well-liked character in the village. He put out a tender for works on two new houses and alterations to the adjoining house in Brewery Lane with the plans on display in the Blue Bell in 1871. That same year Thomas Burn died, aged 78. Thomas had been the ostler – the man who looks after the horses of people staying at an inn – for the late Mr. Maxwell at the Three Half Moons for over 50 years. In 1874 William Lawson had the Three Half Moons, and Andrew Tully the Rifleman.

The resurgent George Storey & Co. were advertising their business as

Brewers, Maltsters, Wine and Spirit merchants, Ale, Porter, Hop and Corn merchants etc. and were also manufacturing soda water, lemonade and gingerade. They stocked whiskys from Old Islay, Glenlivit, Campbelton, and other Highland and Irish whiskies; Old Jamaica rums, white and dark, pale and dark cognac brandies, in casks and cases, Holland's Geneva (Loopuyt's Finest) and Fine Cream London Gin. They were also bottling ales and stouts including Bass and Allsopps Pale India Ale and London and Dublin stout. George Scott had taken the position of the landlord of the Blue Bell and he was up in front of the bench at the Rothbury Petty Sessions in January 1877 for permitting drunkenness in the bar. The local police sergeant had seen a man named Keen stagger out of the Blue Bell so mortal that his wife had to help him home, and on going into the inn later on had found a man called Harris sitting at the bar with his head on the table and a glass near his hand. They were both fined for drunkenness, but the bench – made up of Lord Armstrong, Major Browne, and Messrs Riddell and Weallans – dismissed the charge against Scott. Riddell, of Whitfield, and Weallans, of Flotterton, were both also magistrates on the annual local Licensing Sessions. Two stonemasons, Mark and Andrew Rutherford, were charged with being drunk and disorderly and refusing to quit the Rifleman, run by Miss Tully. They were both fined £1 or faced seven days imprisonment if they didn't pay up.

The Rothbury Petty Sessions were reported in the local papers in the 1880s and had a section called the Drunk List which regularly featured locals and visitors who had over-indulged in the hooch. Adam Hood was drunk and disorderly and creating a 'great disturbance' standing against the Rothbury cross, shouting and swearing and trying to get some money from another man. Lord Armstrong fined him 5s. An old hawker called Peter Rafferty was charged with being drunk and incapable, and the Rothbury coachbuilder Charlton Turnbull charged with being drunk and riotus. It was claimed that he'd punched the Railway Hotel keeper Leightley while steaming in an argument on the bridge. George Tait was called as a witness and said he'd been watching from the school corner, saw the scuffle and them both fall over and that Turnbull was sober as he'd spoke to him after.

The case was dismissed.

George Tait was himself fined 7s 6d at a later date for being drunk and disorderly when he'd made a great disturbance in front of the Sun Inn and went down the street shouting and swearing and wanting to fight another man. George was a Rothbury character; he joined the Fusiliers, then the Borderers, and went out to Malta with that Regiment for a couple of years. He spent a bit time back in Rothbury then thought sod it, and immigrated to Canada. He signed up to be part of the Canadian Expeditionary Force and fought in France in WW1 at the grand age of 43. Somewhat ironically, George went on to become a respected police sergeant in remote rural Canada. His brother Robert was another handful who was charged with being drunk and disorderly on a few occasions – once when he said the policemen were 'squeaking' at him and he threatened to 'smash their b****** faces,' another when he came out of the Blue Bell shouting and swearing, and again when he was charged with being drunk on licensed premises when he fell out with Mrs. Leightley who then had the Sun Inn in 1889. Robert 'Gunner' was a fair sprinter and had taken part at the Morpeth Olympics.

Joseph Wintrip was drunk and disorderly when he stumbled about shouting and swearing and hit the owner of the Sun Inn while his relation Lewis Wintrip was also in the dock that day and was charged with killing an unclean salmon in the Seal Burn with William McGregor. The hawker Issac Miller was drunk and disorderly and was slumped in the mail cart and refused to get out, and when Walter Kidd staggered around the road and refused to go home he was also charged with being drunk and disorderly. Samuel Rutherford also faced a fine for falling over and staggering drunk in the street while the knife grinder Thomas Robinson drunkenly wheeled his scissor grinding machine up and down the village singing at the top of his voice, creating a disturbance and falling down. The farmer John Carr of Walklow Hall came staggering out of the Railway Hotel smelling of whisky and was so drunk that a policeman had to get hold of him and take him home.

A Joseph Costello from Newcastle was charged with being drunk and disorderly when he got into a fight up at Thropton and John Murrell from Percy Main was drunk when he fell through Mrs. Pagan's shop window in the village. Though he first refused to pay for the glass he did eventually and his friends got him away back to the railway station. Rothbury horse race days must have been hugely busy affairs for the local pubs and several thousand visited Rothbury in April 1885 for the revival of the Northumberland Steeple Chase meeting. The steeple chasing appears to have started in around 1853 down by the Coquet with the one annual event, though races had certainly been run on the course since at least 1739. There was a show of cattle in Rothbury on the second Friday in April, which was followed the day after by a horse race for a 'Give and Take Plate.' A byelaw stated that 'no person (was) to retail any liquor on the Race but subscribers,' so the authorities were already hot on the drink then. Races on the Haugh for a purse of gold started up in 1758. The racecourse closed in 1965 to much bitterness.

At an annual Licensing Session in 1879 a Morpeth solicitor, on behalf of a Mr. Gibson of Newcastle, who had an application in for a new license for the new hotel in close proximity to the railway station – the Station Hotel, now the Coquet Vale – opposed the renewal of the license for the Rifleman Inn on the grounds that the premises were unsuitable. So the Rothbury Brewing Company, who had an interest in the Rifleman, hit back and opposed the Station Hotel application. The Rifleman case was adjourned while the new application was thrown out. Storey & Co. still had some clout. Interestingly, their was no black list presented in front of the session, so they must have kept a record of offenders something like a modern pub watch scheme.

The Brewery's luck changed again in 1881 when Ephraim Temple died quite suddenly after a short illness aged 61. He'd worked his way up to managing partner of George Storey and Co. and was regarded as 'one of the most familiar faces and highly respected inhabitants of Upper Coquetdale.' His glowing epitaph in the newspapers spoke of how deeply mourned Temple would be, that he was sympathetic, quick to relieve distress, sincere, honest, highly intelligent and an agreeable companion and friend. Mr. Temple, who was born at Harbottle, was a sportsman and keen on hunting and coursing, was secretary of the Rothbury Steeplechase Meeting and the original Coursing Club. It was said that he'd never in his life made an enemy, was a clever businessman and that his memory would be long cherished. Replacing someone like Mr. Temple would be virtually impossible and it would come as no great surprise when the Brewery was again put on the market in 1883 with R. Donkin and Son hosting the auction at the County Hotel that September.

In 1889 a Mr. John Gallon was manager of the Rothbury Brewing Company. The Gallons were another family with deep roots in Coquetdale. Both a William and Hugh Gallon had appeared at a proof of age case at Newcastle castle for the powerful Gilbert, son and heir of Thomas de Umfraville, to show he was 21 as far back as the early 1400s. Gilbert had been born in Harbottle castle and baptised in Harbottle church and a string of local worthies came forward to testify that. Hugh Gallon said he had accompanied Elizabeth Heron from Rothbury to Harbottle for the baptism, and William Gallon accompanied the godfather Gilbert de Acton from Felton to Harbottle. The knight Robert Lisle had ridden to ask de Acton to be the godfather and the knight Wyncellan Dorstans had gone to ask Gilbert, abbot of Melrose, to be the other godfather. Robert Tempest had asked Elizabeth Heron to be godmother.

Mr. Gallon was involved in a court case row between an innkeeper from Bebside called Joshua Rutter and the Blyth & Tyne Brewing Co. in 1899. The Blyth brewery was supplying the Newcastle House and it seems that Gallon was attempting to strike a deal with Mr. Rutter to supply him with beer from George Storey's Rothbury Brewery. Mr. Carmichael of the Blyth brewery said that the Rothbury Brewery won't brewing their own beer at the time, but were getting it from Newcastle, Northallerton, Edinburgh and other places. The owners of the two breweries, Mr. Storey and Mr. Lynn, were personal friends and it seemed like they were attempting to put business each others way. Shortly after a Mr. A.W. Charlton appears to be the manager of the Rothbury Brewery as there was another reshuffle in the company.

In 1907 Mrs. Mary Stephenson, the landlady of the Turk's Head, was summoned for selling adulterated whisky after watering the nips. Joseph

Cummings must have taken on the license from her as the following year George Wintrip was allowed to take it over from him. Other pub transfers sanctioned by the Rothbury Petty Sessions saw William Smith of Sunderland take over the Queen's Head from Joseph Chatt while the Blue House at Rothbury and the Star Inn at Netherton were transferred from Thomas Farmley to Andrew Tully of Alnham.

The Rothbury Brewery was facing some local competition around the time as Thomas Thompson & Son set up their Lemonade Factory at Well Strand. The pop factory was formally known as the Rothbury Aerated Water Co. and they were manufacturing and bottling fizzy drinks and mineral waters. 'Pop' Thompson was still producing fermented ginger beer in stone bottles in the 1930s.

The local ownership of the Rothbury Brewery was ended in 1911 when the Scottish brewers James Aitken & Co. of Falkirk acquired the business. Mr. W.L. Farndale was the manager of the Rothbury Brewing Company in 1916 and he presided over a meeting of the Licensed Victuallers of Rothbury at the Railway Hotel where it was unanimously decided to put a penny rise on a glass of spirits due to the considerable increase in prices. It was also decided at the meeting to form a Rothbury & District licensed victuallers' association.

The most amazing story of all associated with the Rothbury Brewery occurred in the February of 1920 when two Soviet sailors broke into the building and shot a policeman. The Russian seamen Peter Klighe and Karl Straughtin were lodging in the West End of Newcastle and had travelled up to Rothbury on the train from Morpeth then popped into the Railway Hotel for a drink. Why they were in the country just three years after the October Revolution was never really explained or examined in the packed Rothbury magistrates' court. At 9.10pm PC Francis Douglas Sinton was on the street when he heard a noise coming from inside the closed Brewery building; when he went to the door he heard glass breaking. He sent a messenger to Mr. Farndale and went around the back of the building to investigate.

When he shone his lantern into the bottle shed he saw the dark figure of Klighe in the opening, who shouted something in a foreign language then ran inside. PC Sinton gave chase, keeping his light on the figure as he ran to the back of the large shed. Klighe pulled an automatic pistol from his overcoat pocket and told Sinton that if he came forward, he would shoot. PC Sinton drew his truncheon and charged; when he grabbed the men's shoulder he fired, the bullet grazing his head. Straughtin then came up behind the officer and hit him twice on the back of his head with a crowbar, knocking him to the ground. Mr. Farndale arrived and grappled with a man whose face was covered with a white muffler, who also fired a shot. They fled the scene but were captured in woods at Walbottle Dene on March 1st. The police found fake documents, skeleton keys, drills, some gunpowder, cartridges and a map of Northumberland showing the Rothbury district when they searched the premises at 228 Westgate Road where the men had lodged.

The two men were charged with attempted murder, breaking and entering the warehouse and of also breaking into Co-ops in Ashington and Throckley and an office of the North British Railway Company with 29 other offences taken into consideration. Klighe told the Summer Assize at the Moot Hall Newcastle that he and Straughtin had 'entered into partnership some time ago and they had been engaged latterly in a 'career of brigandage' as they were hard up for money.' They both received 13 years in jail with a recommendation for deportation at the end of their sentences. But there are still loads of unanswered questions about the incident. Had they jumped ship from a Russian vessel following the upheaval or were they spies or on some kind of mission for Lenin? At a brewery in Rothbury? The British Communist Party was formed in the August of that year, so anything is possible. In 1925 a Geordie Communist called Percy Gibson was accused of being a party industrial organiser and having explosives in a tin to blow up Newcastle Town Hall and a Power Station *(see later story)*. It may seem laughable now, but back then anything was possible.

Aitkens, who had also formed in the 1740s, were taken over by Caledonian United Breweries in the 1960s. That company in turn became part of Tennents, but the operation at the Rothbury Brewery was sadly long gone before then - probably by the 1930s.

FIRE IN THE HILLS – ALWINTON AND ANGLO-SCOTTISH STRIFE

The steep rounded hills of the upper Coquet valley aren't particularly high. The rough grass slopes run down towards the silver ribbon of the infant river dotted with the white fleece of sheep where the wind is abated. There is a peace and a silence only broken by distant curlew cries or the babble of the water running brown as Ale with highland wash off.

The tiny village of Alwinton is one of the gateways into the wilderness of the NorthumberlandNational Park set nearby the confluence of the rivers Alwin and Coquet. The nights are dark with star-spotted blackness as you leave the sanctuary of the Rose and Thistle pub, the laughter and light from inside illuminating the pavement a few seconds then slamming back to black.

Although people may face the darkness with some sense of trepidation today, feeling the looming presence of the hills without actually seeing them, there was a time when the black provided a feeling of safety; where if there were no orange flames dancing in the black or the disturbed bleating and braying of animals then everything was alright. For now, at least.

The Rose and Crown is aptly named as the village sits just around ten miles from the Border with Scotland and three incidents that occurred in Alwinton almost 300 years apart can shed some light on the troubled history of the boundary between the nations.

The First Scottish Wars of Independence in the late 1290s had brought destruction throughout Northumberland as armies torched buildings, trampled corn and stole livestock. However, in the November of 1311, it was a gang of fellow Northumbrians that had raided Richard de Horsley's land at Alwinton and driven away over 1,000 of his sheep while he was away 'on the service and under the protection of the king.' Even the church got in on the act with the chaplain William de Bolton being named as one of the thieves.

William de Hateshawes, Richard son of Margery, William le Muner, Roger de Fontayns, William de Beverlagh, Stephen de Clifton, Richard de Sharperton, Gilbert de Whytestane, Vincent de Ellesdene (Elsdon in Redesdale), Gilbert le Forster, Adam son of Gilbert, John and Richard de Beverlagh, John de Farnley, William son of Richard de Felton, Hugh del Park, John le Nedeler, John le Lorimer of Sharperton and William de Yeland, with others, committed the early reiving offence. While many of the subsequent raids that blighted the Border region for three centuries did come from across the invisible line in both directions, many others were as likely to come from one of the barren heather moors of the neighbouring valleys, and English and Scottish riders often rode together to hit isolated farmhouses.

Richard de Horsley was granted a licence to 'impark' his woods at Alwinton and Thirnam (nearby Farnham?) in 1307 and ten years later he handed 100 acres of land and 6 acres of meadow in Linshiels and Alwinton to the church, for a chaplain to 'celebrate divine service daily in the chapel of St. Nicholas in his manor of Aldensheles for his soul and the souls of his ancestors and all Christians.'

His relative Roger de Horsley was the constable of Bamburgh Castle at the North Sea coast and in 1322 has was unable to collect the rents for their lands for the King because everything had again been 'wasted and destroyed by divers attacks of the Scotch rebels.'

As time went on the reivers were encouraged and protected by corrupt officials, relatives and friends in positions of official power in the March Law system that was unique to the area. Lord Dacre, who had been an English War hero at Flodden, received a letter from Philip Dacre at nearby Harbottle castle in August 1522 that 20 Scots riders had 'pricked at the horse' at Alwinton. 14 Englishmen attacked the raiders at Singingside

Swire where two of the important Douglas family were killed and one taken prisoner. Hostages were always handy for ransoming and were taken whenever possible.

In 1601 John Barrow, the laird of nearby Barrow, and George Green of Alwinton – most likely an ancestor of TV's Robson Green – had more than 100 cattle and livestock, a white horse and 20 nobles money stolen by the raider Percy Turnbull and his gang from the Rule water. Percy didn't bother to turn up at the Truce Day to hear the charges against him – amounting to a bumper 254l 6s 6d – and was declared guilty for his non-appearance. These are the kinds of charge that turn up time and time again in the records at the time. Two years later King James came down from Edinburgh to claim the English throne and set about attempting to 'pacify' the borders from 1605.

He failed. By 1618, an Alwinton man called Barty Wilkinson was back in the village. He'd been sent across to Ireland to fight with 149 other outlawed Northumbrians by the King but had deserted.

Looking out across the hills as a layer of cloud and mist snaked around the bottoms and followed the meander of the river, Barty pulling in a lungful of fresh air and sighing; feeling that immeasurable draw, the pull of home.

ON THE HUNT FOR ROTHBURY CASTLE

There's a good reason why Northumberland doesn't feature in the Domesday Book. Although England had been famously conquered by William Duke of Normandy in 1066, the far north wasn't completely taken by the Normans until around 1080 after a long and vicious campaign known as the Harrying of the North. But it wasn't just attacks from the south that the Northumbrians faced as a number of Scottish invasions also left the countryside bloodstained and burned in a time of great upheaval and destruction.

In 1080 the Normans built a new castle on the Tyne near a settlement called Monkchester. A motte and bailey castle had been built by Robert de Umfraville to control Redesdale at Elsdon in 1076. Another was erected by William de Merley at Morpeth in around 1080, significantly for us at a site known as the Ha Hill.

Rothbury's controlling Norman Baron was a Roger Fitz John, who built a motte and bailey castle at Warkworth on the site of today's impressive stone fortress that dominates the village. It can only be assumed that Fitz John also constructed a motte and bailey affair with a wooden fortress to control Coquetdale on the site of the graveyard opposite All Saints' Church today on Rothbury's Haa Hill.

Excavations and digging undertaken by Andy Law on the grass and road near the church have indicated that the village's early Anglian church was originally situated further to the West nearer the houses on what used to be known as Church Gate.

Mr. Law also unearthed significant pieces of an old Anglian stone cross, some of which are today piled up inside the church doorway, while others went down to the Great North Museum at Newcastle. The natural slope with controlling views up and down the river Coquet and a commanding position above the bridge may have been added to, though the graveyard construction in 1869 leaves little evidence of an original wooden castle or the stone one that followed.

Elsdon's motte and bailey was abandoned by around the mid-13th century as it was made redundant by the Umfraville's new fortress at Harbottle. Morpeth was burned by King John in 1216 and replaced by the stone castle behind, again in the 13th century. Working on this premise, it can be assumed that the descendants of Fitz John, who had taken the surname Clavering by this time, had handed control of Rothbury over to a new family and it is likely that they constructed a more permanent stone structure on the site of the motte and bailey castle.

Sir John Ogle held the manor and borough of Rothbury by service of half a knight's fee by around 1315. For a further 1 knight's fee, he held of the king in chief the 'hamlets of Newtown, Thropton, and Snitter, and the forest with the vaccaries of Greenhealey, Pauperhaugh, Thorneyhaugh, Healy, Morrelhirst, and Brockleyhirst.

If anyone is the likely candidate to build the tower, castle, bastle or hall that we can only really speculate occupied the site in Rothbury, then surely Sir John is our main contender.

Ownership of the castle will have passed into the hands of the Percy family in September 1331 when Sir Henry Percy took control of Sir John Clavering's lands.

These few simple lines have led to the Dukes of Northumberland owning all the land in Rothbury since: 'Sir Henry has given and will give him in future, if it pleases God, with the assent of the prelates, earls, barons and other great men assembled in the same parliament, grants for himself and his heirs that the castle and manor of Warkworth, and also the manor of Rothbury, and all the other lands and tenements with their appurtenances in the same county which the aforesaid Sir John of Clavering holds for the term of his life and which, after his death, should have reverted to the king and to his heirs, after the death of the aforesaid Sir John.'

The Ogles, however, remained an important local family and the Percy takeover of Rothbury may have led them to construct their great tower at Tosson. Sir Robert Ogle, possibly the son of Sir John, held land at Hepple and may have also built the tower there in the 14th century. Great Tosson, Trewhitt, Wharton and Flotterton were part of the Hepple barony held by the Ogles in 1363, which were 'held of the king in chief by service of a moiety of a barony.' William Tailbois was the Ogle's 'parcener' of the barony – someone who shared in the inheritance of an undivided estate. Although Hepple tower is reputed to be first mentioned in the records in 1415 when described as the home of a later Sir Robert Ogle, who later moved his court to Great Tosson, it had almost certainly stood for much longer.

In 1346 the manor of Shilvington was held by Robert Ogle, Thomas Fenwick and his wife Joan, while North Horsley was held by the knight Robert Bertram (possibly the hermit in the Warkworth tragedy?), Robert Mauduyt, John Ogle, Ellen the widow of Robert Ogle, son of Robert Ogle, and Thomas Fenwick at an enquiry of knight's fees taken at Morpeth. Six years later Robert Ogle also had land at Thursby near Carlisle and other spots in Cumberland which were held by Ranulf de Dacre. It all gets rather confusing when the document states that 'Robert son of Robert son of Robert de Ogle is heir of Robert.'

What isn't that confusing is how they managed to keep hold of their lands. The Scottish Wars of Independence had led to Northumberland being raided, burned, harried and harassed on an almost constant basis and in May 1335 Robert Ogle, along with Thomas de Heton, Walter de Creyk, Robert de Esshelyton and William de Tynedale (whose coffin you can see today in Hexham Abbey) were ordered to stop gathering men in Newcastle-upon-Tyne for 'the King's service against the Scots who have invaded the realm, to repress their malice' because the Tyneside officials had given the King 'certain men of that town to set out in his service upon the sea against the Scots.' Ogle and his fellows had been appointed to 'array all the men-at-arms, hobblers, archers and other men in county Northumberland, and to cause the men at arms to be placed in constabularies, and the hobelers, archers and foot soldiers in thousands, hundreds and scores, so that they might be ready and provided with competent arms to set out.'

The violence of the times inspired violent means to accumulate and preserve wealth and Robert Ogle was important enough to be one of the judges appointed by Westminster along with Robert Parvyng, Thomas de Fencotes and John de Evere to investigate a complaint by William de Backworth five years later.

William de Backworth had taken some cattle that were 'trespassing at Backworth' and had impounded them, but Alan de Backworth, Hugh le Porter John Dawe and others broke the pound, took away the cattle, stole four of William's own stock and assaulted his men and servants 'so that their life was despaired of, whereby he lost their service for a great while.' The gang also threatened these men and others so badly that William despaired that he 'cannot get servants to till his lands.' The culture of the Border Reiver was becoming deeply ingrained in the local populace.

Robert Ogle, the elder, and William Heron, knight, acknowledged that they both owed the knight Ralph de Neville £60 which was to be levied in Northumberland in 1352 and the extent of old Ogle's estate was revealed at his death in 1363. An inquest at Newcastle found that Robert Ogle held land in Saltwick, the castle and manor of Ogle held by the Baron of Walton, Little Twisell, Shilvington, Aldworth, Longwitton, Seaton Woodhorn, Thirnham (now Farnham), The Colputts, Fulbury, North Middleton, and Dissington South.

The barony of Hepple was his and still included Great Tosson, Trewhitt, Wharton and Flotterton. Ogle also held Aldonshiels and Rouly in the liberty of Hexham, Sewingshiels, the Walfeld, and Thursby, in Cumberland. His son Robert, aged 9 at the time, was his heir. Young Robert shrewdly exchanged land in Hurworth for the remainder of the Hepple estate with Walter Tailbois in 1386. He also had to pay Tailbois 700 marks, to be levied in Northumberland, along with Peter Tilliole and John Thirlwall that year. It is reputed that Sir Thomas Umfraville, lord of Redesdale, built Whitton

Tower at that time.

Just 30 years earlier the land at Whitton was owned by a number of families; Sir Henry Percy held a third of the manor, Roger de Sommerville, lord of Whitton, a third and John Hansen a third. Alice, Thomas and John Clark, Roger Hanson, John Forster, Mariota Pederton and Alexander del Shele all rented land there, so it seems unlikely that the Umfraville's owned the land to construct it – Percy seems a much better bet.

It may be a possibility that Whitton was built to supersede the old tower down in the valley on the river at Rothbury, which would also be owned by the legendary Harry Hotspur, who was serving in the English army in France at that time. He'd been battling the Scots the year before, though, and Whitton may have been constructed to provide some advance warning of retaliatory Scottish raids from its high vantage point on the hill above the village.

Ogle, and his friends John Lilburn, John Fenwick and Gerard Salvain, had to raise a levy of £100 to pay John de Neville, the keeper of Bamburgh Castle, to repair the North side of the castle and the following summer a gang that included Henry and William Lilburn menaced Alan de Heton at his Chillingham castle.

Ogle, Fenwick and William Swinburne were married to de Heton's daughters and had 'made an agreement with him.' It seemed a bit suspect as the Lilburns had locked de Heton up in a tower, kept the castle by armed force and 'committed many other misdeeds and contempts.'

Robert died in around 1410 and his son, another Robert Ogle, inherited further lands in the barony of Hepple including plots at Sharperton, Alwinton and Wharton. He further took possession of a third of the manor of Angrave, and 120 acres of land in Bamburgh, Tynemouth, Felton, and Wooler.

In 1425 Robert Ogle had to levy £200 in Northumberland with the knights John Widdrington and John Fenwick as his arbitrators on his behalf against the knight William Elmeden, with William Bowes and William Chancellor representing him, 'concerning all personal actions, quarrels and debates between them, their men or servants, and shall on his part and on the part of his men or servants perform the same, and every one of his men and servants likewise, so that the award shall be made in the chapel upon the bridge of Newcastle upon Tyne before the Nativity of the Virgin next.' Henry Percy, Earl of Northumberland, John, baron of Graystoke and Robert Umfraville, knight, were the umpires chosen by the parties. Robert Ogle, Henry Fenwick and Thomas Iderton had a like claim in against Elmeden on his lands in Middlesex.

Sir Robert Ogle regained the barony of Rothbury, albeit briefly, in 1461 when Percy was killed fighting for the Lancastrians in the War of the Roses at the Battle of Towton. Depite Ogle's grant of 'seneschal and constable of the lordships and castles of Alnwick, Warkworth, Prudhoe, Rothbury, Newburn, Newburn Haven, formerly belonging to the earl of Northumberland,' being for life, the Percys were back in favour by 1473.

Rothbury castle does not appear on the 1415 list of castles and fortalices in Northumberland, but many of the others do, including Willie Green's Thropton tower, John Cartington's Cartington tower and Robert Ogle's towers at Hepple, Flotterton, North Middleton and Newstead, plus his castles at Ogle and Sewingshields. Great Tosson is also an interesting omission, as is Clennell. Other local fortresses that were included are Robert Umfraville's Harbottle castle, Hugh Gallon's Low Trewhitt, Robert Horsley's Farnham, John Selby's Biddlestone and, of course, the vicar's tower at Whitton.

Rothbury does not appear again in the 1541 list of pele towers compiled by Sir Robert Bowes and Sir Ralph Ellerker. The towers that they listed in Coquetdale were Alnham, where one of the two small towers at belonged to the church and was the 'mansion' of the Vicarage. The other belonged to the Earl of Northumberland (Percy).

The tower and barmkin at Scrainwood belonged to John Horsley while the powerful Percival Selby owned both the tower (with barmkin) at Biddlestone, which would be developed into Biddlestone Hall, and a smaller tower at nearby Cote Walls. The small tower at Clennell belonged to Percival Clennell, who was in the process of building a barmkin wall in 1541 and the small stone bastle house at Alwinton belonged to the Church and was described as the 'mansion of the vicarage.'

Harbottle castle was the main strength in the area and was garrisoned by 100 troops and their horses to defend against both the invasions of the Scots 'in time of War' and the 'defence of the thefts and spoils of the Redesdale men.' It was often used as a base by the Keeper of Redesdale. It originally belonged to the powerful and aristocratic Tailbois family, who had taken over from the Umfravilles in Redesdale, and was approaching disrepair.

Barrow pele belonged to Gerrard Barrow, but by 1541 it had been 'burnt and raised' by the Scots in War time. Garrard didn't have the cash to repair it. The 'great tower' at Burradon was the inheritance of George Fenwick, and Percival Lisle 'in right of his wife.' But Burradon was another building that was in a state of disrepair at the time.

Roger Hangingshaw built the 'strong pele house of stone' at Harehaugh as a means to 'resist the incourse of thieves of Redesdale.' Lord Ogle's tower at Hepple was in need of repairs; the roof, in particular, was in a bad way. The knight Sir Cuthbert Radcliffe owned Cartington Castle; the two strong towers and other stone buildings were in good shape, and Thropton tower was also the property of Sir Cuthbert Radcliffe.

Great Tosson tower belonged to Lord Ogle. The building was requiring repairs in 1541 while Whitton tower belonged to the parsonage of Rothbury and was in a good state of repair, with a little barmkin.

The tower at Eliburn, near the Lee in Rothbury Forest, belonged to the Lordship of Rothbury and the Crown, being on the Earl of Northumberland's lands.

Roger Horsley's tower at Farnham was in good shape. The tower at Nether Trewhitt belonged to Edward Gallon and was in a reasonable condition. Linbrigg pele belonged to Roger Horsley and although the remote tower had been 'burned and cast down by the Scots in times past,' Horsley had taken the stone to build a strong bastle house nearby. As there is no mention made of the proliferation of similar defensible bastle houses scatted throughout the RothburyForest, such as at Bog Hall, Morrelhirst and Brockley Hall, one has to assume that the Rothbury castle was a similar structure.

The Ogles continued to remain influential in Border life and politics and in 1537 the Lord Ogle, Sir William Ogle, John, George and a different John Ogle were all assisting the English Middle March deputy warden Sir John Widdrington in his duties.

There is little sign of the Ogles in Rothbury today; the doorway to the Three Half Moons, the 300 year old pub that bore their family crest on its sign, still stands, and the crest can also been seen in the carriage arch of the early 18th century Ogle House on the High Street. The crest can also be seen with those of other notable families in the All Saints Church.

As for the RothburyCastle itself, even less remains. A few pieces of architectural masonry within the retaining walls of the graveyard show where they were recycled, but the job in removing the structure, foundations and all, was somewhat systematic.

That nothing of the building was recorded for posterity at the time, in 1869, was incredibly short sighted and almost criminal. Just how much history now lies under that consecrated ground we will never know. The sketch in Dixon's *Upper Coquetdale* depicts what appears to be a roofless three-story traditional pele tower in the location in 1843, and the building is shown as two small squares near the top of today's steps in a map of that time, but all that is left is speculation.

CARTINGTON CASTLE IN THE CIVIL WAR

With faces hidden in shadow by the rim and guards of their lobster tail helmets, the line of musketeers fired another volley of shot at the sandstone walls and the heavy grey smoke from their muzzles drifted over the field.

They had no heavy artillery with them so the riders in Major John Sanderson's regiment of horse must have looked on with some boredom as the barrages of small arms fire went on for some five hours without success.

In terms of the English Civil War as a whole, it was an insignificant event. But to show how the conflict between the Royalists and Parliamentarians reached into every village and valley in the country, it was one that should be remembered in Coquetdale, Northumberland.

Major Sanderson had marched from Morpeth to Cartington with 120 horse and 90 footmen on hearing that the castle had been garrisoned by the Royalists under Major Errington and Sir Richard Tempest on Friday 5th May 1648. Cartington had been owned by the Catholic Royalist Sir Edward Widdrington, who fought in the ranks of the King Charles' army during their defeat at Marston Moor near York four years earlier in a battle which saw around 4,000 men in their foppish hats slaughtered. Widdrington was banished, the property sequestered and his wife was fined a hefty £400 for 'giving intelligence to the King's party' in the aftermath.

The Crown had much support among the gentry in Northumberland with not only Widdrington but other wealthy landowners such as Thomas Clavering, of Learchild, the knight Sir John Clavering, of Callaly, Francis

Carnaby, and a number of the Fenwicks, including Sir William of Meldon, throwing their weight behind the Royalists. Thomas Ogle, of Darras Hall, Musgrave Ridley, Cuthbert Collingwood, of Dawden, Edward Charleton, of Hesleyside, and Sir Charles Howard, of Plenmeller, were also all supporters of the Cavalier cause, as were the gentleman George Thirlwall, of Rothbury, and Sir Nicholas Thornton, of Netherwitton.

Widdrington and his kinsman Lord Widdrington had raised a regiment of 2,000 foot and 200 horse at their own expense to serve under Lord Newcastle and to be part of another brigade ahead of the ill-fated Marston clash, so Oliver Cromwell's Parliamentarian Roundheads must have considered him a considerable threat.

In 1639 Edward's father Roger Widdrington had received at Cartington a commissary, two carts and 150 arms from His Majesty's magazine sent by the Master of the Ordnance as the Royalists stockpiled weapons. 1,500 arms, pikes, and muskets were left in the magazine at Berwick at the time along with complete arms for 200 horse. 2,000 pikes and 2,000 muskets were also delivered to the municipality of Newcastle.

With Tempest using Cartington as his headquarters and also as an arms store, Major Sanderson 'summoned' those inside the building to surrender or be slaughtered. When the offer was refused, the crack of shots from 50 footmen echoed around the hills for hours. Just how much fire was returned is uncertain, but with weapons definitely being held at Cartington there must have been muskets poked out of windows and over battlements to shoot back and prevent the building being over-run.

Major Sanderson's footmen returned to Morpeth that evening and the Royalists either fled the castle on the Saturday, according to some accounts, or thought better of it and got out of there on the Monday when they saw Sanderson's troop return with the mounted infantry of the Dragoons from Newcastle.

The commander found the castle abandoned and left 40 musketeers, with 12 other men pulled from the regiments, for Cartington's defence. However, on May the 18th the position was deemed untenable and the men there were called off after taking wrecking bars to the stonework and dismantling what they could of the lead-shot riddled walls in an attempt to prevent the Royalists retaking it.

It wasn't quite the end of the story though as the Cavaliers did return to occupy the ruins of the building. In late June Major Sanderson's men marched and rode from near Chollorford to take Tosson Tower before they were met with two-hours resistance at Cartington on their way to Callaly and a push further on into north Northumberland.

Sir Edward Widdrington had forfeited his lands and estates to the Commonwealth in 1652 for treason but received repatriations in 1660 when the Monarchy were restored. The castle, worth a mighty £8,000 at the time, was wrecked and ruined. Cartington would never be restored to its former glory again.

PHYSIC LONNEN AND THE KNIGHTS HOSPITALLERS

In a list of the Priors of the Knights Hospitallers of Saint John of Jerusalem in England, there are four with unknown dates, but all come from during the reign of King Edward I – the notorious 'Longshanks' or 'The Hammer of the Scots.'

One of those is a Walter. Now Walter of Rothbury was the brother of one of Longshanks most trusted officials – Sir Gilbert of Rothbury, who served as Justice of the King's Bench from 1295—1316, was clerk of the parliament from 1290-1307, and clerk of King's council between 1290-95.

In the November of 1291 the King ordered Thomas de Normanvill, the keeper of the King's Land in neighbouring Tynedale, to gift Walter two bucks and four does. The following year, at Berwick, the King gifted Gilbert of Rothbury four bucks from the keeper of the forest of Bernwood.

So, the brothers were heavy players with influence in 13th century England and that same year, at Rothbury, a document was signed giving 'quittance of the common summons (of the eyre) for common pleas in co. Westmoreland' to the following people - The master of the military order of the Temple in England; Hugh de Louthre (Lowther); The prior of the Hospital of St. John of Jerusalem in England; The abbot of Byland (de Bella Landa); Hamo de Alta Ripa; The abbot of St. Mary's, York; John, bishop of Carlisle; Michael de Hartecla and Roger de Burton.

Walter certainly wasn't the prior of the Hospitallers at that time, as he appears in a similar document for county Cumberland alongside the abbot of St. Mary's, York; John, bishop of Carlisle; Thomas de Multon of Gilsland; Alexander Bonkil; The prior of the Hospital of St. John of Jerusalem in England; Maud de Multon; Robert de Brus (the Bruce); Robert de Harington; Alan de Pennington; David de Torthoraud; The abbot of Jedburgh; Walter de Corry; Isabel de Fortibus, countess of Albemarle -Walter de Rothbury appears next - followed by John de Seton and Walter de Langeton.

Sir Gilbert of Rothbury was the most successful of the brothers, being witness on a number of land documents between 1291, where he is at Berwick and Norham, and 1307, where he is attending the King at Northampton and then to take oath of office in the exchequer.

In the December of 1292 Gilbert owed money which was acknowledged and paid off at Newcastle-Upon-Tyne, and two years later he was again recorded as owing money to co-executors of the will of Isabel de Fortibus, the countess of Albemarle, which were again paid off.

Gilbert and William de Bereford were the King's justices appointed to hear a case of trespass against 8 men brought to the sheriff of York at the insistence of Henry de Percy in December 1298. The men were imprisoned in York until Gilbert and William were next in the area. He makes another appearance in a document of 1302 in London where he appeared as a witness in a land matter of Richard de Baskerville of Thurrock and the King.

While Gilbert of Rothbury was enjoying the patronage of the King as a justice and law man, the other option available to leading a successful life in the 13th century was through the church. It remains a possibility that the land occupied by the Knights Hospitallers of St. John of Jerusalem at Physic Lonnen in Thropton were either granted by, or belonged to, his brother Walter, who may have been a prior in the order, though that remains unproven.

What is fact is that in June 1334, at Newcastle, a licence was granted for John, bishop of Carlisle, to appropriate the church of Rothbury, in the diocese of Durham. The church was no longer ran from Carlisle by 1378 when master John de Appleby was parson of the church of Rothbury 'in the diocese of Durham.'

Another important religious man from the area that preached the word of

Christianity was brother Simon of Rothbury who was a monk on 'the island of Farneisland' – probably at the Chapel of St. Cuthbert on Inner Farne – in 1337.

Simon received payment of 8 shillings from the crown for donning the brown robes among the seabirds and crashing waves. The Scottish King Alexander III had granted the payments to the monks there 'in frankalmoin of the issues of Berwick yearly.' Frankalmoin means free mercy, the church holding land free of a knight's service.

In 1345 the monks were a cell of the priory of Durham and granted 10 quarters of wheat and two tuns of wine along with 13 marks 10 s. payment. The 13 marks 10s. payment was still being issued by the mayor and bailiffs of Newcastle in 1401.

WAS ROBIN HOOD FROM THE ROTHBURY FOREST?

There is something magical about being out in the woods; the dappled light breaking through the canopy of leaves, the earthy smells of mulch and mushroom, the strange silence broken only by the sway of boughs in the breeze. Watching the deer bow to drink from the Coplish burn at dawn in a splash of coppers and browns and golds with a mist moving slowly through the trees.

Rothbury Forest was long a Royal Forest but that seems to have been forgotten along with the felling of the woods that led to bare moor and farmland over the back of Simonside. The trees once covered a track of land seven miles long and five miles wide stretching from Brinkburn to Tosson that were subject to Forest Law, a separate set of rules and regulations to those that covered the rest of the country which had been brought in by the Normans following the conquest.

In the early Thirteenth Century Roger the son of John (Roger Fitzjohn) owned the manors of Warkworth and Rothbury, and the Rothbury forest. He had to pay 40s for the service of one forester with a horse and 60s for three foot foresters 'with their robes'. He also had to pay a yearly sub of 20s 'for sustaining 4 wax tapers about the body of St. Cuthbert' at Durham church. His lands at Rothbury included the village, Thropton, Snitter and Newtown.

It was his son Robert Fitzroger that ordered the deer park wall put up in 1275 that enclosed part of the forest off from the commoners and ensured the enforcement of those Forest Laws to protect the hart and hind (deer), the boar, hare and wolf. It may sound a bit far-fetched but when the Umfraville family, who built Harbottle castle, were handed their land in Redesdale by William the Conqueror, part of their duties were to protect the neighbourhood from wolves. And marauding Scots.

The other laws were to protect the 'vert' – the trees and vegetation itself, so it was an offence to clean land, fell trees and so on, which was regulated by the officers of the foresters and upheld by the justices in eyre and verderers at forest courts.

By 1539, during the rule of the great huntsman King Henry VIII, Rothbury Forest was included in a survey of the royal woods, game, forests and parks north of the Trent. The others were at Sherwood, Hatfield Chase, Galtres, Middleham, Inglewood, and Teesdale. The combined leaders of each forest lordship could muster 3,911 bowmen, billmen, spearmen and able men with horse and harness. The red deer within the forests at that time numbered 2,067 and the fallow deer 6,352.

In the mid-Fifteenth Century the War of the Roses broke out between the Houses of York and Lancaster and brought 30 years of battles in attempts to wrestle control of the English throne. Between 1455 and the final battle of Bosworth Field in 1485 there were numerous sporadic armed conflicts throughout England.

King Edward IV faced a violent insurrection which started in Yorkshire in 1469 as a protest against 'taxes and abuses of power' and demanding the restoration of Henry Percy to the Earldom of Northumberland in place of John Neville. It was led by the mysterious revolutionary character Robin of Redsdale.

Percy's father, also Henry, had lost his title after being killed fighting Yorkists; the Neville's, who had long held land in Durham at RabyCastle, were close advisors of Edward and happy to put one of their own in his place. It seems unusual, then, that Lord Robert Ogle should become a tentative suspect for being the elusive Robin.

Ogle had been a joint Warden of the East March with Sir Ralph Grey in 1438 and also held the title Lord of Redesdale. It has to be remembered that Redesdale, Tynedale and Hexhamshire were Liberties ran by a Lord of the Manor at that time and not strictly part of Northumberland. But Ogle himself was a Yorkist, a white rose man, and although his tower at Muckle Tosson sat as part of the RothburyForest it seems unlikely that Robert Ogle will have been the man who led a rebel army to defeat a Royal force at the battle of Edgecote Moor in Oxfordshire. However, he did die that year and Robin of Redesdale was reputed to have been killed during the conflict. But Ogle was a supporter of the Nevilles and had been created Baron Ogle in 1461 for following the Yorkist cause so the family of the Three Half Moons may not have been involved at all.

Sir John Conyers of Middleham Castle is named as the prime suspect, but it would seem unusual for him to take on the moniker Robin of Redesdale; Ogle was a friend of his who saw action with him, so we have to look towards a man named Robert in the Rothbury-Otterburn area, hence Lord Robert's involvement.

The Ogles had long been influential in Northumberland. In 1316 a Henry Ogle was a soldier at arms of the garrison at Berwick who wanted compensation from the King for a black horse lost 'in the King's Service' at Kelso. He was paid three years later.

A John Ogle was imprisoned at Newcastle-upon-Tyne for the death of Isabella, daughter of Alan son of Martin de Corbridge in 1278. He was bailed by letters to the sheriff of Northumberland.

During the reign of Edward II Sir John Ogle held the manor and borough of Rothbury 'by service of ½ Knight's Fee' with the hamlets of Newton, Thropton, Snitter and the Forest, with the 'vaccaries' of Green Healey, Pauperhaugh, Thorneyhaugh, Healey, Miruldhurst (?) and Brockleyhurst. In 1416 the Knight Robert Ogle also held lands at Sharperton, Alwinton, Bamburgh, Tynemouth, Felton and Wooler as well as Thursby in Cumberland.

By 1580 the Lord Ogle's tenants were at Bothwell, Trittlington, Conneygarth, Ogle, Hepple, Flotterton, Wharton, Muckle Trewhitt, Little Trewhitt, Little Tosson, Lorbottle, and North Middleton, while the Rothbury Forest then belonged to the Duke of Northumberland – but they'd been hit and spoiled so heavily by Scottish riders – generally the Elliots – that they couldn't pay taxes.

So if we're looking for another suspect, then someone that had lost the title Lord of Redesdale might be a much more likely to become Robin of Redesdale. The great knight Sir Robert Umfraville died in 1437. He had served the Neville Earl of Westmorland but was a Lancastrian and his family were married into the Percys (mind, so were the Nevilles, but that never stopped the intrigue and power struggles). On his death the Umfraville lands, which they had held since around 1120 after allegedly coming over with William the Conqueror, passed to distant relative Sir William Tailboys.

But the Umfravilles hadn't died out; the last lineal male descendent of the ancient Umfraville Earls of Angus didn't pass until 1820 when the Royal Navy Captain John Brand Umfraville died aged 36 at Broomhaugh near Hexham. So there would have almost certainly been even more distant relations called Robert Umfraville in Redesdale at the time and they could be the ones to become the legendary 'Robin Mend-All' – and keen to carry the Redesdale tag.

Another possibility is that Robin of Redesdale was 'a villain called Robin of Riddesdale,' an unknown commoner who was able to stir up trouble and inspire violence. That would certainly place him from within one of the reiver families of the area – one the Halls, Potts, Hedleys, Greens, Dunns, Reeds, Wanless', Coxons or Forsters – or, if you're putting money on Robin coming from the Rothbury Forest and becoming an inspiration for Robin Hood, then maybe one of the Redheads.

Could a Robert Redhead of Holling Hill have been the real man behind the famous story from Sherwood Forest? Nobody really knows.

But if you use a bit of poetic licence it's not that hard to re-imagine Little John as John Little, a Scottish outlaw from the Ewesdale family reset among the villains in the Royal woods. That certainly happened. Friar Tuck a wrang 'un from Brinkburn Priory; Alan-a-Dale Alan of Redesdale, Much the Miller's son from the Thrum…the Merry Men indeed.

Robin Hood was an outlaw and thief. Robbing from the rich to give to the poor could have been from poaching the venison in the walled-off woods from the Lord of the Manor to feed the commoners down in the valley while he would almost certainly have undertaken cattle theft and raids both over the border and on his neighbours in the valleys around, then making his way back to the sanctuary of the Rothbury Forest. The very woods that had acted as a camp and base for William Wallace when he invaded Northern England with his army in 1297 - burning Felton Mill, raiding the countryside and harrying Alnwick during a bloody campaign.

The thieves of Redesdale and Tynedale were certainly bad enough to be excommunicated by the Church in both 1498 and 1512. The Bishop of Durham despised the English highlanders and those who were in particular bother with the church then were Sandy Charlton; Christie, Howey and Atkin Milburn, Laurie, Davie and Sandy Robson; Gilly, George, Rowly and Sandy Dodd, George Marshall and Sandy Hunter.

If you're looking for somewhere particularly lawless to put Robin Hood – or Robin of Redesdale – then the RoyalRothbury Forest is as good a spot as any, though the trees are now all felled and the winds whip in off the cold North Sea to chill the very sandstone of Simonside. To blow away the legends across the heather tops.

THE LEGEND OF THE BUCCLEUCH SWORD

It all started with a bloody feud and it ended with a bloody feud. But the real mystery is how the Buccleuch sword ended up in the hands of the Charltons of Hesleyside Hall in North Tynedale, Northumberland.

When Sir Walter Scott, 5th of Buccleuch and the keeper of Liddesdale, rode on a widow's house at Greenhaugh in Tynedale in May 1595 with a hardened gang of around 300 men he couldn't find any Charltons to murder, so in provocation he fired the house and the widow's corn. Eight days later Buccleuch was back at Boughton where killed four of the Charltons, described as very able and sufficient men, and promised to come back soon and kill some more.

The local English officials were quick to point out Buccleuch's reasons for the attacks. Lord Scrope reckoned it was 'for revenge of an ancient feud' and John Carey went much further. He said that the Scotts had been bragging after a raid that had almost beggared Tynedale and Redesdale but the Charltons had taken their goods back and encouraged their neighbours to 'do the same and not be afraid.' That got Buccleuch's back up, but he had another reason.

'Mary! he makes another quarrel, that long since in a war time, the Tynedale men should go into his country, and there they took his grandfather and killed divers of his country, and that they took away his grandfather's sword, and would never let him have it since. This he says is the quarrel,' wrote a frustrated Carey.

Now Buccleuch's granda was Sir William Scott, of Kirkurd and Buccleuch, who died in 1552 – the same year as his father, Buccleuch's great Granda Walter 'Wicked Watt' Scott, who seems a much more likely candidate for having his sword lifted during a raid. Scott's father, Walter the 4th Buccleuch, died in 1574 when a young Walter was only 9-years-old, so he never really knew the men in his line and probably felt a huge weight of pressure to upkeep the name and notoriety. Any stories that he was told could have been changed or forgotten over time. Maybe his dad had told him tales of how his granda's sword had been stolen as a bedtime tale at Branxholme tower.

Wicked Watt was a man of great action and was heavily involved in a notorious blood feud with the Kerrs following the Battle of Melrose in 1526, being locked up in BlacknessCastle under pain of a huge £10,000 Scots penalty. He was pardoned in 1528 and in 1529 was on an indenture made at Ancrum by the Kerrs Walter of Cessford, Andrew of Ferniehirst, Mark of Dolphinston, George, tutor, of Cessford, and Andrew of Primesideloch, 'for themselves and kin, on the one part;' and Sir Walter himself, of Branxholme, Rob of Allanhaugh, Rob, tutor of Howpaslot, John of Roberton, and Walter of Stirkshaws, 'for themselves and kin, on the other.'

The document outlined that: 'All discords to be forgiven. Walter Scott, of Branxholme, 'shall gang or cause gang, at the will of the party, to the four head pilgrimages in Scotland,' and say a mass for the souls of Andrew Kerr, of Cessford, and those of his company slain in the field of Melrose, and cause a chaplain to say mass for them daily 'when he is disposed,' wherever Walter Kerr pleases, for five years. Mark Kerr, of Dolphinton, and Andrew Ker, of Graden, 'shall gang at the will of the party to the four head pilgrimages of Scotland, and shall gar say a mass' for the souls of James Scot, of Eskirk, and other Scots slain in the field of Melrose, and cause a chaplain to say mass daily 'when he is disposed,' wherever Walter Scot pleases, for three years. The said Walter Scott, of Branxholme, 'shall marry his son and heir upon one of the said Walter Kerr his sisters,' paying a competent portion to the said Walter and his heir. Both parties bound to abide the decree of the six men chosen arbiters in all disputes.' The document was signed by the Kerrs. That was how feuds were supposedly settled at the time. Bur Sir Walter had more trouble brewing, and it was coming from the direction of Northumberland this time.

It was a cold and dark night in the February of 1533 when Sir Thomas Wharton, Sir Rauf Fenwick, Reynold Carnaby, and John Horsley with their 400 men met with Lord Conyers and the Tynedale and Redesdale contingent which numbered around another 1,100 at 'Wauhope' in North Tynedale having obtained licence from the earl of Northumberland to invade Scotland.

At around 8 o'clock they crossed the border at 'Whele Causey,' six miles from Jedburgh, heading on with the intention to raid the laird of Buccleuch in West Teviotdale. Before 11 o'clock, the Tyne and Redesdale riders were sent out on a foray to provoke Buccleuch and the rest left in an ambush, or 'bushment' - another word that seems to have its origins on the Anglo-Scottish border. Sir George Lawson reckoned that Wicked Watt had 'always been a common thief and maintainer of theft' in justification of the raiding party as they 'burnt his granges and steads of corn to his gates, with two towns adjoining, and (took) 400 head of cattle, 40 or 60 prisoners, and as many horses, and have come home in safety. Nothing like it has been done so far with such a company,' he wrote from Warkworth.

The earl of Northumberland was even more detailed in his description of the destruction and blatant attempt to draw out Buccleuch, penning how 'they attacked Branxholme, where the lord of Buccleuch dwells, and set a train for him, "like to his accustomed manner in rising to all frays," but he was not at home. They burnt Branxholme, Whichestre, Whichestre Helme, and Whetley, taking prisoners several of the lord's servants who came out of his gates. They did not leave one house, stack, or sheaf of corn unburnt, outside his gates, 'and thus scrimmaged and frayed, supposing the lord of Buclough to be within three or four miles to have trained him to the bushment.'

With the lands and buildings around about smouldering, smoking and charred black and crackling with heat, the men wiped the grime and soot from their faces as the foraying party and the ambush squad met up to make their way home. Beasts being driven and mooing as the breath from their nostrils rose in the weak light of dawn, the grumble from the line of prisoners – one of whom was 'named Scott, of the kin of the lord of Buccleuch.' Not his son William, then, or surely it would have been noted; but tucked in among the folds of a blanket wrapped over the leather jerkin of one of the Charltons, it has to be presumed, was the fine blade of Andrea Ferrara that he'd lifted during the chaos from the burning of the tower at Branxholme. He must have nipped in and pilfered it, or possibly have taken it off the hostage, which may be more likely.

Perhaps it was a special sword that Buccleuch didn't use for everyday activities, hence why he didn't have it on him at the time. An exceptional weapon.

It is believed that the Italian Ferrara had been brought across to Scotland by James V to craft basket-hilted broadswords of just the type that Wicked Watt would want to possess, and the timeline fits well.

The English headed home through Liddesdale, where Northumberland felt that the inhabitants were 'towards King Henry VIII' and also 'to make the King and Council of Scotland suspect them.' A number of the Liddesdalers offered assistance as the English passed through. Tynedale and Redesdale also settled a couple of old scores by burning a town called Newbiggins, killing two Scotsman and leaving many others with gruesome injuries.

Northumberland was pleased with his work and noted that: 'the towns burnt have not been 'enterprised' in any wars at any time within the mind of man. The lord of Buccleuch has always been a mortal enemy to England, and said about 14 days ago that he would see who durst burn him, with many other cruel words, of which my servants knew before their enterprise.' That attack on Branxholme has surely to be the origin for the story of the stolen sword. Buccleuch did respond with an attack on Northumberland – perhaps incensed that his prized sword had been nicked by a bloody Charlton – but in 1535 he was in trouble with the Scottish crown after being accused of the 'treasonable intercommuning' with Sir Christopher Dacre and other Englishmen for the invasion of Scotland and had a couple of spells of imprisonment in Edinburgh.

Buccleuch was a target for the English during the Rough Wooing period and after Watt had been made the Keeper of Newark Castle for 19 years in 1543, his kinsman's lands at Mydshopp and Thirlstane, and some of his own on the Yarrow, were spoiled by the Fosters and Armstrongs.

That December 'Hob's Robin' Foster was commanded to 'get some of Buccleuch's sheep in EttrickForest' which led to 80 men burning Singley within the forest and driving off 1,400 sheep and two prisoners. Two men were also killed. 100 sheep were given to the Scotsmen in the raiding party and another 40 as recompense to a Scotsman whose horse was killed in the action. 'As Buccleuch reports having got much gold in rewards of the Cardinal, he may the better forego them,' wrote Wharton sarcastically. The Liddesdale Armstrongs had also burned Buccleuch's town called Blackgray, 4 miles from Peebles, among others that night.

The following August the West and Middle Marches of England, 'with certain Scotsmen,' invaded Lord Buccleuch's lands in West Teviotdale, burned the barmkin at Branxholme tower and lifted 600 cattle. Buccleuch's Moss House tower was also smoked that night where 30 prisoners were taken and other places set alight. The Armstrongs and Fosters were burning land belonging to Buccleuch and other Scotts again the following month as the devastation continued, leaving little opportunity to apply a little pressure on the Charltons to return the steel which may have now been gone for over a decade.

Buccleuch was one of the Scottish leaders in their victory at the battle of Ancrum Moor in 1545 and that October his son and heir apparent William agreed an assurance with the Kerrs, Douglases and Rutherfords on one part and the Scotts and Cranston on the other. An order taken for peace (that all may concur against the English) was signed in February 1546 between 'Walter Kerr of Cessford, John Kerr of Ferniehirst, Douglas of Cavers, sheriff of Teviotdale, Douglas of Bonjedburgh and their adherents on the one part, and Sir Walter Scott of Branxholme, Turnbull of Bedrule, John Cranston of that ilk, James Pringle of Tinnes, William Turnbull of Minto and their adherents on the other; also between John Rutherford of Hunthill, Nichol Rutherford of Hundalee, Charles and Richard Rutherford and their friends, on the one part, and Walter Kerr of Cessford, Mark Kerr of Littleden, Kerr of Graden and their friends, on the other,' as attempts to cool the simmering bad blood between the important Border families continued. It had little effect, in the long run, and it was to prove Wicked Watt's undoing in the end.

The 57-year-old was walking up the High Street in Edinburgh on the 4th October 1552 when he was shanked by a backstabber. John Hume of Coldenknowes put his sword through Buccleuch and is famously said to have cried: "Strike! A strike for your father's sake!" to one of the gang of Kerrs he was with. They can't have stabbed Scott too many times because when they heard that the chieftain was still alive, slowly dragging himself along the cobbles in a pool of his own blood, they had to send one of their horsemen back to finish the job with his dagger as they got themselves away from the scene of the crime. So while the Kerr feud finished Wicked Watt, the Charlton feud was one that the 5th Buccleuch was keen to keep going and you can only picture him shaking his head now, some five hundred years later, as the Hesleyside family used the sword to cut their wedding cake.

Maybe if a Scott got to hold the Ferrara blade today, blue bolts of lightening would shoot out of it like Highlander, a mad vision of the years of history rolling back across the moors and hills and heather like a high-speed rewind. To feel the quickening, heart racing like that of a horse, the energy humming in a concrete car park. I'm Walter Scott of the Clan Scott, and there can be only one! Cue the Queen music. Fade to black.

A DACRE! A DACRE!

You'd be surprised how many arguments kicked off in church yards during the riding times. Especially among the local gentry who occupied positions in the local power structure that were always bumping into each other around the gravestones and ranting and raving. Occasionally there were even assassinations in the churches themselves.

Richard Dacre was feeling particularly vengeful one Saturday morning when he came to Carlisle with a gang of Lord Dacre's tenants, from the likes of Gilsland and Burgh, and went into the Cathedral. Richard had taken it upon himself to be Grand Captain of all Cumberland at a recent muster, and he didn't remove his cap to Lord Clifford as he confidently stared down and as they met in the church doorway.

Dacre then came across Sir William Musgrave in the churchyard, walked over, grabbed him by the shoulder and pulled a dagger on him. One of the Laird of Featherstonehaugh's sons jumped between them to prevent Dacre stabbing Musgrave, who jumped back pulling out his own dagger. Dacre and Featherstonehaugh then drew their swords from their scabbards but were pulled apart.

You can imagine the crack: "Come on then!" "Leave it, he's not worth it!" muttered threats and curses. Dacre walked around into the market place shouting the rallying call: "A Dacre! A Dacre!" which saw a large mob join him.

The Carlisle city officials were panicked and the Mayor, with Edward Aglionby and others 'commanded Dacre to avoid the market place.' He left leisurely only when the Carlisle men were ordered to harness their horses, went to his lodgings for dinner, then headed off coolly. The Mayor was so scared that he wanted the protection of Lord Clifford in the castle. The following Saturday Dacre was back with 20 Gilsland men 'in harness for some unlawful purpose' and Lord Clifford sent the Mayor and Aglionby to detain him, but Dacre wanted Clifford to make some proclamation from the market cross. This was in 1538.

The infamous Kinmont Willie Armstrong and the gang he was thieving with rode around shouting 'A Dacre! A Dacre! A red bull! A red bull!' when they attacked the Rickergate in Carlisle one night in March 1600, causing confusion and panic – but it was really quite a serious affair. 300 Johnstons, Armstrongs, Bells, Beatties, Irvings and others had ridden a day foray on the Newton of Irthington and Cammock where they burned houses, barns, corn and property, lifted 40 cattle and 60 sheep, took some prisoners and mutilated other people.

On their way back that night around 140 of the gang hit Scotby just outside Carlisle where they again started fires, took prisoners and stole a further 60 cattle and 50 horses. They then rode down into the city itself – a rare occurrence – where they broke and cut up the posts that held the iron chains for the Eden Bridge, grabbed more hostages, and broke up and smashed doors. They then rode up to the city walls near the castle shouting and bawling into the purple night sky as the castle beacon was set alight to warn the wardenry. Some of those involved were named as Christie Armstrong of Barngliesh, Davie, Will and Geordie Kang Irving, the 'English disobedients' Tom and John Carelton and Kinmont himself, who had been famously broken out of the castle by the Bold Buccleuch just four years earlier.

So you have to wonder if the shouting of the Dacre rally was to make the locals think that it was Naworth that was attacking them rather than Scots riders, or just to add to the general confusion and disorder as men galloped up and down in the moonlit street.

As well as their major holdings in Cumberland, the Dacres also held land in Northumberland, at Morpeth, but that didn't particularly impress the other local gentry. When William Phillope of Morpeth unfortunately 'compared the Dacre's blood to be as good as the Ogle's' in the town in 1583, he was attacked by a gang including the brothers George and John Ogle, sons of James Ogle of Causey, Patrick and Martin Ogle of Tritlington, Alex Ogle, Anthony Milburn and others, and given such a kicking that he later died of his injuries. Perhaps they'd been drinking in one of Morpeth's taverns and had overheard him; whatever the circumstances, it was again pure thuggish mafia-like behaviour from a Northumbrian family that claimed decsent from the Anglian Humphrey Ogle and had produced no less than seven lords and thirty knights. A William Ogle, convicted of a felony, escaped from York castle with a fellow prisoner called William Appleby in 1597, but was recaptured and executed.

Despite what the Ogles thought, the Dacre influence is still felt in Morpeth today. The Howard Earls of Carlisle inherited their lands and titles so when you sit in Carlisle Park and listen to the happy twill of the budgies in the aviary, gazing up at the imposing Courthouse, you're on land given over to us plebs by the Cumbrian aristocracy.

KICKING OFF WITH THE POTTS

When people talk about the footballers that Northumberland has produced, it's the infamous Tynedale reiver names that tend to come up in the conversation – Charlton, Robson, Milburn - but there's a lad from a less well celebrated Redesdale riding family that's making his mark in the game at the minute.

And to give him even more of a local connection, he's related to Rothbury skipper Tom Macpherson. Brad Potts was born in Hexham and got started out in youth football at Wark. He signed junior forms at Carlisle United and broke into the Cumbrian's first team in 2012, the year that also saw him selected for an England u19s game.

Potts made 103 appearances and scored 9 goals in his three years at Carlisle before making the move to Blackpool. His time at the Tangerines saw him clock up 87 starts with 16 goals. The midfielder then moved on to Barnsley in the Championship, where he impressed with 9 goals in 59 games. He is currently playing at Preston North End in the Championship where he has turned out 58 times and scored 7 goals so far.

The Potts, along with the Halls, were probably the most troublesome of the families in the Coquetdale vicinity during the time of the Border Reivers. In fact while most histories of the reivers tend to end shortly after 1603 when King James VI of Scotland ascended to the English throne and set about 'pacifying' the area, the Potts were still involved long after, such as when Thomas Pott of Little Tosson rode up to Upperton in September 1629 and stole 16 ewes from Ralph Arleson.

His namesake, another Thomas Pott, was executed at Harbottle Castle in

1518 after the locals had rioted in an attempt to break him free. Pott was described as 'the principal man, for whom the insurrection was made' by Lord Dacre.

Ten of the 'principal thieves among the highlandsmen of Redesdale' were captured and sent with 80 of Dacre's tenants guarding them to the Rothbury gate – possibly Forestburngate now – to be met by the Morpeth jailer. The thieves' friends and relatives met the party, killed the bailiff of Morpeth and took five hostages as they freed the men and fled off across the border into Scotland for sanctuary among the thieves there. William Pott, another 'principal thief of the great surnames of Redesdale' was hanged at Newcastle in 1528 along with 11 others.

Life in Coquetdale had been tough for a couple of hundred years at that point due to the constant conflict with Scotland. In 1333 the King had to order the delivery of a quantity of wheat to the prioy and convent at Brinkburn as their lands and goods had been utterly destroyed in a Scottish invasion. Seven years later a note from Westminster listed John de Fenwyk, Gilbert de Boroughdon (Burradon), Thomas de Heppescotes (Hepscot) and John de Burton, the parson of the church of Rothbury, as commissioners of Northumberland. Fenwick was excused his position ten days later as he was 'appointed as arrayer and leader of men-at-arms, hobelers (horses) and archers, in the county of Northumberland, against the Scots now in rebellion.' Nicholas de Punchardon (Puncherton) took his place in the commission.

The destruction wreaked by the Wars was devastating and the following year Richard de Horsley, the sheriff of Northumberland, was unable to collect any taxes as 'the lands in that county are so wasted by frequent inroads of the Scots lately coming in warlike manner that he may not levy the said rents, farms and profits,' and he wanted some relief from the treasury.

However, it wasn't just the Scots that were a menace and in 1256, in something like an early episode of Vera, John de Plessetis and Robert de Insula had to lead an enquiry in Northumberland as to whether Thomas Carbonel had killed Nicholas de Rothbury 'by misadventure or by malice.'

There were of course attempts to control the countryside by the March

Laws particular to the border area, though the officials that got to do the job were so ingrained with the local villains, or more often than not related through blood or marriage, that a nepotistic, corrupt system ensued. There was plenty of cash involved in both being the law and to turning a blind eye on occasions that suited.

In 1525 the Earl of Northumberland, Sir Henry Percy, as captain of Berwick, earned 2,000 marks in war time and 1,000 in peace. Vice-warden and lieutenant of the East and Middle Marches Sir Roger Heron 'had the accustomed fees and money from the King's coffers for aid as often as he required,' while Sir Edward Radcliffe and Sir Roger Fenwick, as keepers of Redesdale and Tynedale respectively, were earning 1,000 marks a year plus the other fees 'accustomed with their roles.'

Sir William Eure was paying out the following in wages at the time: £40 to his four deputies for the marches. Sir John at Tynedale was getting £40 and John Ogle £5. Hugh Ridley received £3 6s 8d and Thomas Errington the same. In Coquetdale, Percival Selby, George Ogle and Edward Gallon were getting 4 marks; as was John Beadnell. The four un-named warden-sergeants for the Marches were getting £8, a porter at Harbottle got £4 and the constable at Harbottle received £10.

The highest ranking official to bring border justice into Rothbury was Sir Cuthbert Radcliffe of Cartington, who was no doubt feeling quite powerful and influential in 1541 when he was penning letters to the Scottish King James V as the deputy warden for the Middle March.

In the January Radcliffe had met Kerr of Ferniehurst, the Scotish Middle March warden, at Alwinton church and handed over a number of Fosters from Cumberland who had been sent over by Sir Thomas Wharton, the deputy of the English West March, for a great raid 'amounting to £80 sterling.' That led to the redress of two 'attempts by Liddesdale' and the warden of Scotland 'promised to answer for both Liddesdale and Teviotdale' as they attempted to bring the rule of law.

But Radcliffe wrote from Alnwick castle to the Scots' monarch in the July complaining that there had been no justice on bills from Liddesdale (no surprise there) and 'no redress.' He said he countrymen were complaining to him and that a 'heinous attempt' by the Liddesdalers – Armstrongs, Elliots, Nixons and Crosers in the main – 'as robberies, murders, spoilings, and breaking of Haughton castle, scaling it with ladders, riding in great numbers,' and asked the King 'to give straight commandment for redress.'

Later that month he was telling Sir Anthony Brown that he had attended a Day of Truce at Jedburgh and that on Tuesday 9th August he would make the officers of Scotland 'come to Rothbury, where (he will) make them like answer.' So Ratcliffe was holding a Day of Truce at Rothbury in August 1541, the only example that I have been able to find of this happening.

The Scottish officers that he was demanding come to the village were something of Border heavyweights, being Archibald Douglas, 6th Earl of Angus, for the Scottish East March, Andrew Kerr of Ferniehurst for the Middle and Robert Maxwell, 5th Lord Maxwell, for the West March.

Whereabouts they met to do their business in Rothbury is unrecorded and I have been unable so far to track down the list of charges that were brought. What is for sure is that the Potts will have rode into the village to be there and hear what was going on, either in claims they had in for losses or charges of cattle theft laid on them by the Scots. Drinking in a local tavern and setting down their helmets and swords with a clank at the door, laughing and raucous around the tables as the ale flowed in pewter mugs. They maybe even got a ball out and had a kick around on the village green, because the reivers were notable early exponents of the sport.

Perhaps that fighting spirit lives on today in battling Brad.

'BLACK WALTER' SELBY AND THE MITFORD GANG

If you were going to give the Black Walter Selby story the full Hollywood treatment, you'd want to cast someone like Joe Pesci as the main man. Getting some of that swagger and psychotic stage presence would be essential for the big screen, for sure. Stick him in some chain mail, put the black and gold crest on a tabard and chuck a kettle helmet on. Because Black Walter was a character just like the one Pesci played in Goodfellas, albeit six hundred years earlier and set in the moors and heather hills of rural Northumberland.

To understand men like Walter Selby you have to understand the criminal mindset portrayed in all of those popular mafia movies – there is no difference. Be it Black Walter Selby or Sonny Red Indelicato, money, power, influence, respect and intimidation are all that matters. Respect especially. What's the point of walking into a room if you're not going to turn heads and cause a frightened hush? You want to be a presence whether it's in 1970s New York or 1310s Morpeth. No matter.

Black Walter was the chief enforcer in the Mitford Gang headed up by Gilbert Middleton, who was the keeper of the castle whose ruined walls still stand today on a mound above the river Wansbeck.

Northumberland had been subjected to a concerted campaign of devastation by the Scots for a number of years as the Wars of Independence led to burnings, killings and trampling crops. This was done on purpose to starve the local population; take their cattle, burn their corn, kill anyone that gets in the way. It was a series of wars of attrition designed to demoralise and dehumanise.

When the Scottish defeated Edward II at Bannockburn in 1315, it was a trigger for men like Middleton, of Cramlington and Hartley, and Selby, whose property included a fortified tower at Seghill, lands at Felling and Alnham and a hall at Biddlestone in Coquetdale courtesy of his marriage to a daughter of Sir Hugh de Laval, to start taking their destiny in their own hands.

The gang, including the likes of Middleton's brother, John, of Swinburn Castle, his cousin Sir John Middleton, the lord of Belsay, and Selby's brother John started to roam the countryside on horseback asking local farmers if they'd like to join the gang. If they said no or put up any kind of fight, the gang would destroy all of their crops, kill or steal their stock, murder relatives and take them prisoner to the dungeons of Mitford castle until a cash ransom was paid. It was a simple, uncomplicated and effective racket. Black Walter used to hide his cut of the stolen cattle at the rocky crevice known as Selby's Cove at the back of Simonside, conveniently situated between Mitford and Biddlestone.

Gilbert had been incensed when the King, Edward II, arrested his cousin Sir John for 'speaking sharply with him about the Marches,' so he raided Cleveland and 'took all the cattle in Northumberland except for Alnwick, Bamburgh and Norham.' They attacked TynemouthCastle in another incident. But the outlaw gang got cocky and pushed things too far though. Later in 1317 they laid in wait and kidnapped a party of church Cardinals at Rushyford in CountyDurham. Among them were Lewis Beaumont and his brother Henry. Lewis was on his way to be consecrated as the important Bishop of Durham. The gang took money, goods, horses and hostages back to Mitford and threw them in the dungeon as the gang awaited a big payday for their release.

It didn't come, however, and Gilbert – who'd you'd probably have Robert de Niro playing in the movie – was captured along with the bulk of the gang when the King's forces took the Castle that December. Gilbert Stapleton was one of the crew killed during the raid while Middleton and his brother were taken to the Tower of London and hanged, drawn and quartered. The four sections of Gilbert's body were sent to Newcastle, York, Bristol and Dover.

David, the son of Nicholas Middleton, and John Birden were delivered to the Sheriff of Northumberland, William Riddell, as hostages by Black Walter Selby in May 1318, possibly as bargaining chips. David had been a hostage in the Tower but was freed and fought in the Scottish Wars on the English side.

William Middleton was captured in MitfordCastle along with the others and was imprisoned at Newcastle-upon-Tyne. He had been captured by Scots during an invasion but had escaped from them and took sanctuary with a prior before being redelivered to the Sherriff in 1322.

The wily Walter escaped and hid out in Horton pele for a while before flitting over the Border into Scotland. He joined up with the Scots and when King Robert the Bruce came burning and killing in Northumberland again the following year, he took and left Selby in charge of Mitford Castle as his army headed South.

Walter was holed up for three long years in the walls before he surrendered to the Sheriff of Northumberland and was sent down to the Tower of London himself where he was imprisoned until 1327.

Ironically, Lewis Beaumont, the Bishop of Durham, took his lands in Felling – which had been in the hands of the Selby family since the early 13th Century – because his 'enemy and rebel, Selby, had become a liegeman of Robert Bruce' and for his part in taking the Bishop prisoner.

King Edward III pardoned Selby in March 1329 in an agreement with Robert Umfraville, the late Earl of Angus from Harbottle castle, Ralph Graystoke, then baron of Graystoke, and John Eure, that saw his lands reinstated. The Bishop wouldn't let the matter lie, however, and in 1342 he was accusing Selby of several burnings and homicides near Sedgefield back in 1317 and 'adhering to the King's enemies of Scotland.'

Selby had spent this time fighting against the Scots and at some points he was in the service of Edward Baliol. The complicated nature of the Border meant that Scottish nobles such as the Comyns, in Tynedale, the Umfravilles in Redesdale, the Haggerstons, the Hangingshaws and others held land in Northumberland, while Selby himself was awarded land in Roxburghshire for his exploits.

In the March of 1346 Thomas de Lucy, Peter Tilyol, Black Walter Selby, John Haverington (Etherington) of Caldecoates and Clement Skelton were ordered to find out who had carried out a huge cross border raid. A number of 'malefactors and disturbers of the peace, crossing the boundaries of county Cumberland, entered by armed force the town of Blamyre in the barony of Kirkaundres in Scotland,' and had stolen cattle belonging to John Turpin, John Stager and other men. It was a big haul, coming to over £1,000, while other crimes had been committed.

Selby was placed in command of the Liddell Strength, a wooden motte and bailey tower at Carwinley in Cumbria, no doubt to curtail the border raids while the King and the bulk of the English army were across in France at the siege of Calais. There was probably a low lying mist obstructing the views that October when a Scottish army of 12,000 attacked.

A couple of arrows hitting men up on the spiked wooden battlements and slumping them backwards. A strange unease among the cattle in the encampment, a grey and miserable sky; then the shouting, the flames and smoke, the moans of dying men and the crash of swords.

The Scottish King, David Bruce, had Selby dragged to him when the fortress was taken. Probably bleeding and scarred from fighting, his face flecked in blood and blackened with soot, his mail clanking as he was dropped to his knees.

It's said that the old villain begged for his life. To go back to the Hollywood scenario, you'd have Pesci making some big speech about how he'd fought for David's father and Scotland in the past, something atmospheric with crows cackling and a wind rustling trees. Or maybe you'd just get those two seconds of realization that Tommy has in Goodfellas before he gets whacked. An axe instead of a pistol. "Oh, no…." Thump. Beheaded.

BRAVEHEART IN CLENNELL

Given its dangerously close position to Scotland up in the isolated hills of Upper Coquetdale, Clennell Hall was probably little more than a pele tower in the late 13th century, which was possibly constructed from large timbers rather than the more permanent stone that would follow later.

The manor was held by Thomas Clennell by service 'of 1/2 knight's fee, a contribution of 6s. 8d. for the guard at Alnwick castle and 15d. for cornage.' John Burradon held nearby Burradon for a knight's fee, 13s. 4d. for the guard and 15d. cornage. A knight's fee was a unit of land the King deemed sufficient to support his feudal tenants-in-chief.

In Northumberland this was problematic due to the armies that marched over them during the ongoing Scottish Wars. The lands owned by the powerful Umfravilles at Harbottle were regularly worth nothing in rents after being destroyed by Scottish invasion forces and Alwinton had been 'wasted by the Scots' at the time.

Thomas Clennell was important enough of a knight to be gifted two bucks from the King's Forest in the summer of 1283. The next person on the same document is interesting, as Robert de Bruce – father of King Robert - then earl of Carrick, was granted 12 bucks from the same woods that were held by the keeper Geoffrey Neville.

This was, of course, before the enmity that was stirred up between the two nations in the 1290s as King Edward I – Longshanks, the Hammer of the Scots – sought to marry off his son Edward II with 3-year-old Margaret, Maid of Norway, the heir to the Scottish throne, thus handing him control over Scotland.

The poor child died after landing at Orkney that year a series of legal wranglings took place in Berwick and Newcastle until John Baliol, the Lord of Galloway, was crowned King of Scotland in 1292 after swearing fealty to Edward.

An English invasion in 1296 after the Scots failed to provide troops for an English invasion of France led to the long running series of wars that would run in three long spells until 1357, with the borderers on both sides of the Cheviot hills bearing the brunt of the brutality.

In 1301 Thomas Clennell, along with John Swinburne, Richard Horsley, and Nicholas Puncherton, were ordered to choose and assemble 1,300 footmen from Northumberland. Thomas and Richard were to march them to the Monarch at Linlithgow, but the order was rescinded in the December as the King 'did not need them at present.'

There are just a few traces left by the kind of men that made up Clennell's army left in the records, but some local Coquet men definitely served in the Wars. In 1298, following William Wallace's invasion of Northumberland, John, the son of William de Thropton was pardoned for the death of Adam, son of John, son of Michael de Netherwhich, a Scot, 'by reason of his services in Scotland' in a proclamation from Carlisle. Another pardon, issued from Dunipace near Falkirk, excused Michael, son of Robert de Thropton, for the death of Adam de Colewell and his outlawry for the same 'by reason of his service in Scotland.' They were literally getting away with murder.

John de Thropton was arrested in York in 1313 along with his client John, son of Robert of Glanton in a dispute over land in Whittingham and Thrunton concerning his late wife Idonia and Robert de Esslington. John de Thropton was an attorney as well as a war veteran and Westminster ordered the justices of the bench to 'not put them in default' after they'd been locked up for eight days and had missed their appearance before the court.

By 1319 Thomas Clennell and Robert de Thropton were just two of the 'men of the county of Northumberland' who were granted '40 tuns of wine in aid to their maintenance in consideration of the damages suffered by them by the frequent inroads of the Scots and by divers ransoms paid by them to the Scots.'

Others, of names that are instantly recognisable to Northumbrians today, who were handed the aid by Richard de Emeldon, the Newcastle mayor, included William de Shafthowe (Shaftoe), Thomas de Swethehop (Sweethope), William de Herle (Hall) of Redesdale, Roger de Simounbourne (Simonburn), Alan de Erington (Errington) of Corbridge, William Gray of Denum Peter de Urde (Ord) and John de Corbrigg (Corbridge).

Those not so familiar today that had been 'impoverished by the Scots' included Robert de Coventre, John de Normanvil, John Turpyn, John de Shupton, Henry de Akdon, William de Echewyk, Roger de Chemington of Chilbourn, Robert de Merington, Robert de Bollesdon, John de Rollesdon, William Tulet, Richard de Dodhou, William Freser, Nicholas de Eland, Thomas de Normanvill, William de Inghowe, Thomas de Karliolo of Swarland, William de Caldewell, Robert de Milneburn (possibly Milburn?), John de Karliolo, and John de Kynton.

Robert, son of Alan de Seton, was another who received the wine; the Setons obviously became strong followers of Robert the Bruce with Sir Christopher Seton being a brother-in-law that was brutally executed in London in 1306, so the complicated nature of landownership, blood ties and nationality that were so long blurred on the border are easily seen here.

Those lands had been fired and destroyed, crops trampled and animals killed and stolen, but for those such as Thomas Clennell that pulled on their armour in the wars, the rewards could be great. If you've ever tried on chain mail and helmets at an English Heritage day at a local castle then you'll have just some idea of how cumbersome and heavy the kit was and how difficult it must have been to fight in.

Wielding a double-handed broad sword in a battle with just a slit to see through in their helmet and their breathing heaving and laboured, the knights of Northumberland must have witnessed, and played their part in, any amount of carnage. Just keep swinging must have been the order of the day, clanking, slipping in mud and blood, feeling the blade tear through gristle as you forced it in to agonised screams.

Thomas Clennell and Aline Sweethope had a claim on William de Killum's land at Kilham in 1334 ahead of his son Patrick. Thomas was a kinsman of William and Aline his sister, and they had been named his heirs. After two years they were taken by the King anyway, and held by the lord of Wark-on-Tweed – the marvelously named Sir William de Monte Acuto.

John de Thropton was granted an annuity of 10l. by the exchequer of Edward II or the equivalent in land for life around 1340, but he surrendered his letters patent and and they were cancelled and handed to John de Chesterfield 'for good service done.' Sometimes you win, sometimes you lose, and sometimes you look at a small bloke in tartan with long, wild ginger hair, his face painted blue, and wonder: "What's with the mad Australian accent and generic Celtic music?" Braveheart, my arse.

IN THE MAD MEAD HALL AT HROTHGARBURGH

On the Christmas morning of 1980, as I sat in my pyjamas by the tree surrounded by torn paper, I un-wrapped a book gifted by my uncle Henry. It was a beautifully illustrated hardback copy of Heroes & Ogres.

Henna was a great, tall, bearded uncle who wore ex-army jumpers, moleskin pants and brown hiking boots and led us on huge walks over the moors across tangled heather and through woods with sticks, turned over rocks to show us slow worms and ants nests, used a spent adder skin as a bookmark. His hair was shaved short and I recall being unable to grasp hold of it while sitting on his shoulders as a child. His research had led him to believe that the Taits had originated from the mudflats of Jutland in Denmark, sailing across in longboats to settle in Britain with one of the waves of Scandinavian immigration.

He may well have been correct; the personal name Teitr was found carved in runes on a stone in Tveito in Norway dated to approximately 600AD. Jan Teit and the Bear is a Shetland legend, a Teit was a champion of King Harald of Denmark who battled King Hring of Norway, and another an oarsman in an epic Viking poem, while others appear in Icelandic folk tales.

The classic story of Beowulf and the Monster of the Mere appears in my copy of Heroes & Ogres that sits beside me now on the desk some 40 years later as I type. It's the first story and, along with the dark tale of Grettir and the Ghostly Glamm, is probably my favourite. This version has Hrothgar, a chieftain of the Danes, in his great hall at Heorot being tormented by the green and slimy monster, Grendel, coming from the lake to slaughter his warriors and the brave Beowulf who killed the monster and its even more terrifying mother with his magic sword. There are a number of variations of the tale and in one, known as the Hrólfr Kraki saga, it's said that Hrothgar leaves Denmark in the charge of his younger brother Halga and moves to Northumbria.

The first of the Anglians had landed on the Northumberland, or as it was then the Bernician (or Bernaccian to the locals) shoreline across the wild North Sea from Denmark in around 547. They were led by Ida, or Ida the Flame-Bearer as he became known to the local Britons. He is reputed to have burned their hill fort Din Guayrdi at Bamburgh on the rocky igneous outcrop by the beach as he stormed their defences. No doubt a number of round houses and farms were fired too by the sea-borne invaders, though some histories speculate that a number of Angeln warriors had earlier been drafted in to Bernicia as mercenaries to fight the Picts and Scotti from the North, as had happened with the Saxons in the South at Kent where the legendary brothers Hengist and Horsa fought for Vortigern, the King of the Britons, before turning on him. When Ida the Flame-bearer had forced out the Bernaccian British Celtic leader Morgan Bulc, 'Thunderbolt,' he established his own defensible fortress and capital at Bamburgh, then called Bebbanburgh.

If the chieftain Hrothgar was one of King Ida's Danish warrior band that had sailed on Northumbria, then perhaps you'd expect him to be one of the leaders to push on deeper into the country from the coastal beachhead they had established to set up land of his own. To establish a burgh, as it were. Hrothgarburgh. The likelihood is that boats came down the coast and were sailed up the Coquet, as was the tactic of the times, rather than marching across country.

Had he arrived in the Coquet Valley at what is now Rothbury, and it is a possibility, then Hrothgar and his men would have found themselves surrounded by dense woods and Celtic encampments, the ramparts of the ancient Iron Age forts at Lordenshaws, Tosson, Old Rothbury and West Hills high on the purple slopes above the river. They would have encountered a people that followed a Warrior God named Coccid, or Coccidius to the Romans that hadn't conquered them during their earlier invasion and occupation, and a shamanic tradition of applied animism, water deities and totem creatures. A relief carving of Coccid on the grey stone at Yardhope shows the God with a small round shield and spear, so that would give some idea of their weapons. With faces painted blue and dressed in woollen black and white tartans? Who knows for sure. They were earlier known as the Votadini tribe, and their lands had stretched from the Firth of Forth to the Tyne.

If the East Anglian King Raedwald's famous ship burial treasure trove at Sutton Hoo is anything to go by, then the locals can't fail to have been impressed by the glistening helmets with face plates, the metal work on the swords and shields, the sheer dazzling craftsmanship of the weaponry that the men on the boats carried. The small gold square known as the Bamburgh Beast gives us some indication of how spectacular you'd expect Hrothgar and his men to look as they traversed up the misty water, the snap of branches and cackle of crows making them wary at each bend and meander of the river.

Before the Angles erected their intricately carved yellow sandstone cross at Rothbury to mark their conversion to Christianity, they had followed the old Gods of the Heathen religion such as Woden, Thunor and Tiw. It is unrecorded exactly where the 8th century Rothbury cross was discovered while building work was being undertaken at the All Saints' Church in 1850, but the site may still be highly significant. If the intertwined lattice work, magical animals and biblical scenes that adorned the cross did stand some fourteen feet high as has been suggested, then it would have dominated what was then the centre of the village.

It seems logical, then, that the earliest Angles that came down from Bamburgh to settle in the valley would have built their Mead Hall there, at the high point of the Haa Hill overlooking the river. Maybe it was the first big wooden structure that started the village, where Hrothgar and his men sought sanctuary, feasted and drank in the warmth of the flames that flickered orange up the walls on a dark evening leaving them wondering what was in the black of the shadows or the howl of the winds whipping down the hillside. They were, it has to be remembered, strangers in a strange green, wet and fertile land and no doubt they twirled their Thor's hammer amulets just a little tighter in their fingers on a star-splattered crisp winter night as the frosts painted the grass white and the locals launched another attack. Because there was a lot of resistance from the British to the Anglian expansion from their coastal Kingdom of Lindisfarne and Bamburgh; those of Rheghed, Elmet and other native British tribes spent at least 60 years joining in confederations to battle the Anglians of Bernicia, who had joined with the kingdom of Deira by around 613 under to the great leader Æthelfrith as Northumbria started to become a large military power on the island. This power encouraged rivals, and Æthelfrith was killed in one of the seemingly continual battles of the so-called Dark Ages.

When people talk of a 'backs-to-the-wall' fight, it conjures up images of a desperate scrap. But the phrase took on a quite literal meaning at one little-remembered but important battle in Northumberland, where heaven became hell for an invading Welsh/British army. In 635, Hadrian's Wall was still largely intact and an impressive 20 foot tall divisive structure cutting through the heart of the county. The Romans had left Northern Britain a couple of centuries earlier, meaning it was already on its way to becoming an ancient monument. But it was to prove invaluable to the Northumbrian Prince Oswald, who was a descendent of the Angles who had been brought up by Scottish monks on Iona.

The Celtic Welsh and dispersed British, under Cadwallon of Gwyned, had slaughtered the Northumbrian King Edwin and his son at a battle near Doncaster in Yorkshire in 633, which led to the division of the kingdom which at the time ran from the Humber to the Forth and was one of the most powerful in the whole of Britain.

With Northumbria divided into its former kingdoms of Bernica and Deira and the bloodshed continuing for two years in a desperate power struggle, it fell on to the shoulders of 29-year-old Oswald to return to Bamburgh, the ancient seat of power and capital of the kingdom, to re-united the divided lands, claim the crown and bring the new religion of Jesus Christ with him.

Oswald was the younger brother of Eanfrid, nephew of the dead King Edwin, an heir to the throne who had also fallen under the sword of a Celt. Step up our hero, who is reputed to have brought some Scots fighters with him as he prepared for what would be the Northumbrian equivalent of The Alamo. Oswald assembled his army at Bamburgh and marched them across the county into Tynedale to a spot four miles north of Hexham – almost certainly passing through Rothbury on the way.

The Northumbrian army chose a spot in from of the wall to face their enemy, who also included an army of Mercians and outnumbered them, which was to prove a stroke of tactical genius. Not only could the Northumbrians not be out flanked, but the invaders would have to channel through a narrow pass between Brady's Crag and the Wall to get at them.

Oswald was a devout Christian and is reputed to have had a vision the night before the battle where Saint Columba foretold victory. The Prince also led his army with a wooden cross that was placed in the ground among them as they awaited the enemy advance – a spot that is now occupied by St Oswald's Church. Perhaps the carnage made his followers keen to follow new God. The word of the Christian faith was spreading throughout Northumbria and by 674 Wilfred would found the important monastery at Hexham. The Anglian influence has been such that Wilfred would probably catch the Northumbrian accent today – he would certainly understand and while the odd word might be strange, he'd get the gist, the Germanic tone and intonation.

Whatever happened that fateful day with Oswald will never really be known, but the British/Welsh were routed and hacked down as they fled by Northumbrians keen to avenge the two years of suffering that they had endured at the hands of their enemy.

Cadwallon was reputed to have been slaughtered near the Rowley Burn south of Hexham and the Northumbrian victory was decisive. The battle site has forever after been known as Heavenfield and is just off the B6318 Military Road with the St Oswald's tea rooms nearby for a convenient cuppa, should you wish to step back in history and remember a time when Northumbrian's backs were really up against the wall.

So it's just another legend, a tale of wonder and intriguing possibility, a beguiling bedtime story. Maybe there is a Coquetdale hoard just sleeping under patient dark earth to be turned by a plough. Perhaps Hrothgar was the Danish giant of Beowulf legend that terrified the local population from the Elsdon mote hill, rather than the much later Earl Siward the Dane, a Viking whose base was in York. Or could it just be Henna striding over the hills, his beard bristling out under a helmet, taking Billsmoor in two long steps with a spear.

DE NEVILLE, PENRITH CASTLE AND HOTSPUR

You can be sure that Ralph Neville will have looked his best when he met with the Scottish nobles to work out a treaty for the preservation of the towns of Penrith in England and Dumfries across the Border in the November of 1399.

Penrith, in Cumbria, had been especially burned out and completely destroyed on a number of occasions throughout the previous century as invading Scottish armies had repeatedly left the town charred and crackling in glowing, smoking, orange cinders.

So Neville, the earl of Westmorland, will have wanted to make an impression and probably donned his full knights' regalia – carrying his steel helmet, donning chain mail over his shoulders, wearing a full tabard emblazoned with the striking de Neville arms of a white saltire on a red background. He would certainly have strode tall into the meeting with his long hair brushed back and his beard washed carrying, as he did, the licence of King Henry IV as Marshal of England to deal with the matter. But Neville had another reason for wanting to impose himself in matters on the Borders, however - his cousin was the famous Harry Hotspur.

The dashing son of the Duke of Northumberland was probably a personality something akin to *Flashheart* in the Blackadder TV series; you can imagine him making girls swoon at Court, knocking back wine with wild abandon, telling raucous jokes and slapping his knee in a theatrical style. *Huzzar!* It must have been a tough act to keep up with.

Neville had been appointed joint Governor of Carlisle castle with Sir Thomas Clifford in 1385 and the following year was appointed joint Warden of the English West March, also with Clifford. Percy was made warden of the English East March in 1384 and after a number of military expeditions abroad, had famously battled the Scots at Otterburn in 1388. Percy's home was the impressive and stunning Warkworth Castle on the Northumbrian coast, while it is believed that Neville had just started construction of the rectangular, practical defensive red sandstone castle at Penrith around that time to further protect the town, as he knew just how little weight treaties really carried.

It all seems somewhat ironic then that I should take up a volunteer monitor role at Penrith when my maternal great x3 grandfather James Scott and his family had been the last people to live in the gatehouse of Warkworth castle before the Ministry of Works – fore-runner to English Heritage – took over the building in 1921. It completes some strange centenary circle that I don't really grasp, but must have some kind of cosmic bearing, if you believe it that kind of thing. If James had looked after his building for the Percys, then my role would be to help preserve in just some small way the legacy of the Nevilles; the two great rival aristocratic families of the North.

Penrith was in a unique position in that it had belonged to the Scottish King Alexander from around 1249. In 1270 Geoffrey de Neville and Guychard de Charrun were ordered to inquire whether the King of Scotland and his men of Penrith and Salkeld should have had common pasture in the park at Plumpton or any rights in nearby InglewoodForest. When Roger de Lancaster, the steward of the Forest, arrested some of the King of Scotland's men and detained them in Carlisle castle for trespassing in Inglewood, the English King Edward I 'Longshanks' had Adam de Gesemuth and the prior of Tynemouth intervene. Robert de Neville, John de Oketon and Geoffrey de Neville were also involved in investigating the matter which was becoming an international incident.

When King Alexander died in 1286, John Balliol became the Scottish King and he retained control of the English lands in Penrith, Sowerby and Tynedale. Plenty of Scottish lords owned English land – it was little wonder that the local borderers didn't really know who to fight for during the Wars between the countries.

The Scots must really have liked Penrith because when it reverted to the English Crown and the long running series of conflicts that became known as the Wars of Scottish Independence kicked off in 1296, they destroyed, fired and killed in the town several times. It was as if the scorched earth policy was designed to drive the locals of the land so they could reclaim it. But then the English would hit back in the other direction, burning, killing and devastating crops and cattle.

Penrith was burned in 1314 and the King gave £20 and 24 oaks from Inglewood for rebuilding 'two mills, two bakehouses, and a prison burnt and wholly destroyed by the Scotch rebels lately invading that county.' The town went up in flames again in Scottish invasions in 1342, 1345 and 1380 *at least*. No wonder Neville felt it necessary to construct the castle.

And now I have the privilege and responsibility of going down once a month to check over the old walls, to tidy the signage and look out for the old building, acutely aware of Harry Percy snorting in derision, probably making an inappropriate comment, throwing his cloak over his shoulder and swinging away on a rope. But then he'd always claim that Warkworth is the greater fortress. Whatever, Hotspur, whatever.

A BODY SNATCHER IN ROTHBURY?

Old Lewe Wintrip knew how to deal with the devil.

The wizened but wise bloke from the Rothbury forest wasn't daunted when he was confronted by the terrible apparition of the Garleigh Ghost one night on his way over the moors back to his farm in the woods.

He drew a circle in the ground with his walking stick and three times asked what the spirit was and what was its business. The phantom replied once in an eerie low tone then vanished in a flash of light. Remember that; it may save you someday!

The Garleigh Ghost is probably the most famous of the paranormal activities around Rothbury and Coquetdale. David Dippie Dixon reckoned that the ghost had been seen in the vicinity of the railway as 'a gigantic form enveloped in fire stalking noiselessly' in around 1888. He wrote that it had also been seen traditionally as a 'clocker an' burds,' though what that means, I don't really know, though it sounds ominous.

Dixon believed that the bodies of criminals had been buried at the crossroads where the fingerpost stood at the bottom of the first bank back in antiquity, though if the gallows had been at Gallowfield Brae, as you would imagine, it seems a long way to cart a body.

The Garleigh Ghost was still talked about in our youth in the 1970s. We loved to spook ourselves with tales of the Black Dog, of Grey Ladies and headless horsemen, of Druid sects performing rituals in the woods. I asked my father if he'd ever seen a ghost and he said that there had been an apparition on Garleigh once when he was a kid, but it had been dismissed as a prank by students from NewcastleUniversity.

A less famous Coquetdale supernatural event that may also have been a prank was the Burradon Ghost. At Lark Hall in 1800 there was a poltergeist that smashed plates, glasses and teaware from the shelves while tables and chairs danced about the room and scissors, bottles, and wooden dishes flew through the air. Mr. Turnbull, a Rothbury butcher, rented the farm and the hind and his family lived next door. When the Reverend Lauder, a minister at Harbottle visited, a Bible 'moved from the window in a circular manner into the middle of the room and fell at his feet.' Though the hind was suspected, nothing was ever proven in the strange affair.

The ghost of John Green is said to come out and celebrate on the street in Thropton in joyous times. When the gravestone of John Green, an old Thropton family who had the pele tower in the village back in the 16th century, was discovered in some bushes it was incorporated into the modern stonework at the Meadows. The inscription reads:

John Green of Thropton died April 11 1731 aged 92 years.
Roger son of John Green of Thropton died Nov. 30 1765.

It may not be the ghost of father John Green that is restless, but that of another relation, John Green of Thropton, who was drowned and swept away in the flooded Coquet on the 18th November, 1789. He was crossing the Black Burn between Rothbury and Framlington when the gushing brown water from a heavy rain the night before pulled him and his horse under. Though the horse got out, John was lost in the current.

While tales of mysterious and unexplained goings on from the other side can make you shudder, coming face to face with a notorious mass murderer could be just as chilling - and that's just what happened to a visitor to Rothbury in 1856.

While stopping at Mrs. Miller's in the Market Square, a Mr. Lomax of Rotherham claimed that a 'cadaverous-looking old man, who impressed us all as being very strange,' came in asking for a bed for the night.

Although Mrs. Miller said she was full, the old man said he'd walked from Wooler, was 'sair tired' and asked for a chair to sit down in. Mr. Lomax took pity on the man for his 'pathetic appeals' and gave up his child's bedroom, though the man wouldn't be drawn into conversation and wouldn't show his face.

They were woken on a couple of occasions during the night as the stranger firstly gave an 'unearthly yell' and they discovered him with his 'head enveloped in the bed clothes, sighing heavily, and repeating in broken accents the Lord's Prayer.' Later they were woken by 'very different cries—resembling those of stentorian men, women, infants, and others' at different times.

The following morning a neighbouring woman asked if they'd had a disturbed night's sleep. Her husband and another man had recognised the stranger and had followed him that morning to Weldon Bridge where he met, apparently by arrangement, a man who had escaped from the gallows. The man, she said, was 'Hare, the murderer.'

The Northern Irishman William Hare along with his criminal partner William Burke had famously terrorised Edinburgh as the 'Body snatchers.' They were reputed to have murdered around 16 people in 1828 and sold their bodies for medical study. When they were brought to justice, Hare turned King's Evidence for an acquittal and his mate was hanged.

Hare was released and taken to Dumfries, probably en route back to Ulster, when he was recognised and around 800 people started a riot. He was next sighted two miles from Carlisle and heading towards Newcastle by a coachman, then he was gone. That was the last verified sighting of William Hare in February 1829.

Nobody really knows where he went after that; some have speculated back to Ireland, others to Australia, or London, or Canada. Others say he wandered the countryside as a blind beggar.

Perhaps they were right. Maybe it was the notorious William Hare that had spent a tortured, sleepless night in Rothbury 27 years after his release from justice.

Old Lewe Wintrip might have struggled to deal with meeting that one.

JOHN LUNN - SWORD AND GUN

When Robert Bowey died at Rothbury in the October of 1873, there was a three volley salute fired over his grave as they laid the coffin in the ground.

Bowey was a volunteer in the No. 8 (Rothbury Battery) of the Percy Artillery Volunteers. His coffin had been carried by four gunners from the battery, and his busby and belt where placed on top. The firing party was under the command of Sergeant-Major George Grey.

While the men no doubt looked impressive in their uniforms, the Northumberland militias were really something like a 19th Century Dad's Army – though it wasn't the Germans that they feared invading Britain, but the Napoleonic French.

Just like the TV depiction of the Second World War Home Guard units, the officers of the militia were drawn from the local gentry – landowners, farmers and the like. The Captain Mainwaring of the Coquetdale Rangers, a volunteer cavalry raised in 1799, was commander Thomas Selby of Biddlestone. Mr. Clennell at Harbottle was another officer who paraded his troops on the grass in front of the ruins of the castle each week and called a muster roll. When he got to John Lunn, the reply 'sword and gun,' was shouted back by the volunteers. Another unit known as The Coquetdale Troop of Volunteer Cavalry was also raised in the locality. The Rangers were dissolved in 1821. The Cheviot Legion – later the Royal Cheviot Legion - consisting of both cavalry and infantry, were from neighbouring Glanton and the Breamish valley, with their headquarters at Wooler.

William Davy was the bugler of the Coquetdale Rangers in Rothbury and in January 1804 there was a false alarm that had him scurrying to get his jacket and boots on, tripping over himself in his panic to get out of the door and summon up the spit to get the noise out of his instrument. The warning beacons had been lit on the Northumberland coast and spread inland; when the flames at Ros Castle were spotted glowing in the dark, it was time for Davy to spring into action and raise the local troop to muster and assemble.

They had been training every week on the Haugh at Rothbury (and no doubt assembling to sample the ales in the Three Half Moons after), but must have still felt a slight trepidation and unease alongside the excitement as they saddled up with their weapons to go and fight against the French maritime invasion force. Captain Selby rode from Edinburgh to be at the assembly point at Glanton. They needn't have bothered, of course, because there were no French ships and the rest of the following day was spent supping ale in the inns of Glanton with something of a sense of relief.

The following year it was a son of Morpeth who was the naval hero at the Battle of Trafalgar, Admiral Lord Collingwood on HMS Royal Sovereign being an integral part of the British victory over the French fleet on the sea. The wars continued on land and the British were again victorious at Waterloo ten years later.

When the townsfolk of Alnwick had attempted to start an armed association in 1798, the Duke of Northumberland – perhaps mindful and fearful of events unfolding with the aristocracy across the Channel - threatened to throw them off his land and out of their jobs, starting a militia of his own called the Percy Tenantry Volunteers. By 1803 it consisted of six troops of cavalry and 17 companies of infantry throughout the county and including Rothbury. The Artillery Company was formed two years later. When the Tenantry Volunteers were disbanded in 1814, the artillery continued and formed the basis of the 2nd Northumberland (Percy) Artillery Volunteers in 1860.

By the time of the Crimean War the perceived threat from across the seas had not abated and on the 10th January 1868 a group of serious-looking men with lamb chop sideburns, huge beards and intricate moustaches assembled in the village, at the Grammar school, to form the Rothbury Battery of the Percy Volunteer Artillery, under the command of Captain C. H. Cadogan of

Brinkburn.

Around 40 people attended the meeting, including the likes of Colonel Sandford, the Adjutant of the Percy Artillery, Captain Cadogan, who was the commander of the No.3 Battery, Captain C. Ilderton of Tosson tower, W. Dickson of Alnwick, Rev. George West, John Robertson, E. Temple and others of Rothbury.

The cost of the uniforms for the Rothbury battery was £4 4s a man, to a total of £324 for the 77 men, but subscriptions had been assured and collected and the brigade would undertake the clothing of the volunteers. The commissions to raise the corps for the battery were filled by Captain Ilderton and Robertson, Temple, Turnbull and Dixon of Rothbury. Rev. West was made the honorary secretary.

The Rothbury Battery took the Percy Artillery to a complete brigade of eight Batteries with over 400 men involved in the militia raised independent of the regular army and a detachment raised in Glanton in 1872 were added to the Rothbury Battery. The old Gun battery at Alnmouth Links which was constructed in 1881 is still standing, the stone built position including an ammunition store below, though it was altered during World War Two.

The Rothbury men were obviously impressed by the Tynemouth Artillery Volunteers who held an annual week long camp at Rothbury from 1859. It was a big affair; by the summer of 1890 there were 350 at the camp, and they'd fired over 280 rounds of ammunition from both 64 and 40-pounder guns. The volley of fire rolling down the valley must have been immense. There was also a ball held in the village.

The lads of the Rothbury section of what was known by 1887 as the Number 7 Battery of the 2nd Northumberland (Percy) Artillery Volunteers held their own annual carbine competition for prizes. By 1894 the Percy Volunteer Artillery, whose ranks included the likes of Lance-Corporal Taylor, Farr. Drysdale and Troopers W. Richardson, J. Wilson, J. Dobson, T. Wintrip, W.R. Dixon and G. Grey of Rothbury, Trooper W. Howey of Hepple, Trooper E. Hall of Trewhitt and Gunner Mode, P. A. V. of Rothbury, were shooting it out with the Northumberland Hussars in the carbine competition at Addyheugh.

The Hussars, or the Rothbury troop of the Northumberland Hussars Imperial Yeomanry to give them their full title, had been raised in Newcastle in 1819. During the Second Boer War in 1899 the British Government allowed volunteer forces to serve overseas after a number of crushing defeats in Africa during 'Black Week' with the Hussars sending a number of Companies out – they were Dad's Army no more.

A number of Rothbury men served in the conflict, and one was killed in action. Corporal Thomas Pagon was a reservist in the Argyll and Bute Highlanders and he fell at Modder River. The battle was a massacre; as the British troops advanced across open, hot, dusty ground under the blazing sun the Boers, who had dug into trenches, opened fire. With no cover, around 480 were gunned down by the enemy armed with bolt-action rifles.

The others who went across included Sergeant John Robert Taylor, and Troopers Andrew Hedley Dobson, John Davison, William Davison, James Parrage, John Edward Hounan, Arthur Hunter, and Oliver Proudlock of the Northumberland Hussars Imperial Yeomanry. Trooper Thomas Parmley served in the S.A.C., Trooper George Wilson in the 6th Queensland Imperial Bushmen, Trooper George Henry Phillips was in the West Australian M I., while Private William Foreman was a reservist in the 1st Border Regiment and Private William Hamden in the 2nd V.B.N.F. (Northumberland Fusiliers).

Lord Armstrong unveiled a brass plaque to them in 1905, which you can still see in the All Saints' Church in the village today, as 'Oh be joyful in the Lord, all ye lands' boomed out from the choir. The horrors that would follow in the trenches of the First World War for the professional soldiers that came after just could not be imagined then.

A Percy Artillery volunteer.

HORSLEY, HORSLEY DON'T YOU STOP

Mrs. Horsley was our music teacher at school, and she was a bit eccentric.

With her big Elton-style glasses, long hair and ill-matching brightly coloured clothes, you got the feeling that Mrs. Horsley had been something of a hippy, a free spirit in her day. Unusual, then, that she should seem so counter-culture when she belonged to one of the oldest families of the Northumbrian establishment, though she did have an air of Received Pronunciation about her.

The Horsleys had been at Longhorsley since at least the 13th century and probably earlier. The square stone tower that stands in the west of the village was extended by the family in 1490 to further protect them against the raids launched across the border from Scotland, but there will have been a fortification of some description on the site from at least 200 years earlier.

Longhorsley isn't the kind of village that you linger long in; the A697 whips you through in a minute or so, past the Shoulder of Mutton and Green's wonderful family butchers, through and onto the desolate moors. The oldest part of the village is just on up past Green's heading towards Wingates. I painted the interior of the old church there once, a serene and peaceful building, if not all that old.

A notable early member of the family was the knight Roger de Horsley. When he died in 1341 he held lands at Scrainwood (which had been taken by the King from John de Middleton, who had sided with the Scots and was the leader of the Mitford Gang), and Horsley.

Roger had been a big player in signing a Truce between the King and Robert Bruce in 1320. Horsley and Ralph de Neville were appointed to keep the Truce with Robert Bruce and the Scots in Northumberland, with Anthony de Lucy to preserve the truce in Cumberland. Along with Robert de Umfraville, the earl of Angus, William Rydel (Riddell) and John de Penrith he had gone to David, earl of Athol to pardon offences committed during the early part of the Wars of Scottish Independence which had kicked off in 1297.

The following year Roger de Horsley was named as one of the 'keepers of the truce in the marches of Scotland' with William Riddell, Gilbert de Burrodon and John de Penrith. The Riddells also hailed from lands near Longhorsley, Riddell's Quarter being a township that contains the old tower, marked on an 1847 map as a castle. They were also charged with apprehending the perpetrators, both English and Scottish, that had seized the castle of Norham and committed a number of crimes in Northumberland – probably of the cattle raiding and murdering variety.

A Robert Lewer was particularly ordered to be captured and imprisoned after he not only refused to be taken by the sergeants-at-arms, but also threatened some people 'with loss of life and limb, asserting that he would slay and dismember them wherever he should find them, either in the presence or absence of the king.' Just another day on the Border, then.

Roger de Horsley was the constable of Bamburgh Castle in 1322 and was ordered not to take the rents demanded from the poor men in the area as their 'lands, goods and chattels' had been 'wasted and destroyed by a number of attacks from the Scotch rebels.' He himself was paid £40 by the collectors of the custom of wool, hides, and wool-fells in the port of Newcastle-on-Tyne on the orders of the King that year. The monarch owed him the cash for 'the wages of himself, his men-at-arms, and hobelers staying in the company of Robert de Umframville, earl of Angus, for the custody of the castles of Harbottle and Prudhoe.'

In 1327 the prior of St. Oswald's was looking to recoup the bumper £102 10s 0d that Roger de Horsley as constable of Bamburgh Castle had taken for the munition of the castle. The king ordered that the treasurer and barons examine the accounts of William, the Archbishop of York, to find where the liability lay.

Money was again an issue when Roger's son and heir Thomas de Horsley and Roger de Widdrington had to levy £35 in Northumberland to pay off debts in 1359, which they dutifully did.

It was perhaps his son, another Thomas Horsley, who was locked up in Alnwick castle prison with John Ogle in February 1412. A writ from Westminster demanded that William Faucomberge, the knight constable of Alnwick castle, and his lieutenant, under pain of a £200 fine, to deliver to John Bertram sheriff, John de Horton and Geoffrey Langton the prisoners. With such a hefty sum involved, Faucomberge ensured that he delivered them to the sheriff on time.

By 1539 a John Horsley was one of the gentlemen of Northumberland, with Richard Bellasis and Robert Collingwood, who completed a survey of all the Castles in the North for London and they maintained positions of importance throughout the Riding Times. The famous Northumbrian heroine Grace Darling's middle name was Horsley after her mam Thomasin's family. Grace, of course, rode out in a boat with her father on a stormy night from their home at Longstone lighthouse to rescue survivors from the shipwreck the Forfarshire which hit rocks in the Farnes in 1838. Grace died aged only 26 of TB just four years later. It's another tragedy that the family, like so many other local names that had been on the land for many, many generations, seem to start to disappear around the turn of the 21st Century. Rural depopulation, second houses, holiday homes and people buying up properties from the south all contributing to the changing social profile of Northumberland.

Do I clang the triangle now, Mrs. Horsley? Ding.

THE UMFRAVILLES OF HARBOTTLE

It still feels amazing to me that you can walk into the wonderfully atmospheric Hexham Abbey today and see the smooth stone grave effigy of the great Northumbrian knight Gilbert de Umfraville.

Gilbert looks at peace as he lies with his sword and shield, the intricately carved chain mail around his head, his feet unfortunately now missing. It is a peace that Gilbert did not enjoy in the last turbulent decade of his life as the Scottish Wars sent Northumberland up in flames.

He was born in 1245, son to Gilbert the second and his second wife Maud, who was the widow of Scottish lord John Comyn and the daughter of Malcolm, earl of Angus; his first wife was a Baliol, so although the de Umfraville family were English, they had huge ties to the leading families across the heather moors and hills on the other side of the border. The Comyns themselves, though being Scottish, were the lords of the manor in the neighbouring Liberty of Tynedale. Gilbert II inherited the Angus title from his wife and he died in the year that his only son was born.

It is reputed that the de Umfraville family came to England with William the Conqueror in 1066 and that Robert 'With the Beard' was the founder of the line. Gilbert III married Elizabeth Comyn and when his grandson, also named Gilbert, died in 1381, the amount of land the family had amassed was truly spectacular.

The Anglo-Norman Umfravilles held land in York at Newton Kyme, Tadcaster, Paddockthrop, and Hornington while in Suffolk they possessed land in the manor of Hawkden. The Umfravilles owned a huge amount of land in Lincoln and more locally in Cumberland they held the castle and honour of Cockermouth, the manor of Wigton, the manor of Papcaster, grazing in Allerdale and land in Carlisle.

The possessions of the family in Northumberland included the castle of Prudhoe and the manor of Ovingham; Mickley, the manor of Otterburn, Flotterton, Fawdon, and four pasture plots in Coquet moor at the head of the river – 'Hateshawghs, Sholemorelawe, Rashawecote and Kemylpethfeld.' Land at Elsdon, Clennell, Biddlestone, Burrodon, Netherton, Farnham, Angryham, Alwinton and Sharperton, as well as tracts throughout the liberty of Redesdale.

The Umfravilles had also held Scottish land and property, but these were taken from Gilbert III's son, Robert, by King Robert the Bruce after he had often been involved in retaliatory English raiding parties and armies. Robert Umfraville had been appointed Joint Lieutenant and Guardian of Scotland in 1308 and he fought for the defeated English at Bannockburn in 1314 where was taken prisoner by the Bruce, but later released. He was involved in a succession of ongoing peace talks with the Scots during the continuing bloody cross-border conflicts before his death and subsequent burial at Newminster Abbey in Morpeth in 1325.

The family command hub was from Harbottle castle, which was described as the 'chief strength of the Border of the Middle Marches' according to Sir John Widdrington in 1538. It was certainly the guardhouse of Redesdale from which the Umfravilles could lead their forays into hostile Scottish territory, although by that time it was in a bit of a state.

The gate house and the North tower of the outer ward required roofing as the water was obviously running in and soaking the old oak rafters. The wall from the North tower to the dungeon needed rough casting with lime and in many places the yellow Northumbrian sandstone had worn out and needed new stones put in. Several battlements required replacing too.

The inner ward was also in need of repair, with new roofs needed for the hall, kitchen and other offices. An iron gate was needed for the postern and two new windows for the Queen's chamber. The well needed 'wyndes,' stables needed constructing for 100 horses and a barmkin wall needed to replace the old one, four yards high and one yard thick. The estimate for the works came in at £443 3s 4d and '14 fother' of lead.

Appeals for repairs to the castle were frequent throughout the Sixteenth century. It was all a far cry from when Thomas, the son of Gilbert III's other son, also Gilbert, was offered the protection of the crown for one year, along with his fellow John de Mar, as they were students dwelling at Oxford in 1295.

The castle then must have reflected the wealth and status of the de Umfraville family in all of its pomp with bright flags flapping from the towers. The days of relative peace before William Wallace and then the Bruce led their armies to destroy the area with fire and sword. Before Gilbert III had to pull on his mail and swing his battleaxe against them as the countryside was engulfed by burning in 1296.

When he could look at the purple heather running up the slopes to the Drake Stone opposite and smile in the calmness of the valley with the silver Coquet stream gently lapping rounded stones; the contented smile that he wears perpetually in his Hexham haven now. Rest, Sir Gilbert, and be merry, for tomorrow never comes.

PERCY GIBSON AND THE TYNE EXPLOSIVES INCIDENT

The pitman Percy Gibson huddled deeper in his large grey woollen overcoat and pulled his cloth cap further down over his brow as a chill wind whipped down the Tyne. Although it was a cold and fresh Tuesday evening in early December 1924 on the Newcastle Quayside, there was still a bit of bustle around the warehouses and under the web of steel girders that were beginning to be spanned across the wide, dark river to start a stylish new arched bridge. Men whistling, shouting instructions, the grating of chains on stone; the sounds of graft illuminated weakly by street lamps.

Gibson squeezed the brown paper packet tied with string a little tighter to his side with his elbow, feeling the metal bulkiness awkward against his ribs. He glanced over the river, seeing the moonlight stretched long and dancing on the ripples of the inky blackness, and his breath came out like smoke in the frosty air.

The 38-year-old Seghill miner's heart quickened a little as he saw a dark figure approaching. He'd arranged to meet with Harry Shutt that night to discuss his plans for the British revolution and how they'd kick things off on Tyneside. Gibson was reputed to be the organiser of a sub-department of the Newcastle Communist Party's Industrial Committee and perhaps he even wore a subtle small red hammer and sickle pin on the breast of his coat to display his political allegiance.

As the figure approached, their boots clicking across the gleaming cobbles, Gibson was pleased to recognise Shutt's face in the shadows and was even happier that hadn't kept him waiting for too long in the cold. After a brief greeting and a quick shake of hands, Shutt asked Gibson what he had in the parcel under his arm.

"It's a cartridge," replied Gibson.

"That's no use," grumbled Shutt.

"No, it's gunpowder, man…there's a small bomb in the middle."

Gibson had several plans for the explosives; the first was to blow up NewcastleTown Hall. The second was to blow up the cylinders at a power station: "So that the city will be plunged into darkness and the party will loot the shops," he'd muttered conspiratorially. The third big plan was to stop the water supply and the party could 'go into the country and sell water at a shilling a pail.'

"You want to watch you don't blow yourself up while handling that tin," said Shutt, a former serviceman who'd seen action in WW1.

"I don't care," relied Gibson, shaking his head. "It's all for the good of the cause." Shutt took the packet from Gibson and made some excuse to leave, though he'd be back. While he was away, another man called Albert Edward Lewis walked down the dark sloping streets down from the city and met Gibson on the Quayside.

"I've got the stuff," Gibson told him. "I must do something desperate to get rid of it, because my wife is very nervous."

Lewis, stood in a tweed suit and lighting up a cigarette with a match, was another ex-serviceman that Gibson had befriended and was attempting to recruit. He tapped Gibson a Woodbine from the packet and the dog ends glowed orange in the black as they pulled a draw on them.

"I've got lots of gunpowder and guncotton in the house," continued Gibson, blowing smoke into the air. Lewis had earlier thought that Gibson was 'off his head' with his talk of revolutionary acts, but when he'd seen all the Red literature that Gibson kept in a secret meeting room, he'd been convinced otherwise. So much so that himself and Shutt had gone to the police to tell them about Gibson and his plans. They'd been told to play along and that was where Shutt had gone – up to the detective office, where the explosives were unwrapped and inspected under the gleaming lights by a couple of men in uniform, and maybe a handler with his hair stylishly Brycreemed back. There was a coffee tin, and inside that a small syrup tin with a hole in the lid containing gunpowder and small piece of newspaper. There were also cartridges. They re-wrapped the package and instructed Shutt to go back to the Quayside to meet the other two men.

Perhaps his mouth was drying, nervous and certainly apprehensive as he tried to walk casually back towards the two men down at a quieter end the river in the black, the slow sloshing of the river lapping against the concrete sides and the lights of Gateshead twinkling over the other side. Shutt handed Gibson the package back and he tucked it under his arm as the three men talked. After a couple of minutes the police made their move and came out of the darkness to arrest him, Sergeant Walton coming up behind him to take the parcel and ask what was in it.

"If you really want to know, it's gunpowder. I was going to dump it into the Tyne," replied the quick-thinking Gibson.

They took him up to the cells and then went to search his room in Queen Anne Street, where they found subversive literature and a Communist Party card inscribed: 'This is to certify that P. Gibson is a member the Communist Party, Newcastle Local —Signed C. Westgarth, Financial Secretary.' When Gibson was brought before the Magistrates at Newcastle, they spent some time going over the literature, which included such publications as 'The International of the Trade Union League,' 'The Labour Monthly' and what was described as the 'programme of the Communist Bolshevists.' The police, led by Detective Inspector Davidson, had also seized a file of the minutes of meetings, a minute book, a rent book, and a number of nomination forms. They concluded that the literature 'seemed to advocate the rising of the working classes against capitalists' and the Chairman of the Bench remarked that 'there were a great number of passages which advocated force.'

Gibson denied being the organiser for the Communist party in Newcastle, but was of a sub-department, and that he did not have the explosives for any unlawful purpose.

A cashier from the Seghill Colliery said that the cartridges that had been found in the tin were similar to those that Gibson would have used in his work, and that men using explosives at the pit purchased them and the cost was deducted from their wages.

Despite the apparent entrapment element of the case, Gibson was sentenced to three years penal servitude by the Judge.

He wasn't the only Tyneside Communist to get on the wrong side of the Law during the early days of the CPGB and the firebrand orator George William Wheeler was charged with sedition in October 1921. 32-year-old Wheeler, from Newcastle, was a Communist organiser who, it was claimed, was paid £5 a week and £5 expenses by the Third International from Moscow.

"I am a rebel, and I am going to fight the side of the worker. I don't care what weapons we may have to use. Never mind about the law and order stunt. Meet violence with violence. The Communist party are going fight for the unemployed like hell," said Wheeler, who pleaded not guilty. There were again a number of Communist documents produced in the courtroom, including a 'Thesis of Communism,' large tracts of which were reproduced in the newspapers.

It was revealed in 1927 that a Soviet spy called Robert Koling, a 'photostat expert,' had lived in Blyth and had devoted 'much attention to 'Red' propaganda amongst seamen' in the Northumbrian town before moving to London. He'd lived in a quayside lodging house 'frequented chiefly by foreigners' and had left after a larceny charge which was reduced from robbery with violence.

There were accusations of Communist interference the following year when a series of strikes brought out the bulk of the Northumberland coalfields. The Executive of the union, the Northumberland Miners' Association, protested that the work of the Communists in the Minority Movement had been 'interfering with the work and the agreed policy of the Association' and moved to warn branches that 'in no circumstances were outside organisations to be allowed to interfere with work at the collieries.' It was reputed that Communist cells were active in many pits in Northumberland and a newspaper reported that the cells were constituted of 'small groups of young men who are pledged to carry their party propaganda. These men get on with their work, but all the time they are 'grousing' and stirring up unrest among their fellow workers. This sort of thing has been going on for some time—stealthy, dangerous propaganda which is difficult to combat because it is never carried on in the open.'

Pamphlets produced in Birtley in County Durham 'a small town where the Communists are known to be particularly strong' had been circulated amongst the pitmen bitterly attacking the conservative leadership of the union. It was the militant and politically engaged young putters that were bringing the pits to a halt by walking out, much to the chagrin of the union officials, andSleekburn 'A,' Bedlington, Hazelrigg, Gosforth, Montague, Scotswood, Backworth, Dinnington, Woodhorn, Ashington, Ellington, and New Moor were all out.

Two years earlier a communist called T. Aisbitt had caused a storm when he was put forward as a candidate for a Labour council seat in St. Lawrence ward in Newcastle, but was refused as 'ineligible for endorsement as a Labour candidate.' They went for the NUR member T. McCutcheon instead. But the Communist party had long carried a strong level of support among the organised industrial workers of South East Northumberland and in the October of 1933 the Blyth Communist W.H. Breadin was elected a councillor at the County Council in the Northumberland Municipal Elections. In March 1934 Breadin was appointed a member of the Parliamentary and General Purposes Committee.

Comrade Breadin wasn't the first Communist to represent the region, however, and that distinction has to go to the Newcastle-Upon-Tyne MP Joseph Cowen, who succeeded his father into the seat in 1874. Noted in the press that year as the 'Communist member for Newcastle, who represented between four hundred thousand and half-a-million organised men,' a bronze statue of the bearded Cowen stands on a sandstone plinth at Westgate Road/Fenkle Street.

Obviously heavily influenced by Marx & Engels' 1848 Communist Manifesto, Cowen was a radical advocate for the working class who had been born in Blaydon, had worked in his father's brick business, was the proprietor of the Newcastle Chronicle newspaper and brought a public library to the city; he indentified strongly with the miners and took a strong Geordie accent down into Westminster, but he is little remembered or celebrated today.

A Free Communist and Co-operative colony opened up at Forest Hall in Newcastle in 1895, just five years before Cowen's death. The commune was affiliated to the Glasgow Home Colonisation Society and was started up with 24 people on the farm, eight of whom were children. They were dedicated to growing vegetables, had planted a small orchard and started up with strawberries and tomatoes from a glass house. The produce was all taken to local Co-Operative Societies. It managed to keep going until March 1902, when a receiving order was made against the three remaining colonists.

The ideas they had brought weren't completely forgotten or discounted and in June 1909 the Newcastle Communist Club were appealing for comrades to turn out in numbers to 'make the best show possible from our platform' with speakers at a big meeting held on the Town Moor in Newcastle on Race Sunday.

It's not recorded how successful the meeting was - however, by March 1910, the Communist Club had changed their name to the Newcastle Anarchist Club. They weren't particularly dangerous or anarchic mind, and met at 7.30 on a Saturday night in Hall's caff on Pilgrim Street.

Ten years later the Communist Party of Great Britain was formed and party organiser comrade Tom Bell spoke to an audience of over 1,000 in the Palace Theatre in Newcastle on a Sunday evening in October. It was reported that 'the exposition of the principles of Communism and the objects of the Party' were highly appreciated and enquiries made into forming a branch, with Thomas Jackson at the Royal Arcade being the local contact. Bell was at Wallsend the following day at an inaugural meeting of the Tyne shipworker's CPGB branch, of whom J. Cameron of Byker was the chairman, and the names of around sixty interested people were taken. The spectre was rising, and with it working class revolutionaries like Percy Green.

Was he fitted up? We'll never know. He'd been keen to go to trial himself, but the judge as he passed sentence claimed that: "The use and possession of explosives in such circumstances as the prisoner possessed them constituted grave danger to the fabric of society." Maybe, just maybe, the coal miner Gibson had been a pawn used for black propaganda in protecting that status quo, and he'd been set up – or at least further encouraged in his mad schemes – by Shutt and Lewis on the instructions and advice of the local detectives. The establishment felt that this clearly wasn't the case though and Lord Justice Branston, in summing up, said that 'the action of the youths, Shutt and Lewis, who went off to the police, was one which every good citizen would highly commend.'

With events like the infamous fraudulent Zinoviev letter published by the Daily Mail that had damaged the Party's reputation just two months earlier, purporting to order the CPGB to engage in seditious activities, the Tyne explosives incident was possibly just another blow landed in the ongoing Class PR War and Gibson may have been the victim of a dirty tricks campaign.

That war is still running today.

THE BLACK STABLE DOORS OF BAMBURGH

I travelled up in the back of a work van, sat on a dust sheet among the paint pots beside the soft coo of the racing pigeons in their wicker basket. My dad was in the front in his white overalls, his hair golden and curly like Roger Daltry from *The Who*, the radio playing tunes, the smell of turps and gloss.

He was painting the stable block black at Bamburgh Castle, it was a glorious summer's day – the kind where you can feel it coming on through the slight cool of the morning, but the sun high and bright – and I was going to spent it in the dunes and on the beach. A little treat, a cheeky childhood day trip out.

That's one of my earliest and most distinct memories of visiting the old fortress on the top of the igneous outcrop, but it never fails to impress whenever you visit. Coming around a corner then onto the straight stretch of road and you see it, heart just quickening a little, an almost unreal vision. Bamburgh is where my heart belongs.

Robert de Neville was appointed the keeper of Bamburgh Castle in March 1259 in an order from Westminster. Neville was the second baron of Raby, in Durham, though it has been theorised by others that the family may have been part of the Deiran aristocracy pre-Norman conquest and therefore tied in to the ancient Anglians of Northumbria in a family tree going back as far as Woden; but then that was probably just to get one up on their local rivals the de Percys.

Robert was sworn on the Holy Bible to keep the castle loyally and in good faith for the King for 12 years from that date. Earlier constables of BamburghCastle had included John Wascelin, who in 1224 was paid five marks each year by the soldiers that guarded the old stone building for some religious purpose; around that time the church in Bamburgh and the convent of St. Oswald's Nostle were paying 50 marks a year to Pope Honorius and the monastery of St. Sistus in Rome. Talk about a racket.

The English King Henry III visited Bamburgh in 1236 and the sheriff of Northumberland was to check the safety of the building in advance. The following nobles also showed up some 11 days in advance to get things prepared and to provide the security- Adam Tarencun, John le Singe, John Juden, Henry Grafton, Walter Achard, William Blancpomer, Henry Burnell, Gerald de Grosmund, Henry de la Bere and Herlewine Norman.

The following year, Henry put Thomas de Wraucham and Thomam de Wetwod in charge of the operations at Bamburgh, while Robert Newnham and Hugh Burneton were appointed to Newcastle. It was felt that for 'a firm peace to be opened between the King and the King of Scots' that a great expense would need to be spent on the two fortresses, with Hugh de Bolbec commanding the guarding of the camps.

With the stunning and expansive panoramic views over the North Sea enjoyed from the battlements, it was now surprise that in 1260 de Neville would come across a shipwreck and take three of the sailors into his custody in the castle. John Sparcunte had to bail them out. Three years later Robert de Neville was the keeper of both Bamburgh and York castles and he had munitioned both following 'a late disturbance of the realm.' The disturbance was what became known as the 'Second Baron's War' or a long-running civil war between the French-born Simon de Montfort and the Crown. De Neville had been promised his expenses for doing so by the King, and he likewise promised to recompense Eustace de Balliol at Carlisle castle and Adam de Gesmue at Newcastle castle, though the affair rumbled on for a couple of years.

Somewhat ironically, 200 years later it was a relation of Robert de Neville's disinherited but senior lines of the family, Sir Humphrey Neville of Brancepeth, that defended BamburghCastle during a siege where it was pounded it into submission with heavy guns during the War of the Roses in 1464. Perhaps even more improbably, it was Richard Neville, the 16th Earl of Warwick, that commanded the Yorkist forces that took it. Bamburgh was the first English castle to fall to cannon fire as the artillery smashed into the walls.

In the May of 1276 the King, now Edward I, ordered Robert de Neville to hand the castle and lands at Bamburgh over to Thomas de Normanville, but changed his mind and left Robert in control. However, although de Neville continued in Royal service in a number of important roles, by 1288, Robert le Porter of Bamburgh, alias Robert, the porter of the castle of Bamburgh held arable and meadow land in the village and he and a watchman at the castle were paid 2d. daily by the king.

Serious trouble was again brewing and Bamburgh was to become a part of the frontline in the terrible and long-running Wars with Scotland. In 1296 ten Welsh hostages were being held at Bamburgh by Hugh Gubion, the sheriff of Northumberland. Rhys ab Maylgon, Canan ab Mereduth, and Mailgon ab Res were given wages of 4d. daily for their maintenance, and seven months later where to be given safe conduct, without irons, to the castle at Newcastle.

At that time the bailiff of Tynedale handed over the woods and parks that had belonged to John Comyn of Bedenagh in North Tynedale to Gilbert Umfraville, the earl of Angus, and to give him 20 live bucks and 80 live does to stock his park at Harbottle. The burgess of the town of Corbridge was similarly ordered by King Edward to take over the wood belonging to John Balliol, the late King of Scotland, and to take forty oaks to rebuild the houses in the town which had 'been lately burnt by the Scotch.'

The constable of Carlisle castle was ordered to permit Henry Percy and his men to enter the castle and to take provisions for a military expedition to Galway and Ayrshire while the sheriff of Northumberland was commanded to deliver to William de Vescy the land of all his tenants 'dwelling in Scotland who held immediately of him,' and to seize for the King any lands of those Scots being held in prison 'by reason of their rebellion.'

John de Vescy had been appointed the keeper of the King's Castle of

Bamburgh by then and in 1307 an order came to his wife Isabella to release the Scottish prisoners being held at the castle 'taken lately in Scotland against the late King' and to 'allow them to go whithersoever they will.' The men were named as Nicholas Patunson, Fynnus le Suur, Thomas le Clerk, Walter de Lardario, Michael de Momfoth, John le Mareschal, and John de Ethale.

But if anyone thought that the death of King Edward I would lead to any kind of peace with the Scots, then they were wrong as King Robert the Bruce, crowned the year before, continued the campaign of terror, invasion and retaliation that was by now so deeply ingrained on the bloody borderlands.

In 1313 the now constable of Bamburgh castle, Roger Horsley, was ordered to acquit the men of nearby Shoreston and North Sunderland of their taxes for a year as they were 'so impoverished on account of the robberies and fires inflicted upon them by the Scotch rebels, that they are unable to till the said lands or to pay the ferms due to the king, or to support the other burdens upon the said lands.'

Sampson de Mulfen was similarly excused any taxes for the castle and manor of Mulfen 'on account of the robberies and fires inflicted upon him by the Scotch rebels.' Roger Horsley was himself making a tidy profit by letting the inhabitants of Shoreston and North Sunderland build lodgings within the castle walls and charging them rent. The people had fled to the castle when their houses and buildings were fired by the Scots and, 'on account of their frequent attacks,' the Crown ordered Roger to stop charging them. The burgesses of the town of Bamburgh were also pardoned of paying any taxes because they were paying tributes and ransoms to the Scots and they'd suffered a number of burnings of the town and robbery of their goods by the same. The flames were roaring and Bamburgh had suffered so badly that in 1315 King Edward II ordered his butler Walter Waldeshef to deliver six tuns of old wine to the sheriff of York to be taken to Bamburgh and delivered to Roger Horsley.

The sheriff of Warwick and Leicester was to purchase hundred quarters of wheat and a hundred quarters of malt which were to be taken to Bamburgh by the sheriff of Nottingham as relief.

In 1320 the men of the town of Bamburgh were again excused taxes as the Scottish were still inflicting heavy damages and three years later were again allowed respite as they had 'suffered many damages for some time by the frequent comings of the Scots into those parts.' Horsley was ordered to permit the people staying in the castle grounds for protection against the Scottish invasions to take timber for their lodges in the castle and in 'the ditch and moat of the same,' while John de Walton and William de Hevedrawe, both of Bamburgh, were permitted to buy 20 chaldrons of sea-coal in Newcastle and take it into Scotland to secure the release of their sons, Roger and William, who had been 'delivered as hostages to the Scots for certain reasons.'

Roger de Horsley was similarly charged to deliver his prisoner Geoffrey de Heydon to the sheriff of Northumberland. The Scottish raids were still so frequent in 1328 that the people of Bamburgh were again excused by the exchequer. The farms and crops had been burned, their cattle stolen and who knows how many killed, but still they remained and in the March that year William de Herle was dispatched from Nottingham to treat with the Scots at Bamburgh castle. He was handsomely recompensed by the King, who paid him £26 in back wages for 52 days in the May, June and July of the first year of his reign.

Roger Horsley stood down as the constable of Bamburgh castle in January 1330 and was replaced by Robert de Horncliffe. His successor was ordered to pay Roger 40 marks a year for life 'in consideration of Roger's good service.' Horsley was no doubt grateful, but the following year had petitioned the King to get back 'the great sum of money' that he had spent in securing the walls and turrets of the castle himself during the wars. Horncliffe didn't last long in the role and was replaced by John de Kingston in 1332. He had to spend money repairing a number of houses within the castle which were ruinous and blew £20 by the 'view and testimony' of William de Bedenale (Beadnell), while two years later it was a Walter de Creyk that was constable of the castle. He was told to pay the now surely old-aged Robert le Porter, the keeper of the gate of the castle, 2d. daily. Robert had been employed at the castle for over 40 years at least.

In 1336 William de Vescy took over from his mother all of his dead father's lands in Bamburgh with a clause stating that if the lands were destroyed by war then he was released of the 8 marks that he had to pay his mother, Isabella, for them. The document was witnessed by the luminaries in Bamburgh at that time: the clerks Sir Thomas de Bamburgh and Sir William de Emeldon (Embleton?), William de Heppescotes (Hepscot), Thomas de Berewyk of Pokelyngton (Berwick of Pocklington), Henry del Strothre (Strowther) and William le Skynner and Robert Goldewyn of Bamburgh.

In 1338 the knight Robert de Weston recalled in a proof of age case that Thomas, the son and heir of Thomas de Bradford of Bamburgh, had been baptised in the church of St. Aiden by the chaplain Thomas de Corbridge, He remembered it because a Scotsman called Donald de Duns was taken in war and beheaded at Bamburgh that day. Robert Goldwyn remembered because he was given as a hostage in Scotland for the ward of Bamburgh and William Skinner could recall because Robert de Bruce granted a truce to the men of the ward of Bamburgh for six months that seemingly unremarkable Monday.

It seems bizarre then now, as you watch the sun setting low and illuminating the castle in the deepest reds and oranges from the beach with your family, that the peace of the place would have been so disrupted throughout the tumultuous 14th Century. That Bamburgh, the old capital of Northumbria, the gentle seaside village of tourists, ice creams on the green and surfers on the waves, would have been so destroyed by the Scottish Wars of Independence. That you should wander around the walls with your own son today in silence and tranquillity, and see the painters putting a new coat on the stable block and smile at the memory. Black, of course.

SHIPWRECKED IN WARKWORTH

He was responsible for a lot of crimes that went unpunished, but the old rogue Sir John Forster should have been pulled up for causing Warkworth castle fall into ruin and disrepair in 1572.

Forster's disrespect for the properties of Thomas Percy, the Earl of Northumberland, who had been executed by beheading at York that year for his part in the Rising of the North, was palpable. Charles Neville, the 6th Earl of Westmorland, was another one of the ringleaders of the Catholic nobles that had unsuccessfully attempted to replace Elizabeth I with Mary Queen of Scots and he lost all of the family estates and died penniless in exile on the continent in 1601.

Forster's flagrant disregard for the Percy holdings saw him strip out all the lead at HulnePark. He also took the glass, iron and even the lead pipes that brought water to the house. Henry Lord Hunsdon was so disgusted by his actions that he wrote to Lord Burghley that he knew not on whose authority Forster was acting, but that he meant 'utterly to deface both Warkworth and Alnwick' castles. Hunsdon felt it was a pity to 'see how Alnwick and Warkworth are spoiled by him and his' and reckoned that Forster was £500 a year better off since the rebellion, and that he'd taken £3,000 or £4,000 in spoils during that time.

But then I have a strong affinity with Warkworth – both the castle and the village itself. My maternal grandparents lived there, I was christened in the chapel there and the congregation are my Godparents as I was the first child registered when the Presbyterian Chrurch became the United Reformed. I was married there at the Sun Inn opposite the castle and, hopefully, I'll die and have my ashes scattered there.

The big old yellow sandstone walls have long stood on the hill above the village and chances have long been presented for the villains of the county to turn a bit profit. Sir John Forster would have laughed at the opportunists from the village who, in 1316, plundered a ship sailing from Hartlepool to Berwick that was 'driven by a number of attacks by pirates into the port of Warkworth.' The complainers Richard de Kellawe, Adam de Hougat and Richard de la More had sold 82½ quarters of rye of Estland, 3 quarters of wheat, 2 quarters and 2 bushels of rye flour and a quarter of salt to Thomas de Stotford, sergeant of the keeper of the town of Berwick-upon-Tweed.

When the ship docked, it was boarded by Richard de Thirlewall, Robert de Arreyns, Eustace le Constable of Warkworth, John de Aketon, Hugh Gallon and John de Lescebury (Lesbury) who, with others, boarded the ship, carried away the corn, flour and salt and other goods, arrested the ship, and detained her.

Eight years later and a number of merchants from Bruges and Flanders were complaining to Robert Umfraville, earl of Angus, and Gilbert de Burradon that they had been plundered in Warkworth after a storm had driven them aground near Warkworth.

The continental merchants Jacominus de Mark, Lambert Storme, James Touerlate, John Olverdoe, Soer de Colkerk, John le Joefne, Nicholas de Thorout, John Wyndelok and Christian de Malebek said that John Robyn, the master of a ship of Bruges, had landed at the busy and important trading port of Berwick upon Tweed. He was carrying 'wool, hides, wool-fells and other merchandise to take to Flanders' when the ship was 'cast ashore by a tempest.'

The mariners and merchants escaped alive and the ship was not wrecked, but a local gang that included Adam son of Nicholas de Hauxley, Robert de Raynham, Roger son of Robert de Raynham, Robert his brother, William son of Thomas, Roger son of William son of Thomas, Robert son of William son of Thomas, Nicholas son of Adam de Hauxley, Henry de Rihill of Warkworth, William, Simon and Robert Darreise, Richard Tassiman, Adam le Taillour, William Fox, Thomas Egly, Henry le Peschour, Nicholas Scot,

John Cokkebayn, Alan Alegode of Warkworth, Richard le Provost of of Togsten, William son of Robert, Stephen de Togsten, Adam son of Peter de Anebille (Amble), Henry son of Robert, William son of Henry, Robert Ponder, Robert Batyn, John son of Simon, John le Fevre of Anebille, Hugh Wayt of Aclynton (Acklington), William 'Paynesman de Aclynton,' Nicholas Mausone of Neubiggyng (Newbiggin), Alexander son of Elias, Robert Shoute, John Haut, John son of John le Clerk, John son of Juliana, Roger Botting and Robert del Borne of Neubiggyng 'and others of the county of Northumberland' broke into the ship and carried off the goods.

Warkworth is another Northumbrian stronghold with Norman beginnings and it was long the manor of the Fitzrogers, who would become in time known as the Claverings. Roger son of John was granted lands by the King for the keeping of Warkworth castle before 1249 and in 1310 Robert, son of Roger, (Fitzroger) was owner of Warkworth castle and borough. He also owned lands in Buckingham, Essex, Norfolk, Suffolk, as well as huge tracts of land and property at Whalton, Widdrington, Eshott, Horton, Newbiggin-on-the-moor, Glendale, Kirkharle, Newburn, Corbridge, upper Botilston, and the manor and borough of Rothbury in Northumberland. The family had obviously been important followers of William the Conqueror to have been awarded such large amounts of ground in the aftermath of 1066.

By 1311 Robert's son, now known by the surname John de Clavering, granted licence of the manors of Clavering in Essex and Blebugh in Suffolk to Stephen de Trafford, his wife Hawisia and his male heirs, the remainder going over to Edmund de Clavering for life, and then to Ralph de Neville and his heirs.

John de Clavering also granted the castle of Warkworth and the manors of Rothbury, Newburn and Corbridge, and Evre in Buckingham to be held in chief by Stephen de Trafford with similar stipulations; however, by 1313, the castle at Warkworth, the castle and manor of Rothbury etc. with a yearly value of £700 had reverted to John de Clavering and the King at Windsor ordered 'them to acquit the sheriffs and other tenants of the above of the ferms and issues thereof from that day.'

With Northumberland being burned and destroyed by constant Scottish invasion forces at the time, it was probably with some relief that the powerful David de Strabolgi, earl of Athol, Robert de Umfraville, earl of Angus, William Rydel, John de Penrith and Roger de Horsley in 1320 were ordered to 'receive all those of Scotland wishing to come into the king's peace, provided such persons give security that they will attempt nothing against the truce entered into between the king and Robert de Bruce.'

Three years later John de Clavering was ordered to ensure that his castle of Warkworth was to be provisioned and guarded safely, along with the other castles in the marches of Scotland, against all contingencies 'notwithstanding the conclusion of the truce with the Scots.' The Bishop of Durham was to do likewise at Norham and Durham, Robert de Umframville for his castle of Prudhoe and Henry de Percy for his castle of Alnwick.

The earl of Athol was appointed chief warden for Northumberland while Andrew de Harcla commanded Cumberland and Westmoreland as 'head arrayer and conductor of the men at arms and foot thereof.' Henry Percy was directed 'with his entire posse' to do as Stragboli ordered and to 'keep sufficient ward at Alnwick' with Ralph de Neville, then constable of Warkworth Castle, to do the same as were Roger Horsley at Bamburgh, John Lilburn and Roger Mauduyt, the constables of Dunstanburgh, the un-named constable of Prudhoe and Richard de Emeldon, the chief warden of the town of Newcastle-upon-Tyne. Mandates were issued to Percy and Clavering to repair the castles of Alnwick and Warkworth in an order that also stated that magnates having castles and fortresses in those parts should stay there for the defence of those parts.'

Percy must have impressed during the first series of Scottish Wars as by January 1332 an indenture was made between Henry and the King, Edward III, and enforced by John Lowther, that Percy should receive 500 marks yearly for his fee and was granted 'the castle of Warkworth and all other lands in county Northumberland that (the now deceased) John de Clavering held for life or to him and the heirs male of his body and that ought to revert to the King after John's death if John died without an heir male of his body.' Henry Percy obviously graciously paid fealty to the King and must have been rubbing his hands together with glee as he was rewarded for 'good service past and future.' Despite choosing the wrong side on a number of occasions throughout history, the lands are still in the hands of the Percy family today, almost 700 years later.

John de Glanton may have been the constable at Warkworth castle around that time; by 1336 he was the keeper of Carlisle castle, and the King was demanding payment from him not only for 100 quarters of wheat sold to him, but for keeping a Scottish Prisoner of War called William Bard for three years in Warkworth when he was constable there, and for the safe-keeping of Carlisle castle with several men-at-arms and others paid for with 40 marks by the King. John de Glanton was further ordered to spend £10 19s. repairing the 'houses, walls, turrets and other defects in that castle by the view and testimony of Peter de Tilliol' on top of the 60 marks that he'd been ordered to spend on reparation on a number of occasions.

Another ship had ran aground and broken up off Warkworth in 1396 and Henry Percy, the earl of Northumberland, was ordered to set free all of the Scottish merchants on board that his men had dragged splashing from the foamy water and chucked in the dungeons in Warkworth, as well as all of their cargo that he'd lifted. The crown worried that his actions could be a breach of the uneasy truce with Scotland.

By the December of 1545, when King Henry was in the process of 'Rough Wooing' the Scots, a number of Spanish crews under Gamboa were stationed around Northumberland and they must have made for an exotic sight in Warkworth, Alnwick, Bamburgh and Berwick. The Spanish harquebusiers were a cavalry unit and plans were made to post some of them to Carlisle.

But it was the perilous sea around Warkworth that it was most famous for. I recall a ship wrecking on the beach as a child and watching the hulk rust away over the years as it was battered by wind and sand and tide.

Our old friend Sir John Forster had to deal with another ship that had grounded of Warkworth in 1591. He made no mention of any cargo – no surprises there – but complained that the 16 Scotsmen driven ashore who lay there 'in great misery' were costing him money as he had to pay ten men to guard them, plus other charges, and he twined that he had no fit jail to put them in.

'I beg directions either for their speedy trial, or that they may be taken to Berwick within my Lord Chamberlain's rule as vice admiral,' wrote Forster from his house near Alnwick. He had also written to the Privy Council asking if the King of Scots would pay his recompense for keeping them and was keen to get shot of the prisoners as soon as possible. Forster really was something of a 17th Century villain and wheeler dealer - the mystery is how he was never really caught.

THE BRINKBURN HOARD

It was hot and hard work. The sun beat down and birds sang high in the trees as the workmen lifted picks to howk up the hardened ground in brown chunks.

Sweating in collarless granddad shirts and removing their battered tweed waistcoats to set them down and wiping sunburned brows with hankies. Yes, it was hot, and their feet were uncomfortably swollen in heavy hob-nailed boots twisted on the uneven earth and stones.

Cutting through the grass to create a new road near Brinkburn Priory on a quiet bend by the River Coquet, the gang of navvies bent and toiled and grafted. Joking made the day go faster; taking the Mickey, having a laugh and bellowing out the odd curse as rough hands were worn to callous on smooth wood handles. Looking forward to a pint of mild in one of the inns in Rothbury after no doubt, imagining it running cold and fresh down the throat from a pint pot in two glugs.

As they dug on, the men came across a patch of burning in the soil. Black, unmistakable, charred and brittle wood in the earth, a layer in among softer earth that curled like butter to the spade edge. There will have been questions, and no doubt some will have known answers. There's a building been burnt down here, a long time ago by the looks of it. There was also a hearthstone, blackened in the charcoal but still flat, lifted with pinch bars to reveal the flattened soil, smooth as a pool table below. Setting the stone aside and digging on. One fella in his rough work gear dug in and loaded a shovel full up to lob up onto the cart.

"That's the heaviest shovelful I ever threw," he grumbled, wincing at the weight. They stopped and looked among the earth, smoothing off some soil to reveal a small brass pot, around six inches high. It had a real substance to it as it was balanced and bounced gently in a hand. More soil thumbed away to reveal that unmistakable gleam and glint in the sunlight. The pot was packed with gold coins.

The date was the 25th July, 1834, and the workmen had just discovered what would become known as the little-known Brinkburn hoard – between 300 and 400 gold coins of Edward III and Richard II that had been minted in the late 14th Century. It must have looked spectacular as they shook a handful out and laid them on the wooden tail board of the cart and looked on in wonder for just a few moments before the reality hit.

Brinkburn had long been the site of an Augustinian priory and in 1293 William de Felton had a licence for 'alienation in mortmain by way of exchange' with the Priory. That basically meant that he was giving up his claim on any lands there for others belonging to the church. Just three years later the Border country was reduced to ashes as the Scottish Wars of Independence began.

It would seem incredulous that Brinkburn Priory would remain unmolested by the invasion force of William Wallace that camped in nearby Rothbury Forest in 1297, and it is reputed that Robert Bruce fired and destroyed the church in 1315 on another campaign into England. The Scottish Wars were basically a series of terror attacks with armies marching in both directions to slaughter and burn, with a few huge pitched battles thrown in for good measure.

There is a famous story associated with Brinkburn that once when a Scottish raiding party was in the area the monks rang the bells of the priory to sound the all clear when they thought that they'd gone. Unfortunately, the sound of the bells just alerted the Scots riders as to where the secluded and serene churchmen were and they returned to loot and plunder. The monks apparently threw the bells in the Coquet after that, though they are still to be found. And what a find they would be, possibly lying just under the stones in the shimmering orangey water with the spotted silver flank of a trout darting back and then settling alongside.

There is no actual hard date given for the Brinkburn Bells raid but if you assume that it was in the latter 1300s, which is not inconceivable given the turbulence of that century, then perhaps the coins in the hoard had been placed under the hearth in the pot by one of the senior monks as the panicked tales of another Scottish raid approaching went through the area. With the lawless thieving, cattle rustling and murder that followed with local families as well as Scots during the Riding Times, then finding a safe spot for your cash was a must on the Mediaeval Borders.

By 1509 Thomas Carr was the prior of Brinkburn, who was answerable to the Bishop of Durham, the convent of Brinkburn…and God, presumably. But as King Henry VIII's Dissolution of the Monasteries drew closer in 1536, a visit to the Priory noted that Will Hodgson was the prior and that Brinkburn had been founded by lord Burrowe. It paid 100 marks a year and the 'superstition' that it held was the girdle of St. Peter. Other religious icons throughout the region included the bodies of St. Cuthbert and St. Bede at the important Durham Priory. They also held the cross of St. Margaret. Lord Dacre had founded the priory at Newminster and they had the girdle and book of St. Robert. Hexham had the red mass book while Alnwick had the foot of Simon Momford and the cup of Thomas of Canterbury.

Ten years later the gentleman George Fenwick bought some land at Brinkburn off Cuthbert Carnaby for use in his old age and retirement. George had been a 'most notable Borderer within the Middle Marches here, has valiantly served the King these 30 years, in war and peace, both against the Scots and against thieves. His service has not been without effusion of his blood, loss of goods and captivity,' noted Sir Robert Bowes to the Privy Council. The peace and quiet at Brinkburn would suit George down to the ground and his grandson and namesake George would go on to make a real name for himself as MP for Morpeth and a Parliamentarian commander of Northern militia during the English Civil War.

Although George Fenwick was a good old Roundhead when so many of the Northumbrian gentry had taken the side of the King, he was also a bit of an adventurer and had sailed out to America to start a colony at Saybrook on the Connecticut river in 1639. He'd also visited Boston four years earlier, undertaking the huge overseas journey as perhaps something of a trial run.

George returned from America in 1645 and his father's neighbour Robert Clavering, of Brinkburn, was elected to be High-Sheriff of the County of Northumberland by the Lords and granted a commission by the Commissioners for the Great Seal of England, which perhaps had some bearing on his political choices.

The coins of the Brinkburn treasure hoard were handed to Major Hodgson Cadogan, who owned land at Brinkburn at the time. Some of the coins were given to the British museum. Others seem to have been handed to private collectors. It's not really known.

Nobody can definitely account for where the hoard ended up and that's a great shame; it would have made a wonderful display in the beautifully restored English Heritage property today.

BUTCHER BILL, BOOTLEGGING AND GRAIN

If you've ever sat down to the Martin Scorsese movie *'Gangs of New York'* then you'll have watched the scene where Irish immigrants come down the gangplank off the boats and are signed up and enlisted in the American Union army on the spot.

Being handed a blue uniform and a musket and sent to stand in another line as the smartly dressed Bill 'the Butcher' Cutting and his Bowery Boys street gang looked on in some disgust and disdain from the busy, bustling boards of the dock front. Bill the Butcher was notoriously anti-Irish, anti-immigrant and anti-Catholic, but it wasn't just Celtic or Latin migrants that were pouring into New York around the 1850s.

The Rothbury lad Robert Snowdon may just have walked past the notorious Bill in his top hat and coat tails as he was hustled into line to sign up his nationalisation papers and, possibly, his enlistment papers as he looked on in wonder at the tall buildings with a smell of bread, coffee, and sea air mixed with the stench of the sewers in his nostrils, maybe being eyed up and down by one of the Bowery Boys twirling a fob chain as a either a potential recruit or a mark.

Quickly averting his gaze down to his worn boots on the wooden planks, not wanting to draw attention to himself, the country boy Snowdon was jostled along in the mass of bodies towards the Army recruitment table. Perhaps it was a sense of adventure that drove him to undertake the huge sea voyage across the Atlantic; maybe he'd been impressed by stories of Gold

Rushes in the West, or the chance of land and opportunity in America.

There had been riots against the Army draft in 1863 in the slums of the city and the Five Points as the Civil War against the Confederate States raged on and while *'Gangs of New York'* is an entertaining story based on facts, there is no hard evidence that people were actually enlisted straight off the ships as they docked, and Bill the Butcher himself was based on the real character William Poole.

Finding documentary evidence for the date of Robert Snowdon landing at New York has proved tricky – but in 1859 and 1860 a Robert Snowdon was a signatory on a document requesting the Duke of Northumberland to form the Percy Company of the Northumberland Volunteers Artillery, so perhaps it was a taste for action that led him West. Maybe Robert wandered happily across to the recruiting sergeants sometime after the conflict began in 1861. Perhaps his life in leafy, rural Coquetdale just didn't give him the thrills that he craved so he upped and off to fight against legendary Confederate soldiers in their grey kit such as the likes of Bloody Bill Anderson, Jesse James and Cole Younger. The kind of men you'd imagine in a Clint Eastwood movie, bearded guerrillas quick on the draw with a six-shooter in a bar filled with showgirls and card games and shots of whisky. *I'm a good ole Rebel*...the banjo and violin.

The reality that hit Robert Snowdon was somewhat grimmer and obviously had a huge psychological impact on the young Northumbrian. It seems likely that he was at the second battle of Petersburg, in Virginia, in June 1864. The battle raged for three days and Snowdon's saw almost 1,700 of his Federal brothers killed in action and over 8,500 wounded during in ill-fated attempt to capture the city.

With a constant boom of artillery and the smoke and crack of musket shot going off as if in his head, and men falling as lead ripped holes into them and splashed blood and broken bone around, it seems likely that Snowdon was suffering from what would now be described as PTSD as he deserted his regiment sometime between that battle, and the 10-month siege that followed. On the 17th of December 1864 he sent a letter home to Edward Pape in Morpeth from Petersburg. When it arrived in Britain some two months later, the newspapers were quick to reprint the contents.

Robert had been convicted of the crime of desertion and condemned to die by hanging at noon. He sent his love to his family and friends, asked forgiveness of his enemies and hoped to be forgiven in the next world. The wording makes it seem almost like a standard letter that the officers would get the condemned to fill out and sign. Whatever had happened, a wooden gallows were erected and Robert was strung up by his neck. As he took one last look at that Virginian sun, he must have felt a hell of a distance from Simonside.

Robert Snowdon wasn't the only Rothbury man to be done for deserting the army. Robert Allen did a flit from the Second Battalion of His Majesty's 12th Regiment of Foot based in Manchester in January 1757. Described as a 5'5" stocky 17-year-old, with a fresh complexion and a brown wig on his short brown hair, the labourer was wearing a grey coat with broad white metal buttons, a green waistcoat and leather breeches when he absconded from a recruiting party of Captain Grey of the regiment at Newcastle. A twenty shillings award – over and above what was allowed by the Act of Parliament for apprehending deserters – was offered for his capture.

Allen was almost certainly a relation of the celebrated and well-written about Rothbury rogue Jamie Allen, who was the Duke of Northumberland's piper as well as being a multiple times army deserter, horse thief and raconteur himself. The Allens were part of the Faa or Faw gang that had long inhabited the Rothbury Forest, though it may have just been one of their stopping off points as they travelled between Carlisle and Yetholm. The exploits of the Border gypsies are well documented with the Faas, the Winters, Allens and Clarkes all spending time in the gaol at Morpeth – or on the gallows.

It was another man from the Rothbury Forest that was partly responsible for the dog breed the Rothbury, or as it is now better known, Bedlington terrier. Piper, who belonged to James Anderson of the Forest, was bred from a dog called Peachem belonging to the Rothbury stone mason Joseph Ainsley and the bitch Pheobe, belonging to Christopher Dixon of Longhorsley. Ainsley had got his dog from a William Cowen of Rothbury. Piper was described as a slender dog that was about 15 inches high, and 15lb in weight, being of a liver colour and 'the hair being a sort of hard woolly lint.' His ear was large, hung close to the cheek, and was slightly feathered at the tip. He was the first Rothbury terrier and is reputed to have been pupped in the first quarter of the 1800s.

Mr. Anderson may or may not have been a part of the Scottish travelling people of the Forest – they took on local surnames - but the village had a share of radgies and villains left over from the moss-trooping days as it was. The Rothbury butcher Robert Hedley was described as a 'sheep stealer' in the sensationalist 'Hue and Cry' when he robbed a Kelso carrier called John Mien of his pocket book containing money, bills and accounts near Dalkeith in 1776.

And in 1825 the Rothbury native James Napier had only just been released from Durham goal after serving several months when he got himself locked up again. He was adjudged 'a rogue and vagabond' and a 'suspected person and reputed thief' after being apprehended on the Quayside in Newcastle where he intended to commit a felony offence, and was sentenced to one month's hard labour in the house of correction.

While tattie blight and the horrors of starvation drove millions of the Irish westwards into America in 1845, others had settled in England and Scotland earlier looking to start a new life. One Irishman that had ventured to Rothbury was unlucky in 1838 when he was the only man nabbed in a customs raid at a whisky still near Tosson and sentenced to 3 months at Morpeth in default of a penalty of £30.

The still, at Codley Moss, was cleverly disguised and dug into a trench great peat moss so it was completely underground. There was a small doorway to allow the moonshiners in and out, and a hole cut through the ground for the chimney – it was unfortunately the smoke from this that led to its detection.

Two years later another still was discovered in 'a sort of cavern' at the foot of the Tosson hills which was 'capable of producing 100 gallons of spirits per week,' but the Supervisor of the Morpeth district and the riding officers of Felton and Rothbury didn't catch anyone red-handed in that raid.

Tosson was ideally placed for the production of illicit whisky as the springs that ran off the Simonside hills passed through the peat bogs that gave the whisky its unique flavour before it was run into a 40 gallon tank with a fire underneath and some grain added. The Tosson 'gauger-free' could be up to 90% proof and was no doubt freely available in the Royal George Inn that used to stand at Great Tosson and was a notorious establishment for cock-fighting and card playing among its rowdy clientele. There was also a still at Wolfershiel around that time, and the upper Coquet valley also plied the trade to beat the Excise man of duty with the famous still at Wholehope.

Illegal brewing and distilling wasn't just a rural phenomenon, however, and in 1847 an illicit still capable of holding 25 gallons was discovered in a cellar in Pudding Chare in Newcastle. The excise man, accompanied by a policeman, also found about 140 gallons of worts and wash in tubs, besides a quantity of feints, though the owner was not discovered.

When they weren't producing their own illicit hooch, then the locals were involved in smuggling booze which primarily came in at Boulmer. Smugglers from Coquetdale, Bamburgh, Glendale and across the Border in Yetholm, Morebattle and Jedburgh were all involved in landing grog on the coast in ships and carting it away. Some of the names linger on in legend – Blind Wull Balmer of Jedburgh, Jock Melvin, Duthor Grahamslaw and, of course, Wull Faa of Yetholm were all engaged in the gin smuggling racket. At Rothbury it was Bob Dunn of the Forest that brought the spirits back over the heather from the beach and stored it in a double gable wall at Bushey Gap. The space between the bricks was used to conceal the gin and it long baffled the Excise man, who had been after old Bob for a while, until measurements were taken of the inside and outside of the farmhouse and the cavity discovered. The old farmhouse reputedly burned down years ago. An old ballad reckoned that 'Kate the West' was the queen of all the smugglers, but it isn't pointed out where she hailed from. It was reputed that many years later smuggled goods such as silks and casks of spirits which had been hidden and forgotten were dug up in the sands at Boulmer.

As late as August 1882 a Dutch gunboat called 'the Merchant of Scheidam' was seized by coastguards at Boulmer and placed under detention as the crew were suspected of smuggling. The coastguards found 'various kinds tobacco, cigars, and spirits, Eau de Cologne, Dutch drops, and other dutiable goods' when they boarded the vessel.

To give an idea of the scale of the illegal still racket, between 1860 and 1866 there were no fewer than 461 convictions in England, and 64 in Scotland, for the illicit distillation of spirits from molasses, grain or other materials. And they're just the ones that were caught.

Perhaps Robert Snowdon should have considered joining Butcher Bill's gang when he stepped off that ship, instead of signing up for the Army. Maybe he could have taught the old gangster a thing or two about bootlegging.

A Union soldier hanged in 1864-the same year as Snowdon.

BIG JACKIE, THE PITMEN & THE CPGB

Big Jack Charlton was one of our own; a true Northumbrian. Jack loved to come home to the crack in Ashington - sitting in a club with a pint and a hand of dominoes, going around the allotments to see the leek trenches and the pigeon duckets knocked together with bits of spare timber. Watching the whippets run on waste ground and getting away up a river in his waders with a rod in his hand. Flat-capped, Barbour jacketed and with a big grin, Jack might have gone around clumping folk on a football pitch in his white Leeds and England kit, but he was a real gentleman at heart. *You'll catch nowt but cold casting in there, Jackie, lad.*

The Charltons had long been in what was dubbed Britain's biggest pit village and were a part of the fabric of the tight-knit mining communities in the South-East of the county. My own Granda Jack had worked down the pit. I used to marvel at his NCB donkey jacket hung up by the dart board, the heat that came off the kitchen Aga and his motorbike stood in the brick passage by the scullery where the coal was piled up. He was a big influence on me. The Strike of 84/85 came during my formative years - a heady mix of football, teenage girls, Adam and the Ants, writing, the CPGB, the NUM and Arthur Scargill. Jack instilled a sense of social responsibility in me, a hatred for injustice and a strong belief in the trade union movement for both the good of the wider community and for social change.

The long red brick colliery rows of Ashington were a breeding ground for socialist ideas and working class politics and there was plenty of bother in the Northumberland coalfields in the wake of the General Strike back in 1926. A communist called Thomas Bruce was fined £10 at Morpeth under the Emergency Powers Act after he told a crowd of miners at Ashington to stop colliery deputies, who he called 'scabs' from going to work. Bruce declined to take the oath, saying he did not believe in religion and denied using the words. Another communist, John Parks, was sentenced to four months in jail under the same Act at Morpeth when it was alleged that he'd urged the men to fill up a pit shaft at Stobswood and threatened the manager at Ashington. Parks asked the crowd to pull out the safety men and attack the colliery officials. He advised a mass demonstration, with the result that there were scenes at the colliery next day.

A few of the Charltons were involved in organising the Communist Party in Ashington and in May 1940 T. Charlton presided over a meeting at the town's Trade Union Hall where Bill Rust, the editor of the Daily Worker and former International Brigader, was the main speaker. The Ashington branch of the party had some clout and brought up the Mile End communist MP Phil Piratin to give a Sunday afternoon talk, again in the Trade Union Hall in 1948. E.G. Charlton presided over that meeting.

The Ashington miner James Charlton had stood for a place on the Ashington Urban District Council the year before and it wasn't unusual for CPGB candidates to stand for elections in Northumberland. The Reds stood four candidates in the Hirst Ward for the Urban district elections in 1948. The same James Charlton, of Pont Street, received 310 votes and the other communist candidates C. McIntyre 275, D. Fearby 181 and I. Crooks 167.

An unemployed miner called John James Douglas had tried to stand in the Morpeth Borough elections as a communist in 1931 but when he handed in his papers to the Town Clerk, he was advised that he had to make a deposit of £130 as well. It all seemed a bit dodgy, especially as the other two candidates had called on the returning officer as soon as Douglas arrived.

The CPGB was especially strong in the neighbouring port of Blyth, and in November 1933 William Henry Breadin took a seat on the council in Blyth's Croft ward. They almost made it a double with Robert Swinney Elliott finishing fourth out of six candidates. However, in 1934 Elliott did join him on the Town Council as Croft ward returned two communist councillors.

Elliott, better known as Bob, was a man of some conviction and had been an unemployed coal miner himself when he'd stood for local public office. He went on a hunger march with the National Unemployed Worker's Movement down to London and was involved with the Court of Referees and the Blyth Poor Children's outing. His sense of duty saw him volunteer to fight out in Spain as a member of the International Brigade in the January of 1937. Bob Elliott became the Political Commissar for No.2 Company and it is reckoned that over 100 North East men and women went out to fight against General Franco including the likes of Frank Graham, Tommy Dolan, Bill Lower, Bert Overton, Bill Meredith (otherwise known as Ron Dennison, a labourer from Bellingham), John Henderson and Wilf Jobling from Chopwell. Bob had left Blyth on New Year's Day with two other men from the town to enlist in the Brigade. One was declared unfit for service and sent home, but Bob and his comrade Edward Thomas were accepted and set sail for Spain.

Councillor Breadin told a Blyth Town Council meeting in January that Bob was away in the International Brigade fighting for the Spanish Government and said: "However much you can disagree with his opinions I trust the Council will hope he will get back safe, and that he will do his little part for democracy." The Mayor, Ald. J. Reilly, replied: "We wish him well."

The bespectacled Bob Elliott was, however, killed in action near Madrid in the July of 1937. His sister was informed of his death in a letter from CPGB General Secretary Harry Pollitt, and she said: "He died for his ideals."

The letter from Pollitt read: *It is our sad responsibility to have to convey you news received from the headquarters the Spanish Battalion fighting in the Spanish Government Army, that comrade Bob Elliott has been killed in the recent fighting near Madrid. Comrade Elliott and others fell in the course of the victorious advance against Franco's Fascist forces, an advance which is a guarantee of ultimate victory over Franco. I wish to convey you our sincere and deep sympathy with you in the great loss you have suffered in the death of our Comrade Elliott, whose memory as a gallant fighter for peace and democracy will always be honoured.*

Elliott was much loved and respected in Blyth and tributes poured in from all over. His devastated Blyth CP comrade William Daniel of Plessey Road said: "It is sad to think that we will never again hear the voice we loved so well, or look again on his outstanding personality, which commanded the respect of all. He will be missed more and more as time goes on." Daniel reckoned that Bob could 'calm any outbreak of trouble with his persuasive manner.'

"His ideals will encourage many possessed with indomitable spirits like his to achieve the emancipation of the working-class. He left us, pent up with encouragement to keep the working-class struggle to the front at home, while he went to fight with the British section of the International Brigade in Spain," he continued.

"No bugle called him to his task, no bands, no drums, nor banners. His last letter to me was, 'Who had a better right to be in the firing line, than those who professed to be leaders of the working-class, and if he fell, he would be happy in the thought that he had practised what he preached.' All honour to Blyth to be able to possess men like him. My tribute to my fallen comrade: 'A soldier and a man of the working-class,'" concluded Daniel.

Mayor Reilly said that although he did not agree with Elliott's politics in the main, he was genuinely sorry to hear of his death and said he was a young man of whom he thought a great deal.

"I certainly admired the courageous way in which put forward his views, for which he fought and died, with a great tenacity of purpose," he said. Letters of sympathy and tribute also came from the Morpeth MP RJ Taylor, the chairman of the Blyth Labour Party and W. Allan, chairman of Blyth Communist Party. Elliott's friend and fellow communist councillor W.H. Breadin wrote that his death was a 'a profound tragedy and an irretrievable loss to the Trades and Labour Movements in our town and country.'

The rise of Fascism and Adolf Hitler in Germany would of course see thousands more men from the area serve in Europe during the armed conflict of the Second World War and it was very much a Left-leaning Labour Government that returning servicemen and women elected in 1945. The Blyth Communist Party sent many thanks and fraternal greetings 'to all its friends and sympathisers for all assistance given' during the elections that year with W.H. Breadin, R. Waters, T. Mooney, and N. Patrence signing the document. However, in 1949, the veteran Breadin lost his seats on both the County and Town councils. Although the communist influence among the coalfield communities was very diminishing in the electoral field, it was the Communist Party in Ashington that was the driving force behind the plan for a new maternity hospital for the pit town that year.

   I was born in that hospital, the now old Ashington General, which was built with money from the mineworkers, so my first view out on the world was probably of the pit head wheels. My paternal Nana had lived in the colliery row directly opposite the pit gates in Ashington as a child, her father big John Morgan another pitman who took pleasure from simple things in life such as corned beef sandwiches, mince and tatties, bottles of McEwan's Export in a social club. Coal is in all our blood in Northumberland; picture the pigeons flapping in blue skies, fading adverts on the gable ends of buildings and the steam rising off a slag heap with the red and yellow flag flapping behind; maybe the glinting colours of a starling hopping on riveted metal and a proud Jackie Charlton standing in his strip as if in a Paine Proffitt painting with his brother Bobby - our very own World Cup winners. Picture a community now gone.

THE ROTHBURY COLLIERIES

As well as going out under the North Sea, the great North East coalfield extended as far inland as Coquetdale and the seam of 'black gold' under Rothbury was the same as the one at Shilbottle.

They were still digging for coal at Britain's smallest mine, Hesleyhurst Colliery, in the early 1970s. Hesleyhurst was a drift mine that went 350 yards into the hillside was producing between 70 and 80 tons of coal a week in the summer of 1971. It was all being worked by hand and must have been backbreaking work, taking a pickaxe to the coal face and carting it out when their colleagues in the larger National Coal Board owned mines at the likes of Ellington, Ashington, and, of course, Shilbottle, were fully mechanised deep mines putting thousands of tons on the belt in huge operations that employed thousands of men.

The pit belonged to the Wards Hill Colliery Company under license from the Coal Board and employed seven men in '71. Arthur Pick, Tony Raine, Arthur Jackson, Ben Pick, William Gibson, Will Rutherford and James Stephenson were the miners at the tiny operation over the back of Simonside. The company wanted to bring the pit up to ten men and were offering £30 a week wages and free transport in a 20 mile radius so they could get production up to the break-even point of 120 tons. Finding skilled underground workers for the old-fashioned colliery proved difficult, however.

Hesleyhurst had almost been closed in 1969 when an underground spring flooded the works, but it limped on until its sudden closure on March 31, 1972. The pit boss Arthur Pick, who was 61, claimed he was owed over £400 after the colliery was locked up. He had spent 47 years in mine-working but an NUM scheme ensured he got nine tenths of his wage for three years after an enforced closure. The company went into voluntary liquidation, were wound up and the pit completely shut down in September 1973, just shy of its centenary.

John Caisley of Low Lee, near Wingates, had opened up the colliery at Wards Hill in May 1874 and was selling his best coals in the local area at 8s per ton or 6d per boll. He also sold small coals, for burning lime, and shop coal for blacksmiths – the two biggest industries outside agriculture in Coquetdale then.

The first pit opened up in the valley was probably on the moors adjacent to Cragside. Debdon Colliery was situated within the Rothbury North Forest and had opened up sometime around the 1780s. The pit had 16 years unexpired lease in the March of 1791 with John Robinson of Tuggal and Thomas Readhead of the Lee having a concern in the mine working. The lonely Pit Cottage up isolated in the tangled heather on the hills was originally a miner's residence, and there were further pit workings later at Newton on the Moor (Hunter Pit) and Longfram (Fanny Pit). By 1890, when a proposal was put forward to run a train line from Alnwick to Rothbury, Hunter had a seam averaging 32" thick and was producing 34 tons a day, while Fanny put out 30 tons a day, and employed 12 hewers and 25 hands in all.

Debdon Colliery was up for Let in 1803 with proposals to be sent to the Duke of Northumberland at Alnwick Castle, and in 1807 Robert Robinson, the overman of Debdon Quarry, was killed when the rope to get him down the shaft broke.

Robinson fixed a chain around his thigh in order to go down the shaft to work, but when he swung himself from the saddle board the rope snapped two feet above the chain and he fell 18 fathoms to his death. When examined, it was found that the rope had been coiled and lain against a lamp in the barrow way and was damaged. Robinson had been the last man up the shaft the night before.

A similar tragic accident happened in 1831. James Wakenshaw, a 56-year-old pitman, was on his way down the shaft to work at Debdon Colliery at 5 in the morning when he lost his holding and fell to the bottom of the shaft. He was killed instantly and a verdict of accidental death was recorded, though the non existent health and safety laws of the time were obviously protecting culpable mine owners.

Brinkburn Colliery, at The Lee, was offered to let in 1808 so must have been an ongoing concern from just before that time. The advert boasted that the Brinkburn coal was an 'excellent quality, being the same stratum as the Shilbottle seam,' and offered quality ground, pitman's houses and an extensive lime works to be let with the colliery. John Taylor and George Fletcher, both of Shilbottle, seemed to have a managerial concern in the pit at that time.

There was another underground death in the Rothbury coalfield in 1857 when the 34-year-old pitman John Watson was another victim of 'accidental death' as he was suffocated by foul air. Watson had gone down to the coal face without a candle burning to test the state of the air – the overman claimed that he'd warned him twice about this before. He was let down the shaft by a colleague, but didn't shout back up when he got to the bottom as agreed and the alarm was called. By the time they got down to him an hour later, poor Watson was stone dead.

The pit must have been struggling commercially as all of the plant at Brinkburn Colliery was put up for sale in 1876, and it showed what a large concern it was at the time. The gear consisted of '1 Eight or Nine H. P. Horizontal Winding Engine, in first- class working order, is all complete with Boiler and New Wrought Iron Chimney; about 3 Tons of Metal Tram Plates, Trams, Ropes, Horse Gin (neary new); Jack Roller with Stands, Ropes, and Kebbles, Shovels, 4c.; also the Quarry Plant, consisting of about Tons of Iron Rails, Side Tip Waggon, Levers, Mells, Hawks, Drills, 1 Set of Pony Gears (new), a quantity of Scrap Iron and Metal, 4c.' John Jackson at the Colliery could show the engine at work if required with notice given, and it was guaranteed that the boiler was tight and good. It seems that the brothers John and Thomas Turnbull may have put the money up as the following year a concession was offered for leading coals from the Lee Colliery the half mile to the railway line, while Ewesley colliery was also in operation at the time.

But there was another death down the mine due to foul air in 1880, and it was one of the joint-owners who were killed. The 51-year-old miner John Turnbull had gone down the shaft with a lit candle as was the safety practice of the time. Gabriel Hindhaugh, a miner from Hollinghill, had gone down after Turnbull and said Turnbull's candle was out when he got down into the blackness, so he lit it back up for him and sparked up his own wick. Turnbull told him the bad air at a working had put out his candle.

Hindhaugh rapped on the box and another miner, George Mills, came down. John Turnbull, the underground manager, left them to go and get his four-pound pick. The shaft at Brinkburn was 38 fathoms. There was a dip and rise in the workings of a few feet high; claustrophobic, dark and damp. When Turnbull didn't return, Hindhaugh and Mills went to find him and both of their candles were blown out by bad air. They tried to get the ventilation boxes going, but couldn't get to Turnbull for the bad air. His body was recovered the following day after a miner called Matthew Taylor sorted the fan blast in a ventilation box to suck out the foul air. The inquest into John Turnbull's death found, somewhat harshly, that it was 'caused by negligence and foolhardiness of the deceased himself' in that he'd died from 'suffocation by entering a coal mine where there was an accumulation foul air.'

Ten years later Brinkburn was not only producing coal, but ironstone boulders that the colliery was smelting themselves after descending the shaft and running a tramway to the face. Other materials of commercial interest included whinstone, sandstone, limestone, and fireclays. By 1913 a third share in the Brinkburn Colliery, near Rothbury, was offered as a 'splendid opportunity for anyone with capital' and the pit had 21 years left on the lease.

The following year the colliery featured in an animal cruelty case as the Rothbury cartman Robert Anderson was caught by Sergeant Cessford on Knocklaw Bank with a black gelding and a cart laden with coals. The horse was in obvious pain and could hardly walk, its feet being in a terrible state.

Both Anderson and the colliery manager Robert Grunson were fined for cruelty to the horse – Anderson 10s and Grunson £2 plus costs, though he still complained. In the June of 1918 Brinkburn Colliery were advertising for coal hewers wanted at the pit, with single men being given preference, but The Lee, or Brinkburn Colliery, was laid-in due to the depressed state of the coal trade in the February of 1925. The pit, when it was shut, employed a 'fair number of hands' and was just one of the colliery closures that were instrumental in the lead up to the General Strike in 1926.

Hesleyhurst pit

# THE ROTHBURY COLLIERIES

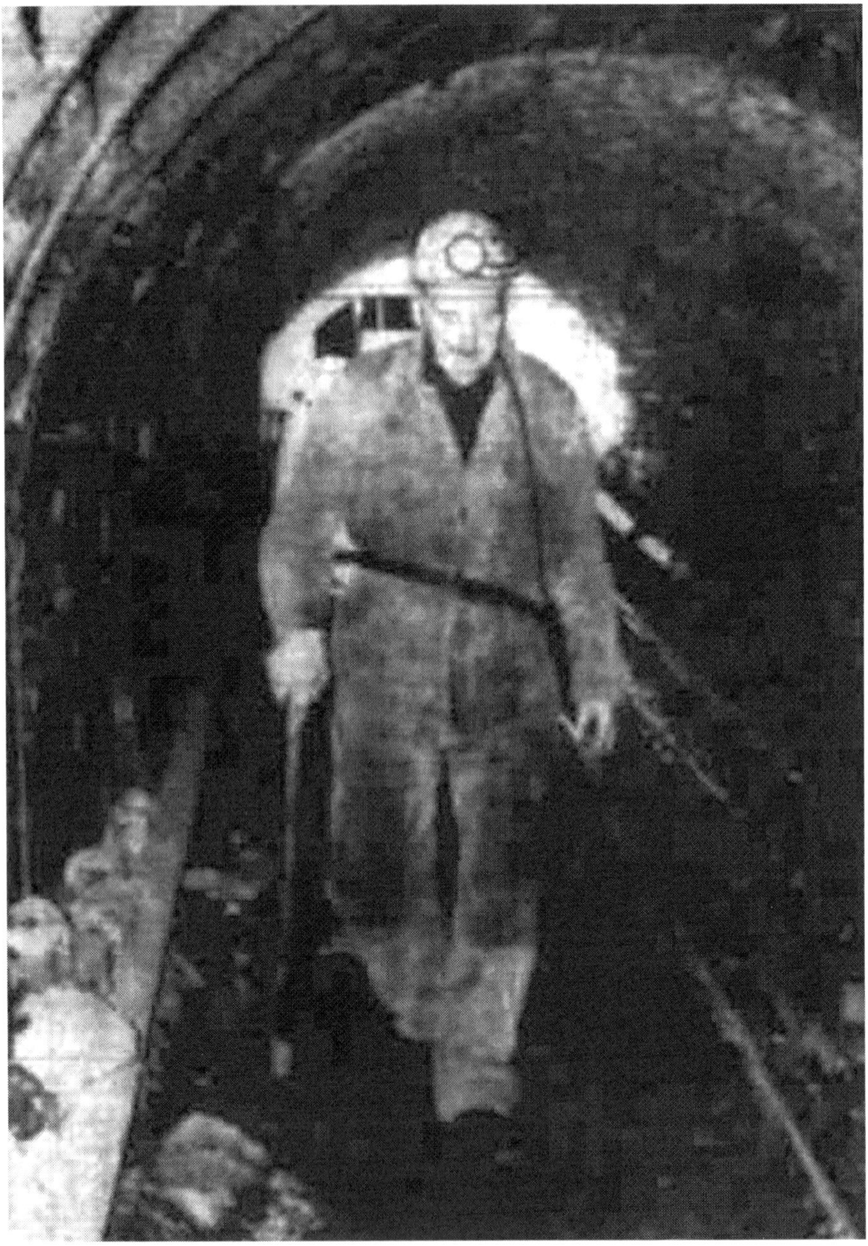

THE UP NORTH COMBINE

The birds sat up in their nesting boxes and cooed softly in the weak flickering light of the paraffin gas lamp. Although it was dark, it was barely tea time in a cold Coquet winter. You still had to go down and scrape the black and white muck off the wooden boards, then fling it on the frosted empty leek beds, and fill the feeding troughs and water trays. Twice a day, every day.

There was a big old rough burst orange armchair and a paint-splattered radio in the far end, with Up North Combine books, plastic eggs and spare rings on the shelving. The ducket had the calming atmosphere of a shed, only better. The wooden stakes on the roof to prevent the birds from settling as they came down – you wanted them to drop straight into the loft and get them clocked. Some of my dad's clocks were wooden boxes, others cold, grey metal affairs. Saturdays were generally race days, when he'd scan the blue skies for the distant black shape of a bird and get the feed tin out and shake it to bring them down.

"There's one, dad!"

"That's a bloody crow, man."

The sport of racing homing pigeons has been in steady decline for a good number of years. You can still pass a few lofts on the train into Newcastle from the west, buckshee ramshackle affairs in the old style, knocked together from any off-cuts of wood but beautiful in their own way. Practical, egalitarian, in candy stripes and practical lifted council colours on the embankments with litter pressed against the foot of the fencing. Flashed past to see men putting birds in baskets, standing on the boards of a cree extended over the years; traditional if a little melancholy.

The Rothbury Homing Society had started up in 1939 and in the first four races flown by the club S.B. Chisholme clocked in first and second in three and third in the other. Chisholme had been an absolute novice until the previous year, so his early success was a little unexpected. Other flyers in the Rothbury H.S. then included Tommy Proudlock and Thomas Rogerson. They were sending birds down to the likes of Peterborough, Selby and Hitchin to race. Chisholme's winner and second from Peterborough came in at a velocity of 1,011 and 1,008, while his Hitchin winner was clocked at 1,028. Proudlock's bird came second at 1,006 and Rogerson's third at 994.3. The velocity is calculated by the distance to the loft and the flying time.

The Coquetdale Federation at that time was made up of lofts at Homing Societies from the likes of Chevington, Amble, Radcliffe, Alnwick and Shilbottle. Hay of Chevington's bird that won the Selby race, with 1,037 pigeons competing, came home at a velocity of 1,455.3.

The sport had its beginnings in private pigeon flying matches such as the one from Newcastle to Dudley between James Emery's Coquet Lad and Michael Salkeld's bird Admiral which was flown for £4 in 1882. Coquet Lad was first home by 1 min 10 seconds, as clocked by Matthew Latty, who acted as the stakeholder and referee.

Three years later the members of the Bedlington Homing Club were sending 11 birds down to race from Peterborough in a pigeon flying handicap held at the Northumberland Arms Inn. The distance was 212 miles and Thomas Stephenson's Flying Scotchman won it. John Harrison's Gladstone was second and Douglas Reaveley's Greenbank third. Thomas Short and George Hay acted as the timekeepers and referees.

By 1905 pigeon racing was getting more organised and the Up North Combine, an amalgamation of all the Northern Federations, sent some 3,000 birds to Weymouth and on to Guernsey in 1905 where they were tossed up from the North New Quay at 5 in the morning by T.J. De Gruchy, the honorary president of the Jersey Flying Club. Mr. De Gruchy had also released the birds for the Scottish National Race which was won by Wyper & Tait with a velocity of 929 yards in the furthest race yet flown for the National in Scotland.

An Alnwick and District Homing Society had started up in around 1899 with Mr. J. Snowdon being the honorary secretary of the club. The officials of the club in 1906, which also ran an annual show of homing and racing pigeons (later adding rabbits), were G. W. Smart, president; W. Buddie, vice-president; Jos. Wood, secretary; John Macfarlane, assistant secretary; and R. Anderson, Alex. Fail, Jas. Hogg, J. Hetherington, J. Gair, H. Thompson, and H. Downey of Longhoughton were on the committee. The Alnwick club became affiliated to the Northumberland Homing Federation the previous year and had paid out £18 in prize money.

The Northumberland Homing Federation to which the Alnwick Club were attached was a large concern and they held an annual show at Morpeth from 1904. There was a record entry of over 500 birds in the 1907 show, though it was held a little early and a number of them were still moulting. Birds were entered into the competitions from clubs at Ashington, Alnwick, Shilbottle, Radcliffe, Morwick, Acklington, Morpeth, Backworth, New Hartley, Christon Bank, Embleton, Ryton, Bedlington, Bates Colliery and as far afield as Greenlaw in Berwickshire, Chester-le-Street, West Hartlepool, BarnardCastle, Thornaby-on-Tees, Clitheroe and Harrogate.The Newcastle House Hotel in Morpeth was the headquarters of the Northumberland Homing Federation.

The Up North Combine organised a long race from Rennes in France in July 1909 where bad weather held the birds over until a Tuesday morning liberation in nice sunshine with a light westerly wind. Clubs at Tynemouth and North Shields had birds in that race and by 1911 the Up North Combine were putting up 20,000 birds in a race from Luton as the popularity of pigeon racing continued to grow in the North East.

J.W. Parkin of Cramlington was the President of the Northumberland Homing Federation and the affiliated clubs by 1912 included the likes of Cramlington, Ashington, Ashington West End, Burradon and West Moor, Bedlington Station, Seaton Delaval, WhitleyBay, North Seaton, East Chevington, Hirst, Broomhill and the North of England Club, who all sent along delegates to the Morpeth AGM.

John Smith of Ashington was awarded a special prize by the Federation for the best averages for old birds all season with an average velocity of 1,198 yards per minute. Thomas Boldon of Barrington won the young birds prize with an average velocity of 1.068.

The officials of the Federation at the time were President: Mr. J. W. Parkin (Cramlington); vice presidents: Messrs. W. H. Endean (Cramlington). R. Fryer (Seaton Delaval), W. Dott (Bedlington), and A. Burton (Hirst); secretary and treasurer: Mr. J. Hennesey, Ashington; auditors: Messrs. T. Potts (Ashington) and R. Dott (Bedlington). The Federation delegates to the Up North Combine were J.W. Parkin and John William Hennesey, who was seeking damages for slander the following year when a pitman called Thomas Tunstall of Backworth reckoned that the balance sheet had shown £3 more in prize money than was paid and 24 for entries in the annual show than had been accounted for. Hennessy said he wasn't bothered about the damages but just wanted to clear his good name, and was awarded £5 in damages after the court found in his favour.

The Cramlington Homing Society was obviously powerful with their lofts competing in Northumberland Federation and Up North Combine races, but the north of the county were also producing some good pigeons and T.R. Ternent and J. Hogg of the Alnwick HS entered three birds in the National Open Race from Bournemouth, finishing a respectable 45th and 49th on the list. Ternent and Albert Smith also sent four birds to compete in the Homing Pigeon National Homing race flown from Jersey that summer. The First World War stopped pigeon racing in 1915

By the end of the conflict, many lofts had squeakers with their bright yellow down with racing looking to make a comeback as life slowly regained some normality. By 1921 a pigeon show at Chester-Le-Street in the Workmen's Club in Pelton Fell, reputed to be the largest in the North of England, attracted 495 entries. Among the birds on show included the legendary 'Mons Hero' bred by Brass and Bruce of Easington Lane that had won the Combine's Mons race in 1911. T. Dent of West Hartlepool also brought along his celebrated pigeon that had won the Mons race that year, been fourth in the Up North Combine and had won the All England.

One of G. Fenwick of North Seaton's birds placed well in the Mons race the following year and had won him pool money of £13 8s. The North Seaton lofts, along with Seaton Delaval, Bedlington, Bedlington Station and Seaton Burn were placing well in the Northumberland Homing Federation races then. The Up North Combine's annual meeting took place at the Crow's Nest Hotel in Newcastle where it was reported that Hindhaughs Ltd of Newcastle had given £20, and Lloyds News £5 for the Mons race in prize money alongside the much-valued Chronicle Cup. The secretary had visited Luton and Nottingham to select the best sites for liberating birds from them for races. Applications to join the Combine were accepted from Chester-Le-Street Osborne, Brandon Colliery, Teams, Gateshead Central and Guisborough Homing Societies. A prominent official in pigeon racing, Robert Fryer, of Stable Row Seaton Delaval, died in 1923. Mr. Fryer had been the secretary of the Northumberland Federation and vice-president of the Up North Combine, and was also a member of the Management and Appeals Committee of the North of England Homing Union.

The old Mons race was gone and other changes were made to the race points and distances for the 1925 season for the Up North Combine. The birds flew from Selby 86 miles, Doncaster 104 miles, Grantham 149 miles, Peterborough 175 miles, Hitchin 217 miles, Hastings 299 miles, Amiens (Belgium) 387 miles, Melum (France) 481 miles and Nevers (France) 589 miles.

The Combine were giving £100 for the Amiens race, as well as a gold medal and the Chronicle Cup. Clubs had to pay a penny a basket for every race into the Combine insurance scheme to safeguard their baskets during transportation. The railway companies, and the LNER especially, offered a grant to pigeon fanciers for special carriages to take baskets of birds for training stages. The trains left Newcastle each day at 10.32 am and stopped at Durham, Ferryhill, Darlington, Northallerton, Thirsk and York. The Up North Combine had drinking troughs at each station in case of any hold-overs.

In the May of 1929 over 20,000 birds from Newcastle and other Northern clubs went down to Selby on a special train of 22 vans for an Up North Combine race. A railway inspector called P. Marshall, of Newcastle, was in charge of the convoy and the birds were liberated from the new goods yard at Selby.

The Up North Combine by the early '30s covered a combination of Racing Pigeon Clubs from at least twenty-four towns and districts in Northumberland and Durham. In 1932 there were 12 old bird races, including four from towns in France, and five young bird races with a total of 15,886 baskets dispatched containing 290,084 pigeons. The season ran from the end of April or beginning of May through to the end of August or the beginning of September. Twenty-eight trains had been used by the Combine to convey birds in 1932. The race points for the old birds were from Selby, Retford, Grantham, Peterborough, Hitchin, Newhaven (twice), Amiens, Newhaven again, Melum and Nevers, while the young birds were released at Selby, Retford, Grantham, Peterborough and Hitchen (twice).

The Combination dealt with organisational matters such as 'race rings (the bird's identification numbers), race registers, distances, timing, velocities, arrangements for convoying the birds to the race points, accounting, and a multiplicity of other details incidental to the successful conduct of pigeon racing on a large scale,' with the railway companies transporting the birds – the LNER dealing with the Combine's baskets. Racing pigeons were flying up to 700 miles at an average velocity, depending on the distance, of 36 miles per hour.

The Combine added another long-distance race in June 1937 when twenty thousand pigeons crossed the Channel in special steamer on the way to Arras, where they were released from, the shutters dropping and a mass of birds blackening the sky with a thunderous applause of flapping wings in an awesome spectacle.

In March 1938 the Wooler HS transferred from the Coquetdale Federation to the Berwick Homing Society, where they joined up with the Spittal, Scremerston and Berwick clubs. William Clark was the Society's Combine delegate and he reported that he'd been elected as the convenor representative for the Borders. Mr. Pirie of Cornhill, a Wooler racer, was elected as a delegate to the Combine with him. The clubs agreed to form a Federation Championship Club which would be flown from the three

Channel Race destinations with a fee of £1 and three birds per race.

Although the Rothbury Club had just started up, the advent of the Second World War again put a stop to pigeon racing, though homing birds proved valuable to the war effort and were used as messengers.

The golden age of homing pigeon racing probably came around the 1950s in Northumberland. A 14-year-old lad from the North Sunderland H.S. called Scott Smith was making headlines as he'd won the Freeman silver cup four years out of five and was the only loft to have clocked in birds on the day the Welwvn Garden City National Race in the Up North Combine. Smith's birds had gained first and second position for the Seahouses-based club, first and sixth in the Coquetdale Federation, ninth and 42nd in the Up North Combine and 16th in the North of England Championship. He had placed third in that race in 1948. There were 2,857 lofts in the North Combine by 1950 and another loft enjoying success at nearby Alnwick were the brothers W. and F. Baston who won every club trophy going with their birds that season.

The popularity of pigeons had always been strong in the mining communities of south-east Northumberland and in 1953 the long-serving Up North Combine secretary Fred Potts assisted T. Holliday, the president of the National Union of Mineworkers (Northumberland Area), S. Nicholson, Divisional Social Welfare Officer, and Games Leagues secretary, John Riddell, all of the Games Leagues Section of the Coal Industry Social Welfare Organisation to start a pigeon racing competition solely for pitmen.

The race was to be flown in conjunction with the second Brussels Race of the Up North Combine held on Monday 27th June and 9,370 birds were sent in 562 baskets.

Davidson Bros. & Kendal (Hirst) won the inaugural race (and came 9th in the Combine), and were presented with a small silver cup with a pigeon attached to the lid. Bland & Sons (Ashington) came second (10th in Combine) and Snowdon and Strutt (Chevington) third (18th in the Combine).

There was an annual pigeon fanciers' supper held at the Welfare Hall in Pegswood and the prizes were handed out by the former Birmingham City, Blackpool and LincolnCity footballer Tom Robinson that year. These were well-attended and popular affairs but as the coal industry declined in the region so, sadly, did the pastimes and recreations that had been provided by the Welfare societies associated with the pits and only a relative handful of pigeon men keep the sport alive today.

But the Up North Combine still has 23 Federations and 120 clubs affiliated, with a dwindling membership of 2614, so when you look up into the blue skies and you may see a small clutch of birds circling over Rothbury - the last of the great racers.

THE NORTHERN ASSOCIATION

While the gentleman Henry Ogle donned the metal breastplate and white leather gloves and joined the Government forces during the English Civil War, John and Thomas Ogle were among the ranks of the more flamboyant Cavaliers that supported the King. For Cromwell or the Crown? Nothing divided families more in Northumberland with fathers, sons, brothers, uncles and cousins all ending up on opposing sides during the violent and bloody conflict.

The Civil War wasn't just one conflict but a long running series of local skirmishes, battles and sieges over politics and religion running from roughly between the years 1638-40, 1642-46 and 1648-51 so it's hard to say who actually won. Although King Charles I was beheaded by Parliament for treason in January 1649, the monarchy was restored in 1660 when his son King Charles II reclaimed the throne. So you have to wonder what the estimated 90,000 combatants lives that were lost to horrendous musket shot, cannonball and cutlass were actually ultimately sacrificed for. Some stood for Parliament and Presbyterianism, others for Royalty and Catholicism, and many others were probably just up for a fight.

Henry Ogle was one of the Northumbrians charged with raising 173 horse and 467 Foot in the county and the City of Newcastle for the Parliamentarian army known as the Northern Association in June 1645. The list of those that were to get the men of the county to enlist alongside him was long and distinguished, too. Algernon (Percy) Earl of Northumberland, James Earl of Suffolk, William Lord Gray of Wark, Sir John Fenwick, Sir Arthur Hazelrigg, Sir John Delaval, Sir Robert Jackson, Sir Thomas

Widdrington and Sir William Selby were all knights, while Michael Weldon, William Fenwick of Wallington, Ralph Delaval, Robert Fenwick, Thomas Middleton, Edward Wright, William Fenwick of Stanton, William Shaftoe, Thomas Laurence (formerly Lorraines), George Payler, Richard Foster, Henry Horsley, Alexander Collingwood, John Hall of Otterburn, Robert Clavering, Ralph Salkeld, William Armorer and Robert Dodsworth were all other important local landowners that Cromwell needed to get onside. Those same gentlemen were also entrusted to form a militia in the county three years later.

Ogle must have wished he hadn't bothered when in 1657 he was served a writ by Sir Robert Collingwood, who was a Colonel in that Regiment of Foot, for payment of £1,500. He, along with the by then deceased William Shaftoe and Sir William Selby, were Commissioners for Raising of Forces for the Parliament in the Northern Association and must have each promised Collingwood a payment of £500. He now wanted his cash and was putting the whole burden of Ogle. The matter was brought to an Assize at Newcastle and Ogle was locked up for two years but released in 1659, so the whole affair must have left a bitter taste for the old Roundhead.

Another Parliamentarian called Lieutenant Colonel Thomas Ogle, and two others, were excepted against, and 'conceived to be unfit Persons to be employed as Commanders' while raising 5,000 men and 500 horse for fighting in Ireland in July 1642, while the Northumbrian Cavalier John Ogle, while being held prisoner in Winchester House in 1645, asked for License to be bailed go to Holland as his friends were either in the Low Countries or Denmark. Later that year a Captain Ogle, who had been condemned for Treason, escaped prison and 'hath since acted against the State.' Other families that were very much divided by loyalties included the Fenwicks, with another Sir John Fenwick being a Colonel in the Royalist Army whose skull and helmet reside in the Old Gaol at Hexham today. He was killed in the bloody battle at Marsden Moor in 1644. Sir Thomas Liddell of Newcastle fought for the Royalists at the Battle of Edgehill and was described as 'one of the most notorious delinquents in the country' while another Royalist delinquent, Sir Thomas Haggerston, forfeited his lands and estates to the

Commonwealth for treason in 1651.

John Swinburne at Capheaton was staunchly Royalist, as were the bulk of the Catholic Selbys, the Radcliffes of Dilston and the Clennells of Clennell Hall.

Northumberland had seen first hand what was coming when in 1640 an army of 20,000 Scottish Covenanters crossed the Border and fought a battle against 5,000 English troops at Newburn before besieging Newcastle. Even closer to home, in 1644, the castle at Morpeth was garrisoned by a party of Scots Parliamentarians and they were able to withstand a twenty-day siege from a Scottish Royalist army 2,700 strong despite a barrage of cannonballs and musket shot.

The strangest Northumbrian story of division among a family during the Civil War concerned the laird of Clennell and the King of the Border gypsy tribe. One John Faw was the early leader of the Faa Gang, known as Lord and Earl of Little Egypt, as he appeared around the Dunbar area and was granted letters from King James V in 1540 and 1553 giving him authority over all the gypsies in Scotland. The Faas established themselves in Kirk Yetholm where the GypsyPalace stands and regularly travelled between there and Carlisle as they roamed the border stopping at places such as Berwick, Wooler, Alnwick, Rothbury, Morpeth, and Hexham along the way. They left a strong legacy in the language itself with Romani words such as jewkle, gadgie, deek and so on still remaining part of the lexicon in the whole Borders area.

Trouble and persecution came in 1609 when a Proclamation banished 'Egyptians' from Scotland. To show they were serious, in 1611 a Scottish Assizes at Edinburgh sent Moses, David, Robert and John, alias Willie Faa to be hanged at the Borrowmuir for being 'Egyptians' (Gypsies) and remaining in the country.

Some four years later a Scotsman called William Auchterlonie was charged with the resetting of Egyptians – especially Johnnie Faw, the 'notorious Egyptian and Chieftain of that unhappy class of people.' Johnnie, his son James Faa, Moses Bailzie and his wife Helen Brown, all Egyptians, were again charged with breaking the 1609 Act banishing them from Scotland in 1616 and were also hanged on the Borrowmuir. The same grim sentence was passed in 1624 on Captain John Faa, along with Robert, Samuel, young John, Andrew and William Faa, Robert Brown and Gavin Trotter, all denounced as Egyptians, vagabonds and common thieves. The females of the tribe - Captain John's wife Helen, James Brown's wife Lucrece Faa, Elspeth and Katherine Faa, Meriore, Jeanne, Margaret and Isobel Faa, Margaret Vallantyne and another Elspeth Faa were at the same time sentenced to be taken away and drowned. Thankfully they all, along with Alexander, John and Francie Faa – the sons of Captain John – and Harry Brown, had their execution superseded and were subsequently kicked out of Scotland 'on pain of instant death' with their children 'never to return' - hence the semi-settlement of what was left of that branch of the Faas within the Rothbury Forest.

By the December of 1628 Willie Faa was reputed to be King of the Tribe and he was married to an Elspeth. Legend has it that Will's travelling family wracked up at Clennell Hall one miserable wet night looking for shelter as they traipsed around the Northumberland hills. Although they were given shelter by one of Clennell's servants, the laird discovered them and kicked them out, cursing them 'as thieves born to the gallows.' Auld Wull cursed that Clennell would rue his decision, and over the next few weeks Clennell's cattle were stolen, horses maimed and sheep killed. He set out with his men and discovered the gypsy encampment in the Rothbury forest, burning it to the ground in retribution. But Willie Faa bided his time, on the advice of Elspeth, and two years later struck back by kidnapping Clennell's young son and heir, Henry, a child of 3-years-old, making the leap over the Thrum Mill rocks to evade the men that gave chase. And with that, it is said, the Faas were gone, away to wander, with Clennell's child in tow according to *Wilson's Tales of the Border*.

Many years later the laird of Clennell was a follower of the King and a Cavalier who was engaged in the street to street fighting in Worcester in 1651, during what was the final battle of the Civil War. Cromwell's New Model Army was well organised, efficient and 28,000 strong, but the King's 16,000 men, the bulk of whom were Scots, put up a stubborn resistance.

Around 3,000 of them were killed and 10,000 captured during the battle.

The laird of Clennell, it is said, rode aware from the carnage and was heading back North when he rode into a troop of Parliamentary soldiers. A ragged-looking, vengeful crew sat around a fire. They captured him and brought him to their leader, who only turned out to be Willie Faa. The irony no doubt tickled the old gypsy and he handed a pistol to one of his men and told them to execute the landowning Royalist. As the young Roundhead was cocking the pistol, Elspeth Faa came running forward and told him to stop. The man who was about to execute Clennell was only his long-gone kidnapped son, Henry, who the Faas had raised as one of their own. The Clennells were tearfully reunited, old Elspeth went back with them and lived into her 90s and as for Willie, well, no-one really knows. What is fact, however, is that his descendents lived in the Rothbury Forest well into the 19th century and they also inhabited Gateshead Fell. 18 of the Faas were transported to South Carolina from Morpeth on board a ship from the Tyne in April 1752 and Patrick Faa, along with seven other gypsies from Yetholm, were 'transported to the Queen's America for life,' but Charles Faa Blyth was crowned the King of the Yetholm gypsies in 1898 in a ceremony that was reportedly witnessed by up to 10,000 people.

THE LAST NORTHUMBRIAN PIRATE

Hoist the Jolly Roger. Who wouldn't want to be a pirate and experience the hot sun beating down on your back as the ropes creak on wood and the waves gently rock the ship side to side. The draw of robbing vessels and digging treasure on palm-lined beaches, gold pieces of 8 and jewellery in chests; setting port in Cuba, Florida, the Bahamas, the suntanned freckled shoulders of girls with wicked hazel eyes slamming down drinks in pewter mugs. Rum, tri-corner hats, bandanas, salty weather-beaten jackets, the skull and cross bones and the blast of cannon, never mind the democracy of an equal share in plunder, the right to choose your captain and the releasing of slaves – yes, it's a pirate's life for me.

Who knows how many privateers sailed out from the port of Tyne during the height of the pirating times? One very early pirate who was raiding around the mouth of the river and attacking the merchants heading out from Newcastle to Lescluses in Flanders was a John de Santa Agatha. In 1335 he had a severe dispute with Thomas Gordon of Newcastle, who killed him and was taken to prison. The English king, Edward III, was probably secretly pleased that Gordon had murdered the 'lawless pirate' who had inflicted 'damage and injuries upon merchants of the king's realm and power upon the sea, and on other subjects of the king in lands beyond, killing some, plundering others, wounding and imprisoning and detaining as prisoners until they should make fines with John, sinking their ships,' and did not want to see Thomas Gordon perish. He asked the merchants of the port to collect together the £60 needed to secure his release 'with speed.'

When you look at some of the names as piracy increased during the late

17th Century, then a few could have hailed from the area – John Coxon, John Graham, William Jackson and Lewis Scott could possibly all have had ties to the Border region. One sailor who definitely came from Northumberland and became a pirate was a man called Thomas Younghusband from Berwick-upon-Tweed. Unfortunately for Younghusband, the ship he was pirating on was sailing around the coast of Holland. And was French.

He was on board the privateer cutter the Velocite which was taken by a Royal Navy frigate in 1811 while cruising around the Texel, an island off the Dutch coast, so forget about the beaches and the sunshine. You can guarantee they'd been sailing in drizzle and storms, soaked through and miserable under grey skies. Typical.

Younghusband, a man of around 40, claimed that he'd been acting as an assistant surgeon and civil officer on the ship but 'had never borne arms against His Majesty.' He was of a respectable appearance and conducted himself 'with becoming modesty and decorum' at his trial for Piracy at the Admiralty Sessions at the Old Bailey in London in 1812.

Younghusband's story was quite amazing – he'd left Berwick in around 1791 for Ostend, in Belgium, with his mother to join his father, a Captain in the British Navy. He had met and married a French girl with whom he had three children but 'misfortune and distress' had apparently driven him to France where he was 'threatened and forced to bear arms, as other men were then obliged to do' in the French Revolution.

The native Berwicker was then forced to serve upon the privateer ship and produced documents that supposedly proved his compulsory means of being forced into French service, though this could not be proved by the court. A men called William Pellison of Berwick was brought down to London and he told the trial that he'd known the prisoner's father very well and that he'd gone abroad 'in embarrassed circumstances' which were not revealed. He also knew Younghusband, as did other witnesses from the Border town.

A midshipman from the Desiree frigate that had apprehended Younghusband's cutter said that he'd told him he was a native of Holland but had been educated in Edinburgh and that Captain Younghusband of the British Navy and other officers were relatives of his. He was charged with being found on board a French privateer, aiding and abetting the King's enemies, he being a natural born subject of the realm. Sir William Scott expressed some sympathy while passing sentence, but Thomas Younghusband was found guilty and hanged by the neck until dead.

While it was unusual enough for a Northumbrian to be raising the Black Flag for the French, what was even more surprising in 1871 was an aristocrat from the area who was caught waving the Red Flag.

The French police arrested a man in Paris that October with the surname Percy, who claimed to be 'a relation of the Dukes of Northumberland, and allied on his mother's side to the clan of the Lord of the Isles, of which the Prince of Wales is the chief.'

Percy, it was alleged, had long lived in France and had been named 'lieutenant d'habillement by the Commune, and was attached to Colonel Brun as orderly officer.' He was nabbed in an elegant apartment in the Boulevard Haussmann belonging to a 'well-known demi-monde lady,' thus adding a bit of sexual intrigue to the strange case of the gentleman Communist, which was reported in Liberti and the Pall Mall Gazette. Who can this Percy be who combines tailoring with the military art? the society papers questioned. Although it's difficult to imagine one of the landed gentry on the barricades of the world's first Communist revolution, it appears that he was actually there and took part in one of history's great moments.

Us Northumbrians get everywhere, man. Do you hear the people sing?

THOMAS BURT: FROM PIT TO PARLIAMENT

It was one of the iconic moments of the Miner's Strike of 1984/85. The elderly American chairman of the NCB Ian MacGregor falling backwards in comedic slow motion over a low wall at Ellington as a wave of angry striking pitmen surged forward.

Blokes in donkey jackets and orange furry-hooded parkas, their faces twisted in rage under flat caps and woolly beanies, shouting and cursing. The shocking images of the police violently charging and battering striking miners on picket lines in Yorkshire will live long in the memory of those who saw them. The memories will live even longer in the rumbling bellies of the school lads who were living on sugar on toast for their tea at the time.

While the 1984/85 strike marked the start of the end of the Northumberland coalfield, there had been at least three Great Strikes in the area during the 19th Century black diamond boom- one in 1831/32, one in 1843/44 and another in 1877/78. The Northumberland and Durham Miners had formed together into a union called 'The Colliers of the United Association of Durham and Northumberland' around 1825 under their leader Thomas Hepburn, who had been working in the collieries from the age of 8. The fledgling trade union was further strengthened by the strike actions in 1832 when scabs shipped in from the Cumberland coalfields were violently attacked by North East pitmen who won shorter working hours and the right to be paid in money rather than tokens.

The 1843/44 dispute was mainly over safety and the introduction of monthly rather than annual contracts in an attempt by the owners to break the union, with over 40,000 men meeting at Sheddon's Hill in Birtley. These actions were less successful, with men that had joined the associations being blacklisted by the colliery owners. The men were starved back to work after 20 weeks by tactics that included being evicted from their homes and seeing blackleg labour shipped in from around the country.

Thomas Burt was born at Murton Row near Backworth on the 12th November 1837, the son of a coal hewer called Peter Burt. He was working underground himself by the age of 10 as a trapper boy at Haswell Pit. Burt became the secretary of the then Northumberland Miners' Association in 1863 and just 11 years later was elected the M.P. for Morpeth. Burt was a Lib-Lab candidate and one of the first ever working-class members to take a seat in Westminster.

So the pitmen had one of their own in a position of power and that was tested just three years into his term in Parliament, in the January of 1877, when a bitter 13-month dispute broke out over a wage reduction demanded by the employers. The bosses wanted to impose a 20% reduction – the union offered to drop 8%.

Delegates representing the union from the various collieries in Northumberland met at Burt's offices in Newcastle in the May to count the votes of the men as to referring the dispute to arbitration and whether to come out on strike; the vast majority (eleven-twelfths) of the men voted to join the industrial action which continued until the 12th of February 1878. A ballot among the colliery districts returned a majority of 943 for a return to work and accepting the reduction, though a large proportion of the men didn't bother voting. The Miners' Association brought the strike to an end and an eventual 12 ½ % reduction imposed by the bosses.

Burt was a moderate voice of reason in a turbulent time and he told a Miner's Conference at Manchester in 1882 that 'one of the suggestions in the programme for bringing about an improvement in wages is that there should be a general strike on the part the miners. That, however, is wild, chimerical, and impracticable, and does not deserve a moment's consideration the part of any body of sensible, intelligent men.'

The delegates, however, voted just for that motion to be carried as militancy grew among the organised working class.

When there was another big strike and lock-out in Northumberland in 1887 the Socialists of the Social Democratic Federation (SDF) were accused of stirring up trouble among the men after speeches were made at a disorderly gathering of around 2,000 in Blyth marketplace asking what the likes of Burt had ever done for them. With responses like 'nowt,' there was some dissention and jostling among the crowd and the speaker back-tracked a bit, saying: "He (Thomas Burt) might be very honest and willing to do good, but be had to fight against a large capitalist class in the House." A local speaker also defended Thomas Burt, saying that he was disappointed to hear his integrity being questioned and that 'Mr. Burt had not many supporters in the House, yet he had done noble work to benefit the working classes.'

With over 16,000 Northumbrian men and boys out of work and on strike, they looked to the other traditional mining areas for support, getting assistance from neighbouring Durham, West Cumberland, Yorkshire and the Welsh miners in the Rhondda. The lock-out had started on January 28th after the masters originally demanded a reduction of 15% in the wages of the men employed at the steam-coal collieries, and of 10% in the wages of the soft-coal miners. The Northumberland Miners' Provident Association had paid out £13,000 in assistance to unemployed members over the proceeding 12 months and was costing around £8,000 a week to sustain the action.

There were further accusations of agitation by the likes of the poet William Morris who told the striking Northumberland miners that they 'were looked upon as a class from which the utmost and best that could expected was that some of them would have the luck to get out of the position of workers, to be thrifty, to save money, and become legalised thieves,' which obviously went down like a lead balloon. They didn't want lectured on revolutionary socialism by someone that earned their living as a capitalist writer and wallpaper and furniture manufacturer, according to a writer in one newspaper. But branches of the SDF were formed in Backworth, Throckley, Ashington and other colliery villages, under the local leadership of John Williams, and a Mr. O'Neil of Dudley Colliery said 'they had taken a large number of names for the purpose of forming a branch of the SDF and he believed they would eventually get the whole of the miners to join. They wanted to join a body that would unite the workers in every part of the country.'

The Socialist League were also getting involved in the dispute and they held a demonstration on behalf of the Northumberland miners on Sunday afternoon in Hyde Park in April 1887. A collection was made for the men on strike and brought in £3 8s 6d. The 17-week strike ended in the May. A two-day conference and negotiation between 'the Wages Committee of the miners and the Strike Committee of the owners' was concluded with the miners agreeing to accept a reduction 12 ½ per cent, in the case of steam collieries, and 6 ½ per cent, in that of house coal collieries. It was expected that the pits would all resume work the following Monday.

There was another demand in wages reduction from the bosses in 1893 but it was noted that there was less stomach for a fight after the 'bitter and protracted' 1887 strikes and the bosses original 7 ½ % demand for a wages reduction was modified to 5% at the request of the miner's representatives. The press claimed at the time that the lessons learned from the 1887 strike were to go for a 'frequent and moderate adjustment of wages' rather than slamming the workforce with a massive 15% hit. The Scottish mine owners were also proposing a 6d a day reduction in their pits, which was received with understandable hostility.

This sense of moderation was continued by the pitmen's MP Thomas Burt and in 1901 the Morpeth member advised the Northumberland Miners' Association that they were acting unwisely in disassociating themselves from the Trades Union Congress (TUC) as 'they have many interests in common, and congresses are of great educational value.' Burt had only spent two years at village schools before going underground but was a keen exponent of continual learning, like so many trade unionists, and was a keen and avid reader. He had also been the TUC President in 1891. It was reported that Burt did not think that 'the permanent cure for industrial conflicts lies the direction of compulsory arbitration,' so was still committed to the industrial action of his Radical youth when he 'sought to remove all class laws.'

However, in the October of 1909, there were remarkable scenes at a meeting in Blyth when a vote of confidence in Burt was carried after he had refused to sign the Labour Party's constitution. The veteran Lib-Lab MP said he could not sign as the constitution 'struck a blow at the reality and vitality of Parliamentary representation.' He was visibly moved by the support he was shown in the outburst and said he would issue a manifesto at a later date fully stating his position to the miners.

The march of Socialism was continuing on however, and Northumberland elected their first Socialist to the County Council in March 1910 when Councillor Robert Gilbertson of the I.L.P. (Independent Labour Party) took the seat for Ashington Hirst Division. A newspaper report stated that 'the teeming population of the largest mining district in Northumberland has once more shown its advanced democratic sympathies by returning the first Labour and Socialist member for Northumberland County Council.'

The I.L.P. had been successful in getting comrade Rae Patterson elected to Ashington Urban Council four years earlier and he had been joined by fellow I.L.P. members Warne and Walter Wilson in subsequent elections, so Burt must have been well aware of a Leftward shift in his electorate as he started to lose their undivided support. The Northumberland miners were out again in 1910 over the Eight Hours Act and by the fifteenth week of the strike, the Northumberland Miners' Association had spent £70,000 in relief pay.

Industrial action rocked the Northumberland coalfields again in 1912 and the Executive Committee of the Northumberland Miners' Association met in their headquarters in Newcastle which they had named after their MP – the Burt Hall. There were 34,362 full members and 5,185 half-members of the NMA at the time and the cost of that first strike would amount to £45,000. The total funds of the union were around £90,000. An official predicted that the strike would run for a further month.

Interestingly, at a meeting of the Rothbury Mutual Improvement Society in the village in January 1913, Hon. W. Watson Armstrong, the son of Baron Armstrong of Cragside – a known Unionist and anti-Socialist said that 'strikes weren't a bad idea.' It caused a bit of a society sensation in the capitalist press as an 'out-spoken democratic utterance' when 21-year-old Armstrong told the hall that he was an 'out-and-out democrat' and 'drastic measures were needed to limit the capitalist. Wages ought be much larger all round, while housing ought to be brought a proper standard, and the State should see to that. We were slow in England in advancing. The oppression of the working man should be done away with. It was absurd that land should be owned by so few, and that it should be so largely used for shooting and fishing purposes, while the farmer suffered high rents and labourers in low wages. Great social evils required drastic measures.'

Just three months later Thomas Burt retired from his post as General Secretary of the Northumberland Miners' Union after 48 years. It was said that he had started with strong convictions and had retained them all the way through his term in office. He died in 1922 in Newcastle at the age of 84.

Burt had spent 18 years working underground before becoming a prominent trade unionist. He was the Morpeth MP from 1874 to 1918 and rose to the position of Privy Councillor. When he and the Scottish miners' leader Alexander MacDonald were elected the Members of Parliament for Morpeth and Stafford respectively, they became the first Labour (Lib-Lab) MPs. Burt was also the first Labour member to accept office member of the Government when he served as Parliamentary Secretary to the Board of Trade from 1895.

Burt has a black plaque at 20 Burdon Terrace in Newcastle where he lived from 1892, a row of aged miners' cottages in Choppington have his name and there is a picture and text on him in the 'Electrical Wizard' Wetherspoons pub in Morpeth. Perhaps it is time to give Thomas Burt more recognition for his lifetimes' work and maybe a bronze in the square outside the Comrades Club would be more suitable.

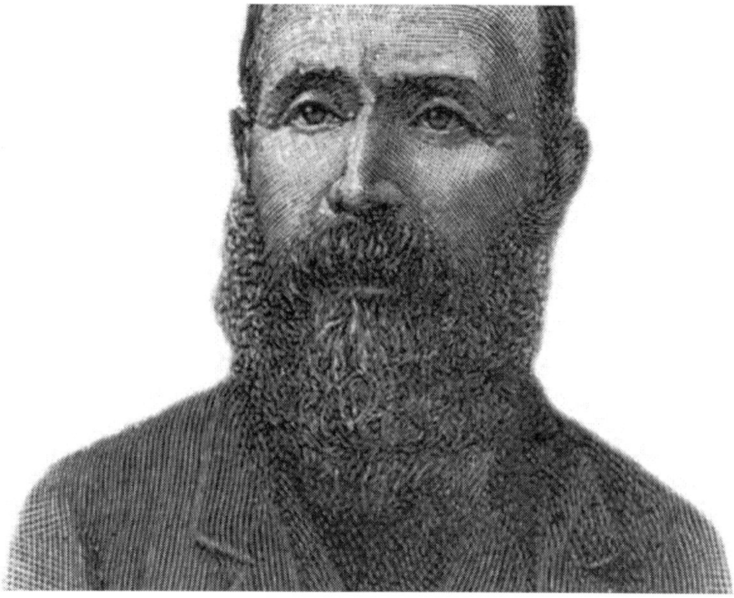

TROUBLE AND STRIFE IN LITTLE MOSCOW

Her husband had just spent three months in jail for illegal picketing during the General Strike and 28-year-old Emily Lawther was on the warpath. She led a gang of women 150 strong from her house on Marx Terrace in Chopwell to a Conservative women's meeting at a church hall in Winlaton where they jeered the speakers, cheered Lenin and sang the 'Red Flag.'

Emily (known as Emmie) was feisty, strong-willed and fierce, and in the February of 1926 had petitioned the Durham County Labour Women's Advisory Council that women should be admitted as associate members of miner's unions. The Chopwell miner's lodge had been admitting women like herself in an experiment that had proved a great success and while the suggestion was met with approval by the meeting, no further action was taken.

Emmie was bound over by the Gateshead magistrates for acting in a disorderly manner after the police were called to the Conservative meeting which was delayed an hour as one of the speakers, a Mrs. Mitchell, said her blouse and hat had been torn off after calling the Chopwell women 'scum' and saying the weren't British.

Emily's husband Steve Lawther was a miner from 'Britain's reddest village' and he was part of a north-east dynasty of coal mining union officials. His father Edward Lawther died at his home, 17 Lenin Street, in Chopwell in January 1936 aged 81 and left behind another 8 sons. Will Lawther was general secretary of the Durham Miners' Association and vice president of tile Mineworkers' Federation of Great Britain, Robert, Joseph, Edward (the general treasurer of the Kent Miners' Association), Herbet, who was an officer of the local branch of the Transport Workers Union, Andrew, who was president of the Swalwell Miners' Lodge, Jack and Clifford. He also had two daughters who, in the style of the time and which will have got Emmie's goat, were named as Mrs. Clifford of Chopwell and Mrs. Wanless of Florida.

Old Edward had been born in Choppington in Northumberland, as were many of his children, and had gone down the pit at 9-years-old. Apart from two years that he had spent in Illinois in the USA, Edward had worked in the coal mines of Northumberland and Durham for sixty years. His brother Robert was the first election agent for the Radical Morpeth MP Thomas Burt, and another brother, William was first president of the Northumberland Colliery Engineerman's Association, and although Edward had been a member of the Northumberland, then Durham Associations, he'd been happy to be a rank and file member.

Steve Lawther had been down at RuskinCollege in Oxford doing trade union studies when he first set eyes on the girl that would very shortly become his wife. Emmie was a Midlander who had gone to work in the Potteries at 13-years-old. She was a bright and active trade unionist and had become the branch secretary by just 18. After she'd met and married Lawther, she moved up to set of home in the notoriously militant mining village of Chopwell, which was part of the Blaydon Urban District Council, chaired by the Communist councillor Harry Bolton.

Chopwell had, in the distant past, been given to Newminster Abbey by Bishop Hugh of Durham and subsequently passed into the hands of landowners such as the Swinburns and Claverings after the dissolution of the abbeys. German emigrants to the area had started a steel factory, but it was coal that was to put Chopwell on the map. There had been loads of bother at the pit before with a series of strikes in the early 1900s which had earned Chopwell a militant reputation, but the colliery first came to the public attention in 1898 with an industrial dispute that hadn't been seen before.

It was one of the first 'lock-outs' of a mine and the local MP John Wilson described it as 'unique in the whole history of capital and labour.' It was felt in the *Stockton and Thornaby Herald* that the men had been forced into the lock-out as it was an attempt by the owners to set aside the Joint Committee rules and procedures after they disagreed with a price for work set by arbitration, so the men had some sympathy after coming out on the cobbles. It was reported that the locality 'to a man will stand loyally at the backs of the Chopwell miners.'

When a man was killed in an accident at the pit in 1904, the men stayed off work the following day and the owners, the Consett Iron Co., unbelievably issued 285 summonses against the miners claiming damages for breach of contract as they hadn't turned in. A huge crowd gathered at Gateshead County Police Court where the summonses were adjourned, though a draconian agreement was made that 'should another fatal accident occur at the pit in the meantime, the men had agreed not to lay the pit idle.'

Another 82 summonses for Chopwell miners to appear at Gateshead County Police Court were issued four years later by the Consett Iron Co. under the 'Employers and work well Act, 1875.' The miners, at number 2 pit in Chopwell, had again walked off the job after hearing of a fatal accident in number 1 pit. They were charged with having absented themselves from work without permission, as only the men in the particular pit where the accident occurred were permitted to stop work. The dispute was settled when the men, under the signatories F. Kirkup and John English, agreed that in future 'No.1 and 2 pits, the Hutton Seam and Whittonstall drifts' would be recognised as separate pits as far as the 'County Fatal Accidents Agreement' was concerned.

Measures such as this obviously led to a bitterness and resentment towards the owners and the Chopwell men were out again in April 1913. 1,300 miners handed in a fortnight's notice to cease work without the sanction of the union, the Durham Miner's Association, and no negotiations towards a settlement had been made. By the September things were getting increasingly tough for the strikers and Robert McFarlane and Robert Whitfield were arrested after being caught by police around the back of a warehouse at night with a hammer, chisel, pincers and screwdriver on them.

The claimed they'd been drinking together and committed a foolish act and were fined 20s each by the magistrates. More seriously their fellow strikers, the brothers John and Fenwick Milburn, and Robert Thompson, were charged with letting wagons loose on the Consett Iron Co.'s line and causing £3,000 worth of damage between High Thornley and Winlaton Mill. They were remanded at Gateshead. Just three days later, on December 12th, the strike was ended and the men returned to work.

Strained industrial relations at the colliery continued after WWI and there was some disbelief at the Gateshead County Police Court in 1921 when a Chopwell miner, appearing as a witness, told the clerk that he wished to affirm as he did not believe in religion. He said he didn't believe in God, and didn't want to argue about it. The Chairman said he found it rather curious when a man said he had no religious views.

But the pitmen could also admit when they were wrong; 901 were out on 14 day's strike in February 1924 from Chopwell, but agreed to pay the company £1,000 compensation after admitting they had got a dispute concerning the measurement of work incorrect. When the settlement was made, the summonses against the men were withdrawn.

Having to pay such hefty costs must have hardened the Chopwell men's resolution, however, and they were back out on strike in a wage dispute the following year. By the August of 1925 there were 'extraordinary scenes' outside the Gateshead Police Court when 52 of the Chopwell miners were charged with stealing coal. Being on strike for two months and with no money coming in, the pitmen had taken to lifting the coal to heat their homes and it was alleged by the court that in one raid tons of coal valued at £45 had been taken. The men marched to the court with a huge procession of supporters and banners reading: 'We have lost the dole, but we still get the coal,' and 'It is a fight to the finish.' The crowd sang the Red Flag outside the court as the proceedings got under way. The miners were bound over and warned that their conduct would not be tolerated.

If that incident had terrified the establishment, they were left relieved in the October after furthers summonses for over sixty Chopwell miners were unconditionally withdrawn. The men were accused of alleged unlawful assembly and the intimidation of safety men at the colliery, which had lain idle for several weeks. The miners and their families, to an estimated total of 3,000, had planned to march the 12 miles to Gateshead and back and were to be met by various contingents of unemployed workers en route. The demonstration was cancelled after the special police court dropped the charges.

The Chopwell miners were still out when the nine-day General Strike hit Britain on the 4th May 1926, and they must have felt that the British Socialist Revolution was beginning. There will have been some nervous excitement and defiant attitudes among the people of the North West Durham coalfield when the national chaos kicked off. William Lawther, who had stood as the Socialist candidate for South Shields in the 1924 general election, and Blaydon councillor Harry Bolton were two of the first arrested under the emergency regulations introduced by a panicked Government.

Lawther had stopped a food lorry in Winlaton Mill and told the driver that he was claiming the right to take over the distribution of its contents. He then fell out with a policeman called Inspector Mark Thompson and said that he didn't recognise Government orders and was charged with attempting to impede the distribution of food supplies. Bolton was accused of threatening to bring in 200 men from Chopwell to stop the lorries. Both were fined a huge £50 and the judge, Sir Alfred Palmer, said that if it had not been 'for the King's appeal to let bygones be bygones' then he would have sent them both straight to prison. They couldn't pay the fines, of course, and were taken down anyway, but not before pandemonium broke out outside the court.

There was a huge disturbance as the labour leaders Bolton and Lawther were sentenced and the 21-year-old labourer Anthony Hession, of Nowhere House, Swalwell, and the 27-year-old miner Robert S. Purvis of Rowland's Gill, were issued fines for disorder and assaulting the police with the alternative of three months' imprisonment. Gateshead Chief Constable K. Ogle said: "It is hard lines have to tolerate such pandemonium in the borough from people outside the borough," referring to the Chopwell contingent. Six days later, on the 21st May, nearly 50 men, mostly miners from Chopwell, were sent to prison for a month for holding up vehicles, threatening individuals, and interfering with the police during the General Strike. On the 16th of June a number of Chopwell men were charged at Hexham with stealing coal after working a drift mine at Hedley Fell and taking around 114 tons worth £100. They were bound over for a year while Robert Charlton, who had been in bother before, was also fined £3.

On the 29th June there were remarkable scenes in Durham when Bolton and Lawther were released from Durham Prison after serving six weeks of their two months' sentence, officially for 'failing to withdraw pickets.' The crowds had come from Shotton, Spen, Chopwell and other colliery areas and a huge roar went up as the two men emerged from the prison doors. The miners had travelled by bike and any other means that they could to be in Durham and Bolton and Lawther were quickly put in two cars and taken to a hotel in the city for breakfast. The crowd assembled in the Market Place and sang the 'Red Flag.' When the two released men went to Hamsterley bank top, they were met by the Chopwell colliery banner - famously emblazoned with portraits of Marx, Lenin, and Kier Hardy – the pit band and a huge crowd of miners that escorted them down the hill into the village.

Will Lawther was born in Choppington, Northumberland in 1889, began working down the pit at 12, was a union official by 18 and was a county councillor and on the National Executive of the Labour Party at the time of his arrest. Harry Bolton was a J.P., the chairman of Blaydon UDC and a card-carrying member of the Communist Party. Other men jailed that May included Lawther's brothers Steve (Emmie's husband) and Andrew, along with other Chopwell miners Charles Haddon and Joseph Bell. Haddon received three months and one month concurrent for illegal picketing and interfering with a fish van that had tried to enter Chopwell, along with Andrew Lawther, who got three months. Bell recieved three months for interfering with a railway clerk who was driving a tri-car and smashing his windscreen with a stick, and all three appeals against the convictions were thrown out in the July. Steve Lawther didn't bother appealing and was also sent down for three months. When the prosecuting Chairman Sir Alfred Palmer had stated that he would 'subscribe to a fund to send the Chopwell Communists to Russia' and asked Lawther if it was him that had written to the press accepting the offer, Lawther replied: "No. I have a better job here."

While he was stuck inside a prison cell his wife Emmie was very active in helping organising the miner's relief fund, visiting and distributing whatever help they could among the striker's families and it was only with the support of the women that the coalfields communities could stick together through the toughest of times.

The bitter dispute, which had lasted 17 long months, finally ended on the 3rd of November 1926 in Chopwell. 18 men, making up the shift at the pit on the second day of resumption at the colliery, were driven home in a specially adapted covered lorry through a crowd of 2,000 booing men, women, boys and girls. There was a huge police presence but no violence broke out. It was over. There was to be no British Revolution.

Another huge row erupted in May 1927, however, when the Blaydon UDC refused to fly the Union Jack flag from the council chambers on Empire Day. It caused a lot of division with ex-servicemen, territorials and the British Legion being stirred up into resentment by letters and inflammatory pieces in the press. A request by the Blaydon Empire Day committee to fly the flag was ordered to lie on the table by Chairman Harry Bolton, who said: "I don't believe in Empire. All empires have been built up by murder, pillage, rapine, and violence. Those supporting Empire Day celebrations are the workers' greatest enemies." And so it all kicked off.

"The only way they will place that Union Jack upon that flag pole as far as I am concerned will be over some of our dead bodies," remarked Councillor Robert Bell, who also commented that the fully fledged Labour members were determined that no flag be flown and he insisted that 'force would be met with force' as the row escalated.

"We are supposed to be red bulls, Bolsheviks, Communists. Revolutionaries, and I don't know what," said Harry Bolton, "But the people who want to float the Union Jack and pride themselves that they are patriots and constitutionalists come along and say 'We are going to have the Union Jack floating on the Council Chamber, legal or Illegal;' they charge us with being unconstitutional when we are demanding justice for our people and accuse us of being Bolsheviks in not respecting the law of the country." He felt that the Union Jack was being prostituted and dragged into the gutter while councillor Anthony Davidson felt that the Union Jack was being used for a political stunt, and councillor James Kelly advised people to keep their children away from the Empire Day celebrations in Blaydon.

The Chief Constable of Durham eventually banned the hoisting on the Union Jack on the council building in an attempt to prevent the danger of a public disturbance. Instead, the flag was unfurled by Colonel A. Henderson, the commander of the Durham Light Infantry during the First World War, in a nearby field. The Pathe cameras were there and a flickering black and white newsreel now captures the rows of men in flat caps and trilbys looking on as a group of men come around the corner with the flag, followed by a load of children waving small Union Jacks, and horse drawn floats. The passion of it all proved too much for 35-year-old James Stephenson, an ex-serviceman himself and Socialist member of the Board of Guardians, and 34-year-old John Prudhoe of Winlaton.

Stephenson met Prudhoe near Winlaton Mill on an evening and said: "They tell me that you are one of the clever ones that are going to run the Union Jack up the council chamber," and called him a scab, continuing; "Neither you nor anyone else are going to fly the Union Jack." When Prudhoe quipped back, saying: "We are going to fly the Union Jack," Stephenson punched him in the right ear and Prudhoe went for him, giving him a real pasting. Even his defence lawyer, Frank Lambert, told the court: "We don't deny that Stephenson got the biggest hiding he ever got in his life."

Later on in the October of that year, a delegation of Northern trade unionists were elected to visit Russia to celebrate the tenth anniversary of the Soviet revolution. Harry Bolton, as a representative of the Chopwell Branch of the Durham Miner's Association, N. Garrow, a NUR man from Bedlington, W. Thompson of ASLEF from Newcastle and J. Douglas, from the Backworth Branch of the Northumberland Miner's Association were voted to go alongside the women Mrs. Foster of the Winlaton Co-Operative

Guild and Mrs. Dunn of the Silksworth Co-Operative Guild.

The meeting at the Socialist Hall in Newcastle was addressed by a Birtley girl called Nancy Hall who had visited the USSR and said 'it was time a revolution was brought about in England.'

The following year it was Emmie Lawther who got the chance to visit the Soviet Union as part of a delegation to Leningrad, Moscow and the Donbass coalfield. On her return she spoke at many meetings about the child welfare that she had witnessed in the Soviet Union, which surpassed what was available in Britain.

There was a sensation in the Blaydon, Chopwell and Spen districts in 1929 when Harry Bolton, still Chairman of the Blaydon UDC, was expelled from the Communist Party. The District organiser, E. Woolley, stated that Bolton's expulsion was for 'indiscipline and political unreliability.' Cllr. Bolton had long been recognised as an ardent Communist and it obviously brought questions from the rank and file members as to what direction the party was taking.

Blaydon's communists were in the news again in March 1937 when an official communication from Spain announced the sad death of the secretary of the local party, 28-year-old Wilf Jobling, who was single and employed in the housing department of Blaydon Urban Council. Jobling had only left England six weeks earlier to fight for the Spanish Government in the International Brigade and had been killed during fighting around Madrid.

The tattered old Chopwell Lodge banner was replaced by a replica in 1954 and the original was given to the Soviet Miner's President Ivan Rossochinsky the following year when he was on a tour of County Durham with two Russian miners. Len Hawkshaw, the chairman of the Chopwell Lodge, handed over the hugely significant piece of cloth and said: "We handed it over in good faith in the hope that it will help strengthen the bond between the miners of this country and those of Soviet Russia."

But that wasn't quite the end of the story. In July 1958 the citizens of Durham woke to find the Red Flag flying from keep of DurhamCastle. It was quickly removed by Lt-Col Leonard Slater, of UniversityCollege, who told newspapers: "The matter is now in the hands of the security branch.

It may be a practical joke but may also be a political stunt." Slater said that the flag had been a 'crude job' of a bedsheet dyed red with a hammer and sickle painted white. It was the first and last time the Red Flag had flown in Durham since the Chopwell miners had proudly raised theirs up the pole.

THE BLYTH CONTINGENT – THE N.U.W.M. HUNGER MARCH

While the Jarrow Crusade set off down to London on the 5th October 1936, another Hunger March organised by the National Unemployed Workers Movement set off from Blyth on Monday 12th October for the capital.

The N.U.W.M. was strong in South-East Northumberland with branches at Blyth, Morpeth and Newbiggin being particularly active in fighting the Means Test and the then newly introduced Unemployment Assistance regulations which saw officials visit impoverished families to assess whether they were entitled to help or not.

T. Mooney was the secretary of the Blyth branch of the N.U.W.M., while J. Rivett held the post at Newbiggin, and the pitman Jack (John James) Douglas at the Morpeth branch of the organisation, which had strong links to the Communist Party of Great Britain though it was officially a non-political body.

Douglas was interesting character who stood as the Communist candidate in local elections on a number of occasions. He lived in Second Avenue up Stobhill Gate and stood in the Morpeth Municpal Elections, for a fifth time, in 1932 where he was again defeated. Jack did gain 585 votes, however, with the four councillors who were elected getting between 1586 and 1220 votes, so he didn't do that badly considering he'd only received 152 votes back in 1928.

Jack Douglas was finally elected onto the Town Council, at the eighth attempt, in a by-election in December 1945, giving him the distinction of being Morpeth's first and only Communist councillor. The by-then retired miner was keen, did a number of Public Debates against his political opponents in the Town Hall and was also secretary, later honorary secretary, of the Morpeth Branch of the Communist Party in which capacity he penned a number of official communiqués to the local paper defending the Left position of the day.

Around 600 people in Morpeth were on the Means Test in 1932 and many had been debarred from claiming, so Douglas was influential and the go-to guy among families that will have been somewhat embarrassed, ashamed and angry at having to let someone into their home to see just how starving and desperate they were, and you can be sure that they wouldn't have allowed the true level of their poverty to be seen by an outsider. The Northumberland District of the N.U.W.M. reported that there were 578 people getting relief in the neighbouring Alnwick District.

There had been a number of Hunger Marches to London from areas of high unemployment in 1922, 1927, 1930, 1931, 1932 and 1934 while even earlier in 1908 a hunger march against unemployment had gone around the country led by the bearded Scottish lawyer Stewart Gray from East Lothian which stopped at Cathedral towns on a weekend asking the churches for special services and collections. But the Jarrow Crusade remains the most famous and well-known of all the walks for social justice that were undertaken during a time of great economic depression and social depravation. The marchers weren't all drawn from the mining community and it was recorded in a Police note on a meeting of the N.U.W.M. in 1929 that 'textile workers, shipyards workers, and many labourers and skilled workers from many trades' were all involved in the protests. The 200 Jarrow marchers were ship workers in the main, affected by the closure of Palmers yard on the Tyne.

The growing mood of public discontent was reflected in Northumberland with demonstrations at Blyth and Ashington on May Day in 1936. The Cowpen and Crofton Workmen's Band led a procession of Labour, Communist and N.U.W.M members to a meeting at the Blyth Welfare Hall where a number of speakers stirred up the packed venue with rousing speeches.

Morpeth's Labour MP Robert Taylor then told the audience at the Miner's Hall in Ashington that: "If we want the abolition of the Means Test we will have to fight for it because we are going to get a means test in the new regulations."

The N.U.W.M. had been formed in 1921 and by 1935 the aims, as declared by Blyth vice organiser A. Ward, were to 'organise the struggles of the unemployed against the central and local government authorities on the principle of 'Work or Full Maintenance.' They also wanted to 'raise the standard of unemployment insurance benefit and Poor Law Relief and to protect the unemployed against loss of benefit or relief, and to defend their claims before Courts of Referees, Unemployment Assistance Board, Umpire and local authorities, and to remove the many administrative grievances that exist in the Unemployment Insurance Scheme and Poor Law.' The N.U.W.M. wanted to 'fight against all attempts of the employing class to use the unemployed to lower the working class standards and conditions, and to actively participate its defending the workers engaged in industrial disputes,' and 'to compel full trade union rates and conditions on all schemes of employment for the unemployed.'

The N.U.W.M. was, claimed Mr. Ward, a mass non-party organisation, that was 'neither an ancillary nor auxiliary organisation of any political party, and its membership was open to all to join.' The N.U.W.M. willingly accepts the support of any or all working-class organisations, and seeks at all times to unify the struggles of the unemployed and employed workers on immediate working class demands, continued comrade Ward, who added that: "The .N.U.W.M. was leading the struggle against the New Unemployment Act, whish has within it many Fascist elements establishing a dictatorship over the unemployed."

In the August of 1936 the Blyth branch of the N.U.W.M. were flexing their muscles and 15 of their members staged a protest against 'starvation measures' being undertaken by bureaucrats in the port town against one of their own. Ahead of the march the following month, T. Mooney, the Blyth secretary of the N.U.W.M., received a massive boost of support and a donation of £10 from the Executive Committee of the Northumberland

Miner's Association for equipping the Northumberland contingent that were to walk to London against the Means Test and the new Unemployment Assistance regulations. The Communist councillor Bob (Robert S.) Elliott was supposed to be the Blyth Council representative on the walk but the council had a late change of heart ahead of the march and withdrew their support. They probably also hoped that Elliott might lose his seat as there was a by-election taking place while he was away. Elliott had also taken part in the Hunger March to London two years earlier when he'd said that the unemployed were 'refusing to starve in silence and the workers are refusing to take the new 'slave Bill' lying down,' and called upon the workers to give greater support to the March with 'every pit, factory, trade union branch, and workers' organisations represented at the congress of action.'

The usual stick and propaganda was dished out in the papers while the local men were away on the March. A wag writing to the *Blyth News*, who signed himself 'Council House,' reckoned that: "Many men in the Blyth district have brought families up to manhood and womanhood and have never done a stroke of work except if they got a green card." His opinion was that 'men are getting more on the 'dole' than they would in the pits, especially the family men.'

But there were also letters of support, such as the one by the Blyth mother Florence Faulkner of Plessey Road who asked plainly if 26 shillings a week was 'any sort of an Income for man and wife to live on This is the very best that can be received even on standard benefit. If the couple have children it makes matters worse,' she wrote in an appeal to 'the citizens of Blyth to assist in every way within their power the gallant men, women and boys who are marching against the despicable Means Test.'

So passions were running high when Bob Elliott and the Northumberland men set off on the walk from Newcastle on Monday 12th October 1936; Elliott was not going as the council representative as had previously been proposed, as the council were strongly critical of the Communist Party and the N.U.W.M. for 'deluding the unemployed for propaganda purposes.' Between 1,500 and 2,000 men set out on the March from a number of different locations around Britain that followed different routes and converged on London. T. Mooney had urged that no action be taken against married men who were on the march but were worried that the benefits for their wives and children would be stopped, and pointed out that Jarrow Town Council was 'in sympathy with paying relief to dependents of those taking part in the march from that town.'

Blyth Communist councillor W.H. Breadin, himself a disabled ex-serviceman, said that: "The Poor Law lays it down that nobody must starve and we would be lacking in our duty if there was any destitution. That cannot be ignored." He continued by saying that there had been previous Hunger Marches to London which had been successful for the unemployed, but that: "If the marchers take to the road and leave their wives and children to the Public Assistance Committee they can be arrested under the law. If that is done, the battle against the Means Test will cease to exist. A tremendous number of married men want to fight the Means Teat but if they are compelled to sit at home the U.A.B. statutory measures will come into force and that will mean tremendous cuts for the unemployed, less money going over the counters in shops and less money to pay rents to enable those who own houses to pay their rates." Councillor R. Bell said: "If we can do anything to smash this Means Test then we ought to do it. It is a hellish thing."

After a couple of weeks the Blyth Hunger Marchers were in Doncaster, looking like they'd stepped off the set of *Peaky Blinders* in flat caps and jackets, and James Ward reported back that the streets of the Yorkshire town had been chalked with slogans and thousands of people had lined the pavements and cheered.

"We feel we can go forward knowing we have the backing of all working class people and organisations in this great effort to smash the Means Test. We wish the Blyth people to know that we are in the best of health and spirits," he said.

The Blyth marchers were on the outskirts of London on the 6th November in Romford, where they were joined by the Jarrow MP 'Red' Ellen Wilkinson, who had come from leading the Jarrow crusade, and walked 8 miles with the men at a cracking pace. Thousands of people again lined the streets with 'deafening cheers' ringing out.

"What we have been striving for in Blyth for a long time was taking shape and working in a practical manner," said Bob Elliott, as he saw trade unions and other working class organisations come together to welcome them. A huge demonstration in Hyde Park on the Sunday saw a sea of banners two miles long converging to hear speakers including Clem Atlee, the leader of the Labour Party.

That December the Morpeth Branch the N.U.W.M. applied for an alternative site to erect their hut and the council decided that further action needed to be taken. Some eleven years later Jack Douglas was on the council himself and was taking down a critic in the local papers who said that he 'hated the Communist policy.'

Douglas pointed out that the General Election of 1945 had been won on Labour's 'Let us face the future' programme which stated that people needed food, work and homes, rising standard of living, improved social services and security abroad. 'Repeatedly the Communist Party has put forward concrete plans to secure these aims,' wrote Jack, 'and has offered to unite its efforts with those of the Labour Party for their achievement.' Surely nobody could argue with the Stobhill Marxist about that.

FROM THE CATRAIL TO CARHAM

It is only 55 miles from Edinburgh to Hawick while it is 169 miles from Edinburgh to Catterick, directly through the main bulk of what was the Bernician kingdom and their seat of power at Bamburgh. I know where my money lies on the site of the long lost and forgotten Battle of the Catraeth being, where the 'native' Vottadini were routed by Anglian invaders sometime in around the years 580- 600AD.

The Catrail is an ancient earthwork dyke that runs for some 45 miles throughout the borders countryside from the slopes of Peel Fell near Kielder right up to the area around Galashiels. The Catrail was banked on both sides, was around 26 feet wide and reputed to have been ten feet high. For a people that had long inhabited hillforts and carved their swirling and dipped cup and ring marks into grey and yellow sandstone rocks, it must have proved a formidable barrier, a marker between worlds.

The Vottadini, or Ottadin, or Y Goddodin, were a reputedly Celtic race that inhabited what is now modern day Northumberland right up to the Solway Firth, and their capital was supposed to have been at Traprain Law near Haddington. There is, however, another possibility that has never really been addressed. The Vottadini, or Y Goddodin, could have been earlier travellers from Scandinavia or Northern Europe themselves and their name might be some kind of a corruption of Woden. Could they have been the people of the God Odin? May a belief in the All Father have been conjured up in pagan faith and superstition more than 500 years before the dawn of Christianity?

Britain is an island and there are no native aboriginal people to speak of as such. Even the Old Britons had to come here from somewhere, most likely the Basque regions of Spain, where they settled in Cornwall, Wales, and the Western side of the island – the so-called Celtic Nations. The prolific construction of hillforts at places such as Yeavering Bell, and the numerous sites in the Breamish and Coquet valleys, point to a culture that is just a little different to the rest of Britain. There are 271 recorded hill fort sites in Northumberland, and 408 in the Scottish Borders. Clearly there is a significant society at work and an indication that there was a need for defence by the people settling the North Eastern seaboard – but to protect themselves from whom? Were they themselves classed as invaders by people that were already settled the land by an earlier Celtic people? Another possibility, of course, is that water levels were just higher and they were occupying the high ground that wasn't sodden and flooded. But the indications point to the Vottadini arriving on these shores from elsewhere and setting up permanent residence.

The early people that walked across the Dogger Bank to inhabit Britain after the ice caps had receded will have crossed from somewhere around the area in the North of modern Denmark around 10,000 years ago. They'll have found land ravaged by the drag of ice sheets and the deposition of large boulders as the freeze retreated. You can see examples of this with boulders such as the Draag Stone at Harbottle and scattered large rocks on the Bilberry Hill at Rothbury. These people settled the East Lothian and Northumberland coastline during the Neolithic period. Humans were certainly hunting and gathering near the rock at Bamburgh around 1,500BC as I myself have found a flint arrowhead from the period in the vicinity of the castle, while I've also picked up contemporaneous flint scrapers and tools at Rothbury in the Coquet valley.

The Coquet is an unusual name for a river and you have to wonder how far back people had been fishing it. The nearby Rothbury Forest had a long tradition of mystery stretching back to the times of the Votadini and beyond. It was known as Cocwudu to the later Anglians, who themselves came over to settle in Northumbria from Southern Denmark under King Ida 'the Flamebearer' when they landed in around 547 at Bamburgh. Ida was the son of Eoppa, but that's jumping the gun.

There is a major study being undertaken by the Bernician Studies Group into the ancient woodland. Cocwudu, coming, they believe, from 'a reformation of the river name Coquet and Old English wudu, meaning woodland.' But why the Coquet? Going further back to the earlier 'indigenous' tribes that inhabited the area, there are shrines dotted around Northumberland and Cumbria dedicated to the local God Cocidius, perhaps most spectacularly at Yardhope where he stands carved in relief on the grey stone with his spear and shield. Cocidius was a warrior God and also, according to Wikipedia, equated by the Romans stationed on Hadrian's Wall with 'Mars, the God of war and hunting, and also with Silvanus, god of forests, groves and wild fields,' which all makes perfect sense. Remove the Latin *ius* from the God and you have Cocid. Could it have changed through time to Coquet? Should the correct name for the upper reaches of the valley be Cociddale?

Add in the fact that an inscription to Cocidius at Ebchester calls him Cocidius Vernostonus, or Cocidius of the alder tree, then you have another big connection to the RothburyForest. The alder tree was much venerated in folklore and mythology.

Rivet and Smith in their 1979 book *Place names of Roman Britain* suggested that the name of Cocidius may have stemmed from the British Celtic word cocco – 'red' – and theorised that statues of the God may have been painted red. The Anglo-Saxon word 'Rot' is red, while 'Rod' is wood. 'Bury' is the Anglo-Saxon for a fortified place. So Rothbury itself may be derived from Rotbury – the fortified place of the red people, or Rodbury – the fortified place in the woods. There is some evidence to suggest that the early people that were encamped at Craster and Howick painted themselves in red ochre. The material is also found in some Mesolithic graves in Denmark.

It seems possible that the early Vottadini could have first landed on the shores up near Dunbar sometime around 500BC and any North Sea voyagers on primitive ships back then would surely have been drawn to the massive rock off the coast. Broxmouth hillfort was established near Dunbar in the Iron Age; maybe that was an early defensive structure before the Vottadini began to explore further inland, spreading both North and South on the coastline foraging, then looking on at Simonside and the Cheviots, which are easily seen from the coast, with the hills proving a point then on the horizon that would be ripe for further exploration. A landing near Dunbar Rock might also point to the similar volcanic outcrops that formed the basis off the Vottadini's later seats of power at Edinburgh and Bamburgh.

There was a Nordic Bronze Age during this period where an advanced culture in Denmark, parts of Sweden and parts of Norway were trading throughout central Europe and the Mediterranean in amber, bronze and gold. They were creating jewellery, artefacts and weapons, and carving petroglyphs of farming, animals, ceremonies, battles and, most importantly, ships. Cup and ring marks have also been found in Denmark, Sweden, Norway and Finland. It is possible that amber traders from Scandinavia looking for new markets found themselves sailing out of the mist onto a strange new island; wet, green and fertile, wooded and habitable with an abundance of boar, deer, and fresh water. Maybe they had been blown off course by a wild, crashing North Sea storm and were grateful for the shelter as they washed up on the sands. You could speculate anything, really, but the Cup and Ring marks associated with the hillforts in Northumberland at places such as Chatton, Fowberry, Lordenshaws and all over the county are indicators of a civilization that was keen to leave a mark on the landscape; to display and hold what was theirs. Bronze Age swords have been discovered at Tosson and spears and round shields in a bog at Yetholm; another example, of similar design to the Yetholm shields, comes, again, from Denmark.

Catterick would have been on the land of the neighbouring Brigantes tribe to the South, who were possibly descended from the Vindelici in the region of the Alps, while the Carvetti occupied the lands to the West, along with elements of the Selgovae tribe and the Damnonii, who eventually formed kingdom of Strathclyde. Therefore the hillforts at the Black and White Meldons near Pebbles would have marked the far West of the Vottadini Kingdom, near to where the Catrail was constructed. Rochester was another important fort to protect the Vottadini from the West, while the broad river Tyne provided a natural barrier to the South, and the Solway Firth marked the edge of the Northern territory.

These were the British tribes that would prove so troublesome to the invading Roman armies in the early first century that they would be compelled to build a wall from the Tyne to the Solway to exclude them from their vast Empire. Don't be fooled by explanations of trading posts and control; people construct massive walls and put mileposts and garrisons on them through fear. The Roman authorities were so perplexed and terrified by the barbarian Vottadini that they simply counted them as beyond the civilised world and shut them out. Yes, they had roads such as the Devil's Causeway that cut straight through the territory, and a Roman fort was placed over the top of an important Vottadini one at Rochester, but patrols out from the Wall into the mysterious Northern lands must have been filled with trepidation. Ask the Ninth Legion. It's easier to say that they were redeployed in Spain than to admit that they were massacred by the Vottadini near Hartburn, if you believe the local legends. That golden standard could still lie buried in a bog, but would more likely have been taken as a prize by the warriors of the Cocid cult. Other local Gods that the Romans incorporated included Veteris, Antenociticus and local water deities of springs and burns. But as the Romano-British culture never actually went beyond the Wall, it is hard to know exactly what the Vottadini religious practices were. There were no baths or wine, olive oil, mosaic-floored villas or central heating this side of the line, you soft Southern gets.

When the Romans eventually withdrew from Britain in around 410AD, there will have been little change to the lives of the Vottadini. They hadn't had a Latin way of life brought to them and they had no imported systems to fall into disrepair and ruin.

Change did come by the year 547 when Ida's ships from Southern Denmark landed on the Northumbrian coast and brought with them fire and sword. The Vottadini may well have shared a Germanic DNA with the Angeln in the distant past, but any links across the North Sea will have been long forgotten by the time of Ida's arrival.

Once settled at Bamburgh, the Angles started expanding inland themselves into the territory of the Vottadini in Bernicia. They took the hillfort at

Yeavering Bell, the hill of the goats where they still roam wild, and built a mead hall below at Ad Gefrin.

The bulk of resistance to the Danish invaders was organised by the Celtic British King Urien, who hailed from the Lakeland mountains around Helvellyn in the Kingdom of Rheged. The Battle of Arthuret, in a field near Longtown, took place in 573AD, where Urien of Rheged supposedly defeated the Anglian invaders and took up his place in Arthurian legend.

The Vottadini themselves, or the fighting men of their warband, at least, must have been forced North and West by the men of King Ida the Flamebearer. The legend in the fabled Welsh British poem states that the Goddodin assembled at Din Eidyn (Edinburgh) and feasted for a year in preparation for battle. Urien's warriors from Rheged are said to have joined them, as, it is reputed, did soldiers of Pictland and Gwynedd. They made up a formidable force of 363 warriors. While that doesn't sound a huge number to be leading into battle, they will have been an elite fighting squad, trained and occupied as a warrior class probably since childhood and used as enforcers by the local tribal chiefs. These weren't a rag-tag farmer's army, they were the Celtic British equivalent of a Special Forces unit; chain-mailed, heavily armed and battle hardened. The tale gets a little confused as some say the battle was against Theodoric, a son of Ida, and that the Britons assembled at a fortress called 'Guinnion' for battle at either at Peel Fell, the head of the Stanhope Burn, near where the Tweed and Gala waters meet, at Catterick in North Yorkshire or even at the Milfield Plain in north Northumberland.

A mighty battle cry went up from Urien's army when they attacked at the 'White Stone of Galystein' and clashed with the well-organised shield wall of the Anglians. The Celts were smashed by battleaxes, swords and spears in a bloody and violent clash over several days of fighting against the odds and only two gore-splattered and exhausted men returned home from at the end - Aeron Brave and Conan Strong.

Around fifty years after their victory at the Catrail, the increasingly powerful Angles of Bernicia and Deira (the area between the Humber and the Tees that they had also settled) established the Kingdom of Northumbria when they united and incorporated the former lands of the Votadini, the

Brigantes, the Carvetti and the Selgovae together under the one ruler, King Æthelfrith.

The paganism of the Angles had began to fade in around 623 when King Edwin was converted to Christianity by Saint Aiden from Iona and a monastery established at Lindisfarne by 634 after the defeat of the Welsh Briton Cadwallon by King Oswald. It was another pagan, the fellow Anglian Penda of Mercia, who had joined forces with Cadwallon to devastate Northumbria after killing King Edwin during a bloody battle at Hatfield Chase the previous year. Penda's army also had their revenge when they defeated and killed King Oswald at the battle of Maserfield nine years later as Bernicia and Deira broke into separate states. Penda was also at war with the East Anglians, but was finally hacked to pieces and beheaded himself at the Battle of the Winwaed in 655 by the Bernician army of King Oswiu. It was described by the venerable Bede as a victory over the 'heathen peoples,' but then he was a Christian monk and scribe, so he had an agenda, though the victory did reunite a divided Northumbria.

The Northumbrian kingdom extended its influence North and West into Dal Riata and Strathclyde but suffered a heavy defeat when King Ecgfrith's forces were decimated by Picts at the Battle of Nechtansmere in 685. That Northumbria would, however, produce such treasures as the Lindisfarne Gospels, the beautifully illuminated scripts that were produced at the Holy Island in around 715-20, giving a wonderful insight into the art and culture of the people at that time. Why they are kept in London and not on the island permanently is nothing short of cultural appropriation. The Picts and Irish were certainly influencing the Bernician tastes at the time and were a settled part of the religious population as well as mingling in with an increasingly cosmopolitan general society around Bamburgh.

The momentous events in 793 when a Dragon was seen in the sky over Northumbria - which would indicate some lingering Paganism - that preceded the first raid on Lindisfarne by Scandinavian ships on a Viking brought about huge change for Northumbria from the North Sea. Deira, and York especially, were invaded by the Great Heathen Army, became part of the Danelaw by 876 and were completely conquered by Norse fighters in 914. Olaf Guthfrithson became the first Viking overlord of Bernicia in around 939 as the old Anglian control was put under increasing pressure from Northmen in the South. You have to wonder if Guthfrithson's legacy lives on in Coquetdale today in the Gutherson family, while similarly the likes of the Ormston's and Ord's may have an ancient Scandinavian lineage.

When the whole of Northumbria was eventually absorbed and annexed into England in 954, the writing was on the wall for the old Kingdom. They did, however, assemble another great army to do battle with what was by then Scotland over the Northern Bernician territories between Berwick and Edinburgh in 1018.

The Battle of Carham is of major significance because it essentially draws the line of the modern border between England and Scotland. You may have seen Uhtred of Bebbanburg in the Netflix series *The Last Kingdom*; Uhtred was a son of Waltheof and the earl of Northumbria, with a reputation as a great warrior and leader. There has been some debate as to whether Uhtred had been killed in battle two years earlier and his brother Eadwulf led the Northumbrian warband; the Danish King Cnut had invaded England in 1016 and made Eric of Hlathir the earl of Northumbria, so it does lend some weight to the claim that Uhtred was already dead.

The leaders of the Scottish army were King Malcolm II of Scotland and Owen the Bald, the King of Strathclyde, as the Great Golden Age of Northumbria was butchered on a field near the banks of the Tweed. Some sources state that the combined Scots/Cumbrian army assembled around the Ettrick Forest – probably near the Catrail, where the Northumbrians had won that famous victory over 400 years earlier – and they were intercepted by a Northumbrian army before they crossed the Cheviots.

What is more likely is that the Alba/Cumbrian army marched from the Catrail somewhere around Selkirk, through Newton St Boswell's and Kelso on the north bank of the Tweed and were met by the Northumbrian army at Carham where they forded the river. The invasion force were heading straight for Bamburgh and the Bernician seat of power; while people say that the Scots victory won them Lothian, it also importantly won them all of the lands of Teviotdale over the Cheviots that had belonged to Northumbria.

The men formed up into their time-honoured shield wall, knocking sword pommels on colourful wood, shouting and swearing, wearing helmets with long nose protectors, chain mail, carrying long spears, and battleaxes and no doubt deploying archers to blacken the sky with a volley of arrows. They had comprehensively defeated an invasion from Alba in 1005 when led by Uhtred, and no doubt hoped to drive the invaders back into the deep, slow moving river and run its waters red with blood.

The portents in the sky had not been good again; a comet was visible for the 30 nights preceding the battle and the Christians will no doubt have told any men with enduring heathen beliefs to put their superstitions and premonitions aside and that God would look out for them on the battlefield. Marching forward across the grassy land and holding together as blows rained down on their shields, a narrow range of vision as a helmet slipped down and sweat stung the eyes, jabbing and thrusting a sword through the gaps between the wall. Eventually the terrible realisation that the shields had crumbled and a boar's head formation of the enemy pushed through – the loss of discipline as desperate hand to hand combat broke out all around. The slaughter of the Bernician warband that day saw the great old Kingdom of Northumbria shrink to practically what are the bounds of the modern county of Northumberland from that fateful day onwards.

The Northumbrians, however, never really did lose their sense of identity and belonging. When Copsi was created the Earl of Northumberland by William the Conqueror following his devastation of the Northern lands that initially held out against the Norman occupation, Osulph, the man that had held the position before him, took his revenge by beheading him at Newburn in 1071. Vengeance, passion and fighting are in our blood so when you travel north to Newcastle for a Premier League game and are hit by a wall of noise and accents that don't quite ring true in your ear and you question whether you are still in England – your England - believe me, you're not. We're Northumbrians - and proud of it.

WHERE IS THE NORTHUMBRIAN SUTTON HOO?

Æthelfrith Iding, the last great heathen king of Northumbria, was killed in battle around 616 when fighting an army of the East Anglian king Rædwald. While the famous excavation of Rædwald's boat burial at Sutton Hoo in Suffolk in 1939 revealed an abundance of treasures reflecting the skill and zoomorphic art of the Anglo-Saxon Age in Britain, no grave has yet been found to indicate his fellow pagan Æthelfrith's final resting place.

Perhaps his body was hacked to pieces as the spoils of war, a fate which befell his son Oswald after he himself had been defeated by the Mercian pagan king Penda and the Welsh Britons at the battle of Maserfield in 641. Oswald had converted to Christianity and became a Saint, his battle-battered skull and severed arms and hands becoming important holy relics that were recovered at great danger from the victors.

So while Rædwald's impressive treasure trove of glittering gear including the famous face helmet, a sword, axe-hammer, circular shield, chain mail and spears, silver dishes, gold buckles, drinking horns and a purse containing 40 gold pieces that were dug up from the tumulus in a field not that far from Ipswich, nothing has as yet been found to indicate the wonderful treasures possessed by the Bernician kings far to the North.

There are a couple of tumulus marked on OS maps of Bamburgh, though these are believed to originate from much earlier. The cemetery at the Bowl Hole in the dunes down from Bamburgh castle contains the bodies of people but, as yet, no royal burials. Yeavering could also be the place used to burn or bury the remains of the ancestors of Woden in Bernicia; the Cheviots were important to Ida's grandson, Æthelfrith, and his moot, or place for giving justice, was at Yeavering Bell where an amphitheatre capable of holding 350 people in 16 tiers was discovered by Brian Hope-Taylor in 1954. There was also a great mead hall and other wooden structures.

Bamburgh was named after Æthelfrith's first wife Bebba and was the capital of his Bernician kingdom. It was known to the Welsh Britons as of Din Guaire, then Bebbanburg, and later becoming Bamburgh. Bernicia stretched from Durham to Edinburgh; Æthelfrith later added the neighbouring kingdom of Deira, from the Tees down to the Humber, to become king of all Northumbria, though the cost of this was his life. Æthelfrith became king of Bernicia in around 593 and extended his power base in around 604 when he exiled Edwin, who had a claim on the throne, from Deira.

A year later Æthelfrith led an army to Chester and slew the outnumbered Welsh British in what became an absolute slaughter, including the killing of a reputed 1,200 Christian monks who were on the battlefield praying for a Welsh victory. Æthelfrith was a man with pagan beliefs and some of his Gods mark the days of the week now – Tiw, for Tuesday, Woden for Wednesday, Thor for Thursday, Frija for Friday. If the monks from Bangor planned to use the power of their God against him then they were fair game, he reasoned.

Edwin had fled south and was given sanctuary by the East Anglians. Although Æthelfrith offered Rædwald substantial bribes of silver to kill Edwin for him, he refused, supposedly on the counsel of his wife. The next attempt was a bit less subtle and was to threaten force; if Rædwald didn't hand over Edwin, then Northumbria would declare war on East Anglia. They were the same people culturally, ethnically and spiritually, so Æthelfrith's possessions, weapons, and jewellery would have mirrored those belonged to Rædwald that were so spectacularly uncovered and now feature in the story of the Netflix movie *The Dig*.

But where are they? Rædwald's army marched North and met Æthelfrith's warband just south of the Humber in what was then Mercia and is now modern Nottinghamshire. Perhaps neither army marched, and both sailed the rugged coast to the mouth of the Humber before travelling inland.

If Æthelfrith's army had travelled by ships, then perhaps they were destroyed in the aftermath of the conflict, fired and burned to blacken the skies with smoke, just as their blood had run the river Idle red. That could explain why no ship burial has been found for Æthelfrith. His body will have been stripped of all his weapons and clothing. He will have been almost certainly decapitated and mutilated. There was effectively no reason for what was left of Æthelfrith's blood-splattered and butchered corpse to lie in the cold soil of Mercia. He had fought and died well. He had taken his place in Valhalla.

As for his treasures in the fort at Bamburgh – his sons Oswald, Eanfrith, and Oswiu fled into exile as the victorious Edwin travelled north to reclaim not only the Deiran crown, but that of Bernicia too, making him the new ruler of Northumbria. Perhaps they took as much of what they could with them to their island retreat with the monks on Iona. What was left would have certainly been appropriated by his rival Edwin.

His protector Rædwald was the first pagan king to explore, if not embrace, the ideas of Christianity and is reputed to have converted before his death in 624, around the time that bishop Paulinus of York was converting Northumbrians at places such as Holystone and Yeavering. Rædwald didn't die on the battlefield. He didn't die with his sword in his hand.

The person that was buried at Sutton Hoo was obviously important, a king or warlord, and they were hedging their bets on the afterlife by combining elements of their long-held heathen beliefs with the new Christian religion. Two tiny gold foil crosses were found in the mound, and it is believed that they may have covered the eyes of the grave occupant, whoever they were – Rædwald being the popular choice.

Maybe the best chance of finding the lost treasures of Northumbria will come from the chance discovery of a hoard somewhere in the fields that sweep down to the volcanic rocks and white breakers of the North Sea.

Perhaps there is a pot containing spectacular gold and silver items lying underground that will illuminate our understanding of the Dark Ages in Northumbria in bright and gleaming glory buried on the sands of

Lindisfarne, the Holy Island.

Until that day, we have to celebrate the great treasures of the Great Northumbrian age that we do possess – one being Cuthbert's cross, the gold and garnet crucifix discovered in the Farne Island monk's wooden coffin at Durham Cathedral, and the other, albeit in the hands of the British Library in London, being the celebrated Lindisfarne Gospels. Eadfrith's early 8th century spectacularly illustrated vellum Hiberno-Anglian book, reputed to have been produced in honour of Cuthbert, is occasionally loaned back up North. We should all take the chance to see them when they are home.

THE ASSASSINATION OF DAVIE THE CARLING

He'll have been a low-ranking member of the Ogle family – a soldier or associate, someone who worked for them or had married in – and his eyes will have lit up at the news. Perhaps he would have been sitting somewhere public like a tavern in Rothbury or Morpeth, and the informant will have chosen his time to sidle up quietly, maybe offering a drink in a mug. It will certainly have been someone he knew.

"Are youse still after Davie Elliot?" the informer will have muttered, his gaze drawn to the orange flames dancing in the fire as he stood by the large mantle.

"Aye are we!"

"Well, I've heard tell where he is if you're interested."

The Ogle will have shushed him, drawn him closer and asked what the tout wanted in return for his information. Payment? Protection? It could have been either. Maybe the informer had an axe to grind with Elliot himself and just wanted him out of the way. Possibly he was giving up the information on the orders of a superior that didn't want to be identified; a March official or such like.

When the exciting news was fed up the chain of the Ogle family structure, it will have gone as far as the Headsman and the plot will have been drawn up with their friends and neighbours, the Shaftoes and the Fenwicks, to put a hit-squad together.

The lush green fields and rolling farmland of mid-Northumberland around the Scot's Gap area doesn't feature heavily in most reiver histories, but the Ogles of Ogle Castle, the Shaftoes of Shaftoe Hall at Little Bavington and the Fenwicks of Wallington Hall would all soon be implicated in a plot to assassinate the notorious Scottish rider Davie 'the Carling' Elliot. Mr. Shaftoe of Bavington, Oswald Mitford of Ryle, William Fenwick of Bitchfield, Roger Fenwick of Cambo, and William Shaftoe of Gunnerton were all knocking about together in a crew in 1585. This was their area of operation, in the farmland just to the east of the notorious north Tynedale and below Redesdale. The Scottish reivers knew it well. Davie the Carling knew it especially well.

The Carling was a violent career criminal who had been locked up as a pledge in Blackness castle in 1569 by his own Scottish crown and Lord Maxwell in a rare clampdown on the Border crime families. Davie was a brother of Elder Will the Tod Elliot, who was also locked up in Blackness with Adie 'Cowdais,' Wilcock's Hob, Gavin's Jock in Rammsigill Elliot, Eckie Armstrong, the son of Andrew of Gingles, Tom Armstrong, Willie Armstrong, Archie Kene, Clement's Hob and Dand of Braidley.

He was in trouble on the Scottish side again in 1575 and was a fugitive stopping with the Fenwicks and Shaftoes in the area of Kirkharle along with John 'Todsfoot' Elliot. The arrangement was unusual because it was taking place just one month after the infamous Raid of the Reidswire when the Scotsman Martin Croser fired an arrow at William Fenwick of Wallington, and all hell broke lose.

Two of the Fenwicks and a Robert Shaftoe were killed almost instantly after and the Scottish Warden Carmichael swore that he 'would hang 100 for that day's work,' but as they were leaving the Truce Day he swung his horse around and the Scots charged, killing Sir George Heron and others, and taking a number of gentlemen prisoner. For gentleman read high-ranking gangster, because that's what the landed gentry on both sides of the frontier were; ruthless, opportunistic, keen to earn, high on notoriety and protected by officials.

While the Carling was being sheltered by the Fenwicks and Shaftoes, the families went into Liddesdale and killed one of the Elliots. One of the

Tynedale Robsons was killed in an ambush on the Scottish side while raiding, and the Regent Morton wrote to the English Middle March Warden Sir John Forster that he felt that, regarding fugitives, it would have 'been better for the common peace and quietness of both the realms that more had been hanged and banished long since.' William Douglas was charged with getting the fugitives back, but old Forster will have been keen to use the thieves for his own ends – he was long engaged in corrupt practices with the Elliots. (*Please see the author's book Dick the Devil's Bairns – Breaking the Border Mafia for a full and comprehensive reiver history.*)

Whatever deal was worked out, in 1584 Sandy Hall of Yardhope complained that Davie 'the Carling' Elliot was with over 100 other riders including Francis and Hobb Armstrong of Whitehaugh, four of the Gingles Armstrongs, Eckie Armstrong of Harelaw, Dickie Armstrong of Dryhope, Eddie Elliot of Shaws, and Nebless Clem Croser who ran an open day foray at the Slymefoot and lifted 300 cattle, 40 horses, spoiled 30 shielings and took 20 prisoners.

Davie the Carling was the ringleader of the huge day foray on the Tarset valley later that year when himself and Nebless Clem Croser, Kinmont Willie Armstrong, and 300 others took 40 score cattle, three score horses, 500 sheep, burned 60 houses and killed 10 men. The bill was sworn by Jenkin and Gerry Hunter, Michael Milburn, Bartie Milburn of the Keam and Lance Milburn of Tarset.

Davie was named as one of the main players in six unanswered bills of complaint made by the English Middle March in the February of 1587. The complaints had been lodged for raids on Haydon Bridge, Featherstonehaugh, Biddlestone, Prendikes and Thornburn, and another at Mindrum in the East March. The complainers were Harry Collingwood, Jenkin Hunter and Christian Fenwick. The English authorities were still seeking justice for those crimes three years later and the Earl Bothwell and Earl Moray were charged to present Davie along with some of the worst outlaws and villains of Liddesdale including Sim Armstrong of Mangerton, Sim Armstrong of Whithaugh, Kinmont's Jock Armstrong, Will Elliot of Hartscarth, Martin's Archie Elliot, Archie Elliot of the Hill, Archie Armstrong of Whithaugh,

Ninian Armstrong of Tweden, and Andrew and Francis Armstrong, both sons of Lancey of Whithaugh.

In 1589 the Carling was in a gang that included the fellow Elliots Will of Fidderton, Alexander of Fallon, Rinion of Dodburn, Robin the laird of Burnheads, Hob Bully, Rinion Armstrong of the Harelaw and 80 others that hit Percival Reed of Troughend in another brazen day foray for 51 cattle, 3 horses, 60 yards of 'lynncloth' and killed two men. The Carling was back at Troughend later that year to kill another two men, take two prisoners and steal 100 cattle, 5 horses and £10 worth of 'lynncloth.' Also on that raid, which also hit James Hedley of Garretshiels and others, apart from those named above which rode again, were Tom Turnbull of Hopsburn, Davie Laidler, Archie, John and Rowie Croser and 100 others. The Carling's son Eddie was also involved in some large scale raids into Northumberland during 1589/90.

He was certainly implicated in many more crimes, though most of the bills of complaint will lie un-transcribed as yet in the dusty archives. In 1598 Davie the Carling Elliot was with other Scotsmen who murdered William Ogle, Reynold Shaftoe and others in the mid-Northumberland area. The Carling was named as the principal murderer and he had long been a thorn in the side of the Northumbrian families. It puts to bed the revisionist histories at present that suggest that many reivers 'only ever went on one raid' as a 'right of passage.' He had been involved in a life of crime for at least 27 years, as had all of those other Liddesdale men that he was riding with.

But the Northumberland families were just as violent and organised themselves and when the informant revealed that the Carling was being sheltered by an English official, Thomas Carlton at Gilsland, they probably weren't that surprised. Carlton was implicated in the Kinmont Willie Armstrong breakout from Carlisle castle two years earlier. He was also in up to his neck with the notorious Grahams and was another who was accused of conniving, inefficiency, corruption and consorting with the criminal reivers of both nations.

When the Headsmen were told where the Carling was staying they did a lot more subtle digging about themselves, probably pulling in favours from families that they knew in Cumberland, and found the exact house that Elliot was staying in.

They put together an assassination team of fourteen men – Ogles and Shaftoes in the main, though some members of the crew may have had other surnames – saddled up and made their way across the barren tops to the Northumberland/Cumberland border.

The hit-men were professional and effective – they'd probably done it before – getting into the house and killing Elliot without much fuss. Martin's Gibb Elliot had been similarly executed by a hit-team of the Tynedale Dodds in Liddesdale the previous year as the gangland violence and reign of terror continued.

The Ogles obviously left witnesses, though, as while they were quietly riding home, seven riders came galloping towards them. The crew will have seen them from a distance and reeled around slowly to explain what they'd done. Killing a Scottish murderer in a blood feud in England shouldn't have really been a problem, but they hadn't banked on the Carlton factor.

He charged up with his men going absolutely nuts, swearing, red-faced and enraged, cursing that they had killed a 'man in his charge who he had given protection to.' The Ogle gang wanted nothing to do with him, and probably told him where to go in no uncertain terms. Though Carlton had a bit of power himself as the land sergeant and Queen's officer, he came from a family nothing like as big and influential as the Ogles and Shaftoes; to them he was nothing. An irritant. The more they told him to get lost, the angrier he got, and he smashed his spear against one of the Ogles which knocked him off his horse and left him winded on the deck. He then fired his pistol at another which just missed, the lead whistling by his head.

One of the Ogles thought sod that, drew his own pistol and fired. The ball hit Carlton square between the eyes and blew a gore of blood and brains out of a large exit wound at the back of his head as he slumped backwards off his horse, killed instantly. The death of their boss just spurred on the men that he'd brought with him, however, and they chased the dismounted Ogles to a small old castle which offered little defence.

After a while of shouting back and forth the Ogles said that they'd give themselves up and face the Law if they were unharmed – but once they had given up their armour and pistols, one of Carlton's men whacked one of them on the head with a sword short, causing a horrendous injury. Seven of the Ogles were taken to Carlisle castle and put in jail by Henry Leigh, who said he would 'commit (them) to safe keeping till her Majesty's pleasure be further known.' Where the other seven went is unsure.

Sir Robert Carey, however, backed the Ogles and wrote that 'the Scotsman that was slain was a notable notorious thief, and had been at the killing of many a true English man, and a happy turn it is he is so well gone.' With such an influential official as the former Middle March Warden giving them his support, it ensured that the Ogles would get away with murder – as had happened so many times before.

Such was life on the Border.

BADGER BAITING, COCK FIGHTING AND BLOOD SPORTS

There can surely be no sadder sight than a big old silver Tommy Brock curled dead on a roadside. I recently passed one on a grass verge near Housesteads and my heart sank as I drove by.

The badger is an elusive and passive nocturnal creature who just wants to be left alone to get on with its business in the forests and fields, and they're not really that widespread in the county. The badger is an omnivore that eats earthworms, beetles, roots, vegetables, berries, fruits, frogs, rats, mice, small birds, and rabbits, as well as being partial to the honey from bees, while wasp grubs are a great delicacy to them. They are creatures of habit and wander the same paths over generations, even it that means crossing a busy road, which leads to the numbers we now see hit and killed.

Back in 1898 it was reckoned that the badger was extinct in Durham and virtually gone from Northumberland, where it was reputed to have 'been common enough fifty years previously.' Badger baiting at that time had largely stopped due to the scarcity of the animal rather than any concerns for its welfare. But there must have been a larger population in the Coquet area in times gone by as the oldest existing house in what was RothburyForest is Brockley Hall at Hesleyhurst. Brockley has a lintel in the yellow sandstone walls with the date 1666 and the name Thomas Wharton on it; the general feeling is that Brockley was probably once a bastle house and to gain its name there must have been an abundance of badgers about – similarly with Brockley Park near Hepple, brock being the Old English word for a badger. That other native woodland creature the fox was also similarly well represented in the area to give the names to Foxhole wood and Foxton Hill in the Forest, as well as Todsteads near Brinkburn (todd being the Middle English for a fox.)

As far back as 1263 one Philip Basset was granted a licence for life to hunt with his own dogs throughout the forests of England 'the hare, the fox, the cat, the badger and the cony (rabbit), except in fence month; so that he do not take the great deer or course in warrens; and grant that he may stretch his nets wherever he will to take the said creatures to wit, hares, foxes, cats, badgers and conies.' In 1303 every free man could course 'to take hares, foxes, cats, or badgers' with those animals enjoying nothing like the privileged protection afforded to deer throughout the land.

The balance between humans and nature is a delicate one and the last Earl of Ravensworth was said to have shot the last wildcat in Northumberland in 1853 in the woods of Barmoor Castle. Although that was alleged to be the last seen in England, wildcats were thought to be around Twizell in remote north Northumberland as late as 1862. They similarly had isolated homes at Cats' Crag at Spindleston Hill, the Cat's Loup up beyond Langleeford on the Harthope Burn and the Cat Cairn near Kielder.

Unfortunately, the wildcat, pole cat and pine marten were treated as vermin by gamekeepers in the 19th century and when a badger was similarly reported as being killed by keepers and foxhounds in Northumberland in a newspaper report in 1907, there were genuine fears that they could also be heading for extinction.

There was certainly a shift away from condoning animal blood sports at the time and along with the decrease in badger baiting, the once-popular cock fighting was also on the demise - though they may have actually just been driven underground. Rothbury had five cock-pits around the 1830s, according to D.D. Dixon. There was one in the Blue Bell garden, which was at that time called the Malt Shovel; another behind the Turk's Head (then called the 'Fighting Cocks.') A third was at the west end of the village up near the Catholic Church, and a fourth was in a yard behind the Fox and Hounds. The most important cock pit was at the Haa Hill near the Church.

50 or 60 birds fought there in four mains in 1838, their steel spurs gouging, cutting and tearing as they clawed at feathers.

Cock fighting was prohibited by the law by around 1891, but a visitor witnessed a fight, or 'main', at Shilbottle that year. The umpire was a rabbit-catcher who had a reek of whisky fumes coming off him and the two 'well-known sporting characters in the lower walks of society' brought along their birds to a secluded nook down by the riverside where five miners, who had bets on, and a publican were waiting. One of the men had a champion fighting cock and he challenged the other to bring three birds to take it on; the first was killed almost instantly by the formidable three inch sharp spur that the champion wore, driving it into the other's head. The second was caught in the eye, blinded and withdrawn by its owner. The third put up a huge fight, the writer describing how his crafty master had 'kept the best till the champion was exhausted with his previous work.' Although the bird was beaten, the champion himself died an hour or two later while on his way home due to some injury that had gone un-noticed in the heat of the fight. They were still organising cock fighting mains across in Cumbria in 1913 and a large fight took place and was reported in the papers on a Saturday evening in mid-Cumberland. The battle was Town v. Country and was fought in a grassy glade, with the birds again wearing sharp-pointed steel spears which were fitted by experts in the game. After 14 rounds of savage clucking and squawking the country bird landed a fatal blow and won the betting for its owner.

There was gambling involved in badger baiting too and men with wiry terriers dug them out of their setts to fight to the death for savage fun and wagers. But then the ignorance around the native wild animals in 1897 was quite staggering. A writer in *Field* tried to dispel some of the myths surrounding the badger such as being accused of killing lambs, of infecting foxes with mange, that they hibernated in winter and the persisting fallacy that they had legs longer on the right side than the left so they could move better along the side of a hill. There was also a common belief in the countryside that a badger lived to a great age and was blind for the last years of its life. The writer noted that a man took a badger with three cubs at Bywell, near Riding Mill, in April 1883 and that 'badgers were fairly numerous in Northumberland then, although they prefer the warmer soil and climate of the southern and midland counties.'

By 1909 the numbers of badgers in Northumberland were increasing greatly, especially in Coquetdale, and a gentleman with an estate near Swarland 'strictly preserved the badger from molestation and had a strong holt on his estate.' It was reckoned that the fox was in scarcity due to the prevalence of mange while it was also wildly suggested that 'the cock pheasants have been eating them.' Whey aye. Two boar badgers had been trapped in the village of Swarland itself and were described as 'exceptionally fine specimens.'

However, while the badgers were being protected if not encouraged at some places in Northumberland, they were being persecuted again in other parts of the county, Yorkshire and Cleveland by the early 1920s. It was felt that the efforts of some estate owners and the fact there were fewer gamekeepers during the First World War had helped the badger to increase its numbers but they had been 'dug out, shot, trapped and done to death by other means with the avowed intention of extermination' by 1922 and it was noted then that 'the badger in the North seems doomed.'

The following year was no different with the 'wanton wholesale destruction' of the creatures in north Yorkshire as it was reported that 'as soon as they endeavour to come near the haunts of men, and particularly ignorant gamekeepers, their death warrant seems to be sealed. It is to be feared that this is even the case in some districts whose principal landowners are anxious to preserve badgers. So is passing one of the most interesting, picturesque, harmless and least understood the wild animals of England,' despite some efforts to preserve the animal.

One badger met an untimely end near Gosforth in 1926 when he wandered across a railway line and was electrocuted. While there were a dozen or more well-known badger haunts in Northumberland at the time, it was thought that the unfortunate Brock had been sheltering in Gosforth Park woods and it was 'exceptional' to find one so close to the City.

The sad tradition of badger baiting was still quite common in the countryside before World War Two but in the twenty years after the population of greys had again increased and a survey in 1961 by the Natural History Society of Northumberland, Durham and Newcastle-upon-Tyne found that the animal was well established throughout the district and they were far more numerous than people realised, while the Badger Act of 1973 gave some protection to the nocturnal creature around farmlands. The persecution began again in the 1980s and 90s, however, as the secret horrific 'sport' of badger baiting was increasing in Northumberland as men with terriers went about digging (under the pretence of digging out foxes) or smoking out setts. On some occasions badgers were thrown to dogs around the back of pubs for 'entertainment.' It was claimed that baiters broke a badger's leg or jaw ahead of the contest to give the dogs a better chance. Hexham Police were hunting a badger baiting gang in 1994 and it was estimated that 10,000 badgers a year were being killed by baiters and diggers, even though they had been declared a protected species under a 1992 Act of Parliament.

The badger was given another torrid time when a cull was ordered by the Government after a link was purportedly discovered between them and bovine TB in 2013, though this caused some anger as the cull was said to be 'scientifically unsound' and the free shooting of badgers was shown to be an 'inhumane method of killing.' Northumberland's badger population escaped the cull despite the threat of a cap being lifted in 2018, and in 2020 the Northumberland Wildlife Trust were delighted as a programme of vaccination that they had been pushing for from the beginning was given priority by Westminster officials. The badger, it seemed, could go back to its night-time wanderings free of hassle and the imminent threat of a miserable death at the hands of people.

I'm a countryman and I've been lucky enough to lie on my back with a blade of grass in my mouth and see some of the most wonderful sights in British nature; otters, kingfishers, hedgehogs, stags, stoats, red squirrels, boxing hares…I've even seen a pine marten jump up a dry stone wall and take off up a tree. But I've never seen a live badger. I have seen a few setts around Rothbury over the years - as kids we played in a place we dubbed

'Badger Wood' after finding fresh dug holes near a cave, and I've noticed the deep red soil thrown deep out of other holes in secluded spots while out for a walk over the hills. A good few years ago a workmate complained that he'd been woken on several successive nights by a strange sound of scraping coming down the Woodlands bank in the wee small hours. Looking out of the window across the moonlit road he saw him coming down between the cars – a big badger dragging his claws on the tarmac, grunting as he headed down from his home somewhere up along the Coplish Burn in the woods to wander into the village looking for food. The image made me smile.

One night, maybe, I'll have the good fortune to see one myself out there under the stars in the wild, in its native habitat, safe from the threat of unwarranted persecution. For what's a badger ever done to you?

THE PAINTED WALLS OF COCKLAW TOWER

You can see it in a field by a farm in the distance as you come around the corner at Chollerton by the church before dipping down under the arches of the old railway bridge. The yellow sandstone on the square peel tower at Cocklaw was reputedly robbed out from the nearby Roman Wall to construct it when the Errington family moved in around 1372.

When you look at the square shape of the stones in the construction, it seems fairly certain that the stones have originated from Hadrian's frontier. The Erringtons were said to have occupied Cocklaw tower until 1567 and it was possibly John Eryngton who appropriated the stone to build it. He was 35 in 1372 and a powerful and influential enough man to ride with Henry Percy, earl of Northumberland (Harry Hotspur's father), to Shawdon in 1387 as he recalled in a proof of age case for Henry de Lylburn of Shawdon at Corbridge in 1407. Robert Elryngton said in the same case that he saw Henry Percy acting as godfather. A truce between England and Scotland in 1453 was signed by Thomas Heryngton, who you would imagine might hail from such an impressive defensive residence as Cocklaw.

Despite its distance from the sea perhaps it was another one of the family, a cousin maybe, named John Heryngton who was the master of the ship 'Seinte Marie' of Newcastle-upon-Tyne that was arrested among others ships and vessels in the port of Sandewich after dropping a load of sea coal in 1389. And it may have been a descendent of his, a 'common smuggler' called Lancelot Errington, and his nephew Mark Errington, who seized the castle on Holy Island for the Jacobites in 1715. Brandy was involved, of course, as he incapacitated the corporal, sergeant and 10 or 12 men garrisoned there with drink before the magistrates of Berwick with 20 soldiers came the next day and re-took the castle – and seized the brandy that was on Errington's ship.

The surname has many spellings including the likes of Erington, Erinthen, Erryngton, Herington, Hernithen, Heryngton, Hetherington, Etherington, Harrington and despite their exploits on sea they were found throughout the border in Northumberland and Cumberland, but Cocklaw was their main pele. The name pele tower is said to come from the Cumbric word pil, for a fort. That theory includes pele being a variation of 'stockade' and a tower being built within a paling becoming known as a pele tower. Given their location, the Erringtons were obviously involved in border reiving. The reivers committed two crimes repeatedly in Scottish Law called reif and stouthreif. That's where 'reiver' comes from. Reifer. They weren't called reivers at the time, though - they were known as outputters and intakers and then regularly just 'thieves.'

A Thomas Errington either came from Cocklaw or nearby as in 1528 he and his sleuth hound, assisted by William Charlton and other Tynedale men, he tracked down the rebels Will Charlton of Shitlington, Jasper Noble, Roger Armstrong and Archibald Dodd near Haydon Bridge. Errington killed Charlton, whose body was hung in chains on a gallows near Hexham, while Noble got the same treatment at HaydonBridge.

In 1537 the Erringtons Nicholas of Bingfield and his sons, and John Errington of Buklee, with the townships of Byngfeld, Halleden, and Colwell refused to 'rise to the hue and cry' regarding the outlaws Edward, Ninian and John Charlton, John Heron, the bastard son of John Heron of Chipchase and others after the murder of Roger Fenwick. It was no real surprise as an Anthony Errington was later implicated in the affair himself and indicted at Newcastle.

The Erringtons were involved in all the reiving activities of the North Tynedale families, though they are rarely credited, despite family members turning up in Hexham gaol on many occasions. One misunderstood crime that the reivers undertook was the taking of blackmail. It was described in 1596 as that because the borders were very poor and didn't own much silver, they paid their rent in meal, corn, etc. The payment to the landlord was called greenmeal, and that to a gang doing extortion blackmeal because 'it was taken foul and dishonest.' Sir Robert Carey wrote in 1598 that 'the times are such that every gentleman in Northumberland seeks the Scots thief's favour and have long paid 'blackmeale' as they call it; while the poor men that cannot, are continually spoiled.' Another official document around the time complained of the 'intolerable exaction of 'blackmeale'' by the Grahams and others. It was a protection racket.

A branch of the Erringtons may have moved to Cocklaw during the turbulent 1300s from their estates in Yorkshire; certainly, in 1403, a deal was made between Richard de Aske and John Haryngton, both of Yorkshire, and Thomas Heryngton and William de Halywelle of Northumberland for the abbot of Alnwick that he 'shall make no suit in the court of Rome which may tend to prejudice of the king or crown, or to impair the laws, ordinances, statutes or customs of the realm, nor go himself, nor send any man thither for the purpose,' which certainly suggests a family relationship, especially as the bond for breaking the deal was 100 marks.

With its yellow sandstone and squat, rectangular build, the Grade 1 listed Cocklaw could almost be a tower plucked from one of the great county castles of Alnwick or Warkworth and dumped in the fields. It has that kind of a grand look despite its utilitarian feel, and with over 40 feet of stonework still standing in among the sheds and buildings of a working farm, Cocklaw is an impressive ruin.

Inside the three storey tower it is reported that the floors have collapsed in but the shell is largely intact. There is said to be traces of a 16th century mural painted on a wall in a first floor chamber above something of an oubliette prison below, which was originally only accessible from a trapdoor in the painted room, though at some time a hole has been knocked through the wall. There is a vaulted lobby possibly something like that which can be seen at GilnockieTower today, a fantastically preserved and restored tower on the Scottish side near Hollows. A doorway to the right leads to the newel stair up through the building; the lay-out consists of a single large chamber, smaller chamber to the south and the stairwell in the south-east which is the same throughout.

From outside, vegetation can be seen sprouting from the cavity on the top parapet where roof trusses will have once been tied in, with yellowish lichen and mosses on the gable faces, while some stonework has tumbled off from here in the past. Cocklaw had a spiral tower at one time, which had broken down by around 1860, and was long used from around that time as a cow byre. The fact that the tower is on private land right beside a farmhouse has probably gone some way to preserving it in the condition it is in and while it is nice to catch a glimpse as you head on over the A6079 heading west, one can only wonder what faded fresco is painted on the plaster of them walls. It's an intriguing mystery.

I only really delved into the history of the tower as a researcher for Robson Green's popular TV series *'Walking Hadrian's Wall'* got in touch regarding the reivers in the area and I thought it tied the two together nicely, a Roman defensible structure being recycled into a defensive structure for a riding family. But she never got back so I had all this on my computer, which I have handily recycled myself.

While Cocklaw would have made a fantastic base for reiver tourism in Northumberland were it not situated on a working farm, the Old Gaol at Hexham just six miles away, which was built in 1333 to house the miscreants of the liberty of Hexhamshire, is the main centre for telling the story of the Anglo-Scottish raiding families today. The big rectangular building of yellow sandstone right in the middle of the town is well worth a visit if you want to explore that history further…or even just to stick a family member in the stocks outside for a laugh.

EBB'S NOOK AND THE GREAT HEATHEN ARMY

The unusual straight rays of light that filled the horizon ran in parallel lines away to a vanishing point in the North Sea and persisted for a good half hour. It was a strange natural phenomenon and with the peace provided by the tranquil repetition of the sea rolling in an and out off the rocks below, you could almost pass it off as a religious experience; especially while sitting with a flask in the small hollow of a 12th century chapel that almost certainly sits on the remains of a much earlier Christian building.

The promontory at Ebb's Nook in Beadnell has a magical atmosphere as it is and it felt even more special to observe the rare anticrepuscular or antisolar rays, a meteorological optical event showing the opposite of the sun, which certainly made you contemplate the Northumbrian Princess Æbba at least, if not God.

TV's *Time Team* had done a dig on the site a few years earlier and Mick Aston in his brightly coloured jumpers had discussed the early Northumbrian conversion to Christianity with Tony Robinson and the crew as they exposed a few remaining stones of the tiny church, hence the dip in the grass.

Æbba was a daughter of Northumbria's last Pagan King, Æthelfrith of Bernicia, who was described by the monk Bede in his *Ecclesiastical History of the English People* as 'ravaging the Britons more cruelly than all other English (Anglian) leaders' and 'over-running a greater area than any other king or ealdorman, exterminating or enslaving the inhabitants, making their lands either tributary to the English or ready for English settlement.' It may have been Æthelfrith's army that attacked and burned the Mote of Mark, a small hillfort near Kipford in Galloway (what was then the Briton's Rheged) with a wonderful cockle shell beach down at the Firth of Forth many miles to the west during that period of expansion and domination.

But when he was slain in battle by the East Anglian king Rædwald and the Deiran exile Edwin in 616 (*see story 33*) his children had to flee into exile themselves from Bamburgh to the court of the Dal Riadan king Domnall Brecc in what is now modern day Western Scotland. It was during that enforced exile far from home that Æbba and her brothers were converted to the Christian religion by the followers of Saint Columba.

It is told in some accounts that Æbba became a nun to avoid the attentions of a man called Aiden, who was a Prince. But could it not be more likely that the man who was smitten with her was Saint Aiden, the monk that had trained up both her and her brother Oswald on Iona? The same Aiden that came to Lindisfarne around 633 when Oswald retook his Kingdom by force and after the first missionary who was sent to preach, a monk named Corman, said the Northumbrians were a 'savage and un-teachable race.' Aiden had certainly been a massive influence in turning the beautiful Æbba to the path of one God and she established a monastery with her brother's help at Ebchester, in the Deiran (near Consett) part of the kingdom around 635. She then moved to northern Bernicia to establish the monastery at Coldingham near St. Abb's Head that she is best known for. It is possible that Æbba constructed her small chapel on the sea front at Beadnell as a precursor to the bigger monastery as she made her way back north and the location was the inspiration for her bigger ecclesiastical building as both are near similar rocky outcrops that run into the sea.

Æbba may have drawn spiritual inspiration from the water and being right on the North Sea coast drew obvious parallels to the main Christian religious centres of Iona and Lindifarne. While the alluring Æbba may have tempted Aiden, it is also possible that she proved sexually attractive to Saint Cuthbert, too. He spent his time up at Coldingham swimming in the bitterly cold sea at night to avoid getting involved in the fun stuff and a legend that two otters swam out to join him in the sea comes from that time period. Perhaps Æbba never really forgot her Pagan roots and the worship of the feminine force and sexual energy. Certainly, looking into the sky and reading signs from it have roots in a older heathen tradition, and before the first Viking invasion of Lindisfarne in 793 it is well recorded that 'immense whirlwinds, flashes of lightning and fiery dragons were seen flying in the air' in the months leading up to the attack which saw the church plundered of its silver and its monks slaughtered.

While that first hit and run was a precursor to the Viking Age in Britain and although the north of Northumbria remained outside the Danelaw for much of it, another beautiful nun named Æbba, who was the Abbess of Coldingham almost 200 years after the original Æbba's building had burned down during a wild wake for her, would have a horrendous run-in with the terrifying Northmen, or Norse. Although they were known as Danes to the Anglian, Saxon, British, Irish and Pictish people on the island, the sea-borne Viking invaders hailed not only from Denmark but also from the other Scandinavian countries of Norway and Sweden.

In 865, in what either prompted, or was a fourth invasion of the Great Heathen Army, depending on the source, a woman was raped by a Northumbrian King called Osbert, who had been deputed by the West Saxons. He had been out hunting when he found the lady home alone and forced himself upon her. The un-named lady was the wife of a nobleman called Beorn Bocador, a Dane by birth, and he would travel back across the sea to ask for help to deal with the treacherous warlord that had committed the vile sexual assault.

What the Danes delivered to avenge Beorn Bocadar's wife was unbelievable; 20,000 armed men led by Ingwar and Ubba, with Berno, Halfdene, Oskitel, Bagseg, Hosten, Eowils, Hamand, and Guthrum loaded their ships and set sail for 'East England' (East Anglia) to teach the Wessex-puppet ruler rapist a lesson he would never forget. Unfortunately for Northumbria, a storm blew the awesome flotilla of longships off course and they ended up being driven ashore at Berwick-upon-Tweed. The Vikings destroyed everything in their path; they burned every town and village that they came across, killed people indiscriminately with both old and young all falling under battleaxes, especially Christians, and took particular joy in smashing any monasteries to pieces.

When they advanced on Coldingham, the terrified nuns inside looked up to their abbess Æbba (the younger) for help. They had obviously heard the stories of the Norsemen and their appetite for cruelty and violent abuse, be it sexual or otherwise, and were no doubt clinging tightly to their wooden crucifixes with tears in their eyes and a sickening fear in the pits of their stomachs. Some may have even witnessed what the Vikings had done in the past before following their calling to the church.

Æbba took a knife to her face and cut off her nose and top lip to make herself less attractive to the bloodthirsty raiders while advising her nuns to do the same to try and save themselves from the absolute brutality of rape. The Vikings burned Æbba and her nuns inside the monastery. Some records state that the also fired 'Landaff, Tynemouth, Wearmouth, Streveshall, and several other great monasteries,' while 'deflowering the nuns and committing all manner of rapine and cruelty.' It was a savage and inhumane time.

While some authorities give the date of the attack as 865 and others as 870, what is for sure is that in 866 the Great Heathen Army were back in tremendous force again to take control of the southern part of Northumbria, controlling York after a pitched battle that saw them slaughter the two Kings Osbert – the alleged rapist - and Alla. Other histories tell that Alla had killed the legendary Ragnar Lodbrok by throwing him in a pit of snakes and the 866 invasion force was lead by his sons Halfdan (or Hvitserk), Björn Ironside, Sigurd Snake-in-the-Eye, Ivar the Boneless, and Ubba. When they took York they subjected King Alla to the 'blood eagle' – severing the ribs and pulling the victims lungs over their shoulders – to avenge their father's death. The devastating Viking attacks continued every year until 871 and on as the Scandinavian warriors plundered, murdered and established themselves a foothold in Britain. In 874 Halfdan Ragnarson led half of the Heathen Army northwards with him from York and spent the winter camped around the river Tyne before battling with the Picts and the Strathclyde Britons the following year. He then headed back to York and divided his Northumbrian lands among his men for them to farm, though these were for the most part in the Deiran section of the Kingdom.

In an age remembered for bearded, helmeted men in animal hides wielding swords and axes in shield walls, the fact that remarkable, inspiring women were also able to make their mark is testament to their unbelievable spirit and devotion. Æbba the younger was Sainted after her terrible death; Æbba the Elder died at her monastery at Coldingham in 683 and was later made a Saint herself with her feast day being the 25th August.

The site of her chapel near the small harbour and lime kilns at Beadnell remains a place of great tranquillity and contemplation, even to someone who sees strange geometric shapes in the sky and wonders what the portents are. Sometimes you don't need a Seer to throw the bones and look into the strange phenomenon; sometimes nature just feels right and the presence of God, or Odin, or the Princess Æbba can be whatever you want in your head or heart. Sometimes you just enjoy the experience for what it is.

THE ALNWICK RIOTS

The tobacconist young Crawford was a popular lad in Alnwick. His father was most likely the publican and day labourer Thomas Crawford from the Ducal town and the family were well known and well liked. If there was any doubting that, the police were to find out very forcefully in the June of 1866.

Crawford had been arrested with two other youths in Alnwick by the sergeant of the police, a man called Watson. Crawford had allegedly been maimed and maltreated by the officer, while the other two had just been fined. Despite his kicking, Crawford had also been summoned to appear in court the following month on a charge of 'resisting and assaulting the police in the execution of their duty.' Unfortunately for the boys in blue, Crawford was also a rifleman in the Northumberland Light Infantry Militia, and there were a great number of them in the town and locality busy training at that time.

The Northumberland Militia had been formed in Alnwick in 1759 and was led by Sir Edward Blackett; just two years later the North Yorkshire county Militia were involved in a scandalous massacre in Hexham when they opened fire in the Market Place after the reading of the Riot Act, killing more than 50 men and women and injuring hundreds of others who had marched to protest about a ballot to select men to join the ranks of the Militia.

Known as The Buffs due to the colour of their uniforms, the Northumberland Militia was raised separately to the regular British Army after the Seven Years' War conflict (1756-63) in North America and the men were selected by the deeply unpopular ballot in each county. The numbers to serve were 'based on a return made by the county authorities of men of eligible age between 18 and 50.' That was initially 560 men in Northumberland. The increase in the local constabularies by around 1859 meant that the Militia were used less and less for keeping order and were more of an auxiliary unit for the Regulars serving in conflicts such as the Crimean War.

On a hot Saturday night around midnight, perhaps telling after the pubs had kicked out, the menacing atmosphere that the militiamen had been generating exploded into a violent riot on the streets of Alnwick 'such as has never been known before.' The police had been aware of a sense of trouble brewing and a Superintendent Harkes had brought in officers from around about to assist if it did all go off as they had worried. And did it ever.

The streets became more and more crowded as people gathered in an excited rabble with the militiamen in their shirts sleeves and various other bits of military kit forming the main part of the group. One militiaman came down Clayport with several pokers under his arms and called out: "Now lads, who wants a poker and who wants a bayonet?" He threw them down with a clatter near the Corn Market and they were quickly taken up by his comrades, who then rushed the police and attacked them in little pockets wherever they encountered them.

Coppers were pelted with stones and whacked with pokers as they ran in little groups, totally outnumbered. They hid and locked themselves in the militia depot itself, in Thompson and Davison's brewery, and anywhere else they could find. Sergeant Watson was handed out a particularly severe beating by the rioters, and the Superintendent was wounded in the neck. The main body of the police were driven back up Hotspur Street and into the police station where they hurriedly locked the doors.

A simultaneous volley of stones smashed every window in the building and the sound of shattering glass no doubt encouraged the towsfolk who joined in tearing down some railings and lifting a large stone to batter the station doors in with. The militiamen, however, told them to leave it to them as 'they would be known and fined.' They gave up after a while and dispersed. When they were gone, at around One o'clock, the police formed up four deep with drawn cutlasses and marched to the top of St Michael's

Lane and around the town, but couldn't find any of the rioters.

Twelve years later, in 1878, the Northumberland Light Infantry Militia became the 3rd (Militia) Battalion of The Northumberland Fusiliers and they saw action out in South Africa in the Second Boer War. They travelled across in December 1899 and 23 men of the Regiment were killed by both disease and fighting the enemy.

Another serious riot occurred in Alnwick in March 1875 during the hirings for farm workers, and it cost a policeman called Sergeant Hatley his life. There were over 2,000 strangers in the town looking for graft when a drunk farm labourer called John Wait started a fight in one of the pubs. Two policemen came in to arrest him and there was a major scuffle when Wait was knocked to the ground with a truncheon and taken outside. There was a large crowd of people shouting and yelling waiting and Wait's brother waded in to save him. As more police came into the crowd, reckoned to be around 3,000 strong, they all got embroiled in vicious street fighting in tightly packed groups as they surged forward. At the peak of the riot, with stones being thrown and fists flying, Sergeant Hatley fell. The officer that went to his assistance was given a right hiding before Hatley's body was taken to a nearby butchers stall were he was found to be dead. The disturbance also went on for an hour. Anyone that has ever been in a riot will know that sixty minutes is a seriously long time to be involved in disorder; with bottles flying and smashing on the street, shouting and swearing and a heaving surge of bodies squeezing and pushing forward, the initial pump of adrenaline helps to fuel the fighting. But after an hour the body's chemical fight or flight responses have been long burned out and you're running on pure hate or vengeance.

They certainly weren't the only riots in Northumberland during the Nineteenth Century; drunk Irish reapers at Wooler in 1863 fell out among themselves and starting fighting. When Sergeant Murray of the Northumberland Constabulary intervened, he was punched and kicked senseless. Irish iron workers at Shotley Bridge were accused of drinking spirits and starting a serious four-day riot against their English workmates in 1858 which had to be put down by the 'Sherwood Foresters' militia from Newcastle, while a detachment of infantry also had to be dispatched from Newcastle Barracks to quell a riot among the colliers at Bedlington in 1852 where stones were again thrown. There was another pitman's riot at Cramlington in 1865 which saw the miners Thomas Dodd, Alex Barras, David Moore, Thomas Pringle, Thomas Wanless and Thomas MacLean all jailed for six months.

Some serious disorder erupted near Hexham in 1870 with the bizarre 'Derwentwater Riots' at Newlands South Farm. 19 men were charged with riot and conspiracy to commit riot in a strange land and property dispute on behalf of the eccentric 'Lady' Amelia Radcliffe, who styled herself Countess of Derwentwater. Those charged were the auctioneers John Murray and Henry Brown, John Nicholson (joiner), John Drummond (collier), John Allison (miller), George Robson (carrier), George Harrison, Isaac Turner and William and George Lovatt (butchers), Robert Cole (cab proprietor), John Brown and John Parker (blacksmiths), William Todd (flour dealer), Michael McNally (beer house keeper), James Hunter (farmer), James Miller (plasterer), Robert Glendinning (labourer) and Henry Carss (rate collector).

They had used great force with arms and 'with other evil disposed persons unlawfully, tumultuously, and riotously made great noise, tumult, and disturbance to the great disturbance and terror of the Queen's subjects and against the Queen's peace, and did then and there unlawfully obstruct the passage the liege subjects of our lady the Queen upon and along a certain public Queen's highway there.' Basically, the farm had been given to the Admiralty following the execution of the Earl of Derwentwater for his part in the 1715 Jacobite Rising and Radcliffe claimed that she was a relative and that the land was rightfully hers. She wore a sword by her side, a military cloak and a cap with white plumes and had taken possession of the old ruined castle at Dilston. The court was told that when she was removed from there, Radcliffe had 'occupied a sort of sentry-box for some time the highway, but was re-moved by the highway authorities,' to much laughter.

Henry Brown was acting on behalf of Mrs. Radcliffe in going to the farm lifting all the cattle, demanding the rent, making threats and saying that the farm was hers with the others all backing him up. It was a complicated legal case but the long and short of it was Brown was sentenced to imprisonment with nine months hard labour, the others were all fined £50 each, and the mysterious 'Countess' left the court being followed by a noisy crown and had to 'seek refuge in a shop in St. Nicholas Buildings.'

In a less high profile case, the fishermen George Allison and Thomas Cromarty were arrested for a riot on Holy Island in 1889 when they, and others, attacked the police station after the lone local policeman had arrested Matthew 'Dugald' Cromarty for throwing a stone through the bobby's window. He'd been unpopular for informing the Receiver of Wrecks at Berwick that a number of the villagers had unlawfully lifted flour from a shipwreck that they'd recently salvaged. It was hardly 'Whisky Galore' but the policeman obviously felt he was just doing his job, and the locals (nearly every man on the island was actually involved) disagreed.

There was also some kick back against authority with a poacher's riot on the Coquet near Harbottle in November 1817. When the water bailiffs went to apprehend some men poaching salmon with the light and leister, a whistle was blown and around 16 men came out of the blackness armed with leisters and bludgeons and beat the hell out of them. Only two were caught and prosecuted; John Emans of Netherton and William Black of Trewhitt were charged with riot - Emans was fined 20 shillings and confined to Morpeth Gaol for seven days while Black was fined 3s 4d and released.

The rest of the gang just vanished back into the night.

ROTHBURY CARNIVAL

It seems quite unbelievable now given the current nature of the sport, but five Newcastle United stars spent their Bank Holiday Monday running a football sideshow on the Haugh at Rothbury Carnival – just three days before the first leg of the UEFA Fairs Cup Final against Ujpest Dozsa at St. James's Park.

Pop Robson, Iam McFaul, Bob Moncur, Frank Clark and David Craig spent two hours signing autographs down by the riverside among the throng of marquee tents with the smell of candy floss and hotdogs in the air despite the rain that threatened to put a real dampener on the 1969 event.

The day out in the country certainly didn't do them any harm as on the Thursday night at Newcastle the United stars were in dreamland when Moncur struck twice and Jim Scott got the other in a second half blitz that gave United an amazing 3-0 lead to take across to Hungary. They then won that game 3-2 when Moncur, Preben Arentoft and Alan Foggon were on target to lift the Inter-Cities trophy 6-2 on aggregate. Wendy Wilson, a 22-year-old from Jubilee Buildings, was the Rothbury Carnival Queen that year and thousands lined the streets despite the gloom and drizzle.

United goalie Iam McFaul with his young son at the Rothbury Carnival.

Although it rained in '69, most recollections of the Rothbury Carnival bring back happy memories of the sunny Seventies with T-shirt tans and beer in packed pubs, the Pipe Band marching down the High Street and floats on flat bed trucks, children sitting their father's shoulders as they wandered through the crowds in a procession cheering. It wasn't exactly Notting Hill or New Orleans, but the annual Coquetdale Whitsuntide Bank Holiday event was one of the most eagerly anticipated on the calendar.

The Carnival had run pre-World War Two, was restarted in the April of 1959 with the simple goal to raise funds to make a children's playing field, and the event kept going until to 1984. Many will remember the park that the funds from the first two years built, down on the riverside behind the bus station. There was large slide with narrow metal steps leading up steeply and the shiny gloss of the slide than ran down quick then levelled off onto a worn bit of grass at the bottom; there were the metal climbing frame monkey bars, the six person wooden horse, the see-saw, the old steam engine and the lethal spinning top. There was the sand pits and the swings, which would all be retro chic now no doubt and bought up as salvage by some antique dealer.

The whole event was organised by the Coquetdale Round Table and although it was cancelled in 1961, chairman William Storer commented that they planned to hold other events throughout the year. "We cancelled the Whit Sun carnival held for the last two years because we do not want local people to become bored with the idea. Next Whit we may renew it," he said. Those first two years had raised £360 for local charities and £400 for the riverside park.

The Whitsun celebrations sprung from a much earlier tradition and it was long a legend that the Knights of the Round Table had witnessed a divine vision of the Holy Grail on a Whitsunday, which prompted their quest to find its true location. Perhaps that is why the Tablers got involved in the first place. The Coquetdale Round Table was chartered in September 1954. It is an international men's organisation but has always seemed something of a closed shop like the Freemasons; you know people in it, but you don't really have a clue what they do.

Though the earliest examples of the Rothbury Carnival are vague, the event certainly took place during the 1920s and George Nichol was the honorary treasurer from the first event until he stood down in 1936. An almost surrealist black and white image from 1924 shows a man in a top-hat on a bicycle with adverts for products such as Heinz tomato chutney outside the newsagents, with Lee's garage in the rear, and smartly dressed men in flat caps and trilby hats stood around on the street. It has the feel of a Man Ray.

Lord Armstrong was at the Carnival in 1930 and crowned Miss Oliver the

May Queen. The 'Mayor' and 'Mayoress' handed over the keys of Rothbury to Lord Armstrong who handed them to King Carnival and his Queen. There is some grainy, flickering amateur footage of the 1931 Carnival held in the Armstrong Family collection, and you can view it online at https://www.yfanefa.com/record/19800.

It is best described by the note which accompanies it and explains that: 'This brief film opens as the Rothbury Carnival procession moves down the High Street. Crowds of onlookers line the street. Various shots of the carnival route include an individual wearing an eccentric white Michelin Man costume hopping along the road. He is followed by a number of children in best clothes or costumes, which include nurse and American Indian outfits. A troop of children in Scottish pipers' outfits march down the road. A man pushes a cart on two wheels. Two lads in school uniforms and flat caps walk beside the procession. A horse-drawn covered float passes. A woman dressed in harem trousers walks between two men in sailor outfits. There is a shot of the covered float with beer barrel load as it passes by Soulsby's Café.'

In 1936 the Whit Monday carnival was held to benefit the Newcastle Infirmary and local charities. Before the NHS was formed in 1945, charity cup football matches and carnivals were held as a way to raise money for providing health services. The Carnival committee at that time comprised of the Chairman, Councillor J.P. Clark, the honorary organising secretary, John Phillips, the assistant secretary, George Carr, and the treasurer W. Pattison. The event that year 1936 raised £130 and the finale was a whist drive in the Jubilee Hall.

Once again the events were marred by rain but there was a wide selection of things going on and large crowds attended. The carnival 'Mayor' was T. Carruthers and the comedy dame 'Mayoress' was Tommy Ballantyne. The events started on the Saturday up at Union Park where there were flat races, a three-legged race, and an obstacle race. There was also a clay-pigeon shoot. The big carnival procession took place on Whit Monday and a huge number of visitors bustled on the busy streets before some heavy thunder showers will have driven them into the pubs, no doubt. The Carnival King was

George Davison and the Queen Dorothy Ford, while the skirl of bagpipes and rattle of drums of the Rothbury Pipe Band filled the village between the rolling rumbles of thunder down the valley.

A six-a-side football competition with eight teams was hotly contested and won by the team 'Maltings' of Rothbury, obviously made up of lads from the Malting Yard. Their homes on Coquet Terrace had been placed under a compulsory purchase order just a few months earlier, and those at Ritton White House near Ewesley were given a clearance order under the Housing Act. A case of scarlet fever had occurred in the Malting Yard in the April and the Rothbury Urban District Council and the Ministry of Health were involved. The properties were vacated and set for demolition by February 1939 and the Woodlands was built to replace it. Twenty-two homes were affected and 95 people were moved out of the Manor House, the Malting Yard and some buildings the strip of land at Well Strand. There were 23 workman's huts demolished and 81 people dispersed from Ritton White House. There was even more serious upheaval that year when War broke out. Perhaps a feeling lingered after what was witnessed and experienced by many of the men in Rothbury and Coquetdale, especially in the Far East where many were prisoners of war at the hands of the Japanese, that the frivolity, fun, and sense of community at the Carnival should be put on hold and it didn't appear again until the resurrection in 1959.

With no event in 1961, there was no Carnival again in 1965 but it was back in 1966 where it raised over £300. Around 20 Thropton men were pulled underwater in the Coquet to cheers from the reigning Champions in the tug o' war. The following year saw a continuation of the popular of the tug o' war over the river as well as the addition of more side shows, while the money raised was to go towards a new play park in Thropton and other local charities.

The Gateshead FC manager, and former England international, George Hardwick opened the Rothbury Carnival in 1968 and the former Sunderland boss joined the team in judging the floats. The committee hoped to give half of the money raised to the Olympic fund to help send the British team to Mexico City and the rest to Rothbury Recreation Committee. The main organiser at the time was Alan Parkin, the director of a local building firm and past Chairman of the Coquetdale Round Table, as well as other Round Table members.

TV personality Tom Coyne from Nationwide opened the Rothbury Carnival in 1972. The organisers, the Coquetdale Round Table, said that at least six other neighbouring Round Tables had joined in to man stalls at the biggest event to date and they hoped to raise money to buy a mini-bus for the Hillbrow Children's Home in Morpeth.

The following year four parachutists from the Red Barons free-fall display team leapt from a plane above Rothbury as one of the top attractions – as well as a drinking competition from the 'Rothbury Pot.' The five-and-a-half pint pewter tankard was bought by the wife of the landlord of the Queen's Head, James Embleton, at Corbridge seven years earlier. It had sat on the bar in the Queen's since about 1969, but nobody knew much about it. "My guess is that it's about 200 years old," Mr. Embleton told the press ahead of the 'who can drink 5 ½ pints the fastest' competition. "It's difficult to tell unless you're an expert but it is certainly very old." Carnival Queen Marjory Jackson, crowned for the second time in three years, appeared at many of the carnival events, including the drinking competition. It had been hoped that the Red Barons would jump with the pot, but the team leader Gordon Fernie said it was impossible to jump with it in the conditions.

Around 20,000 people turned up for the then two-day event in aid of local community projects and charities and the attractions included the parade of floats, the tug-of-war contest and a chain-saw competition, along with 60 displays and exhibits. "The carnival has been a huge success," Alan Parker, secretary of the organising committee, told the newspapers. "This must be due partly to outside help, and the whole village has really got together to make the carnival a success."

There was also Cumberland Wrestling contests, Geordie Comedy Theatre, Canoe and Archery displays, Pipe and juvenile Jazz bands, Crazy Contests, and a Children's Pet Show, while punters had the chance to win holidays to Costa Brava, Istanbul and Paris.

The prizes were certainly decent and by 1975 the winners of the Carnival raffle were Mrs Mitchell of the Pinfold in Rothbury, who bagged £75 in premium bonds. Mrs Willis of Rowland's Gill won a portable television; L. Veach of Newcastle bagged a mini weekend In London and Mrs M. Rowland of Walkergate took a case of wine. In the March of 1976 40 men (and their oversized 'babies') were involved in a pram race from the Queen's Head in Rothbury to the Cross Keys at Thropton to raise funds for the Carnival, which had itself raised £9,000 for charity over the previous four years. The Carnival was attracting over 30,000 visitors to the village by then as it peaked in popularity. Entry to the show field cost 40p with events happening on both the Sunday and Monday including the escapologist Hardeenii, fire eating and sword swallowing from Stromboli, and comedy trick cyclists Silvia Scarri and Dot. The grand parade of floats left the bus station at 2pm on the Monday, and I have a feeling that I may have been on that one, though my jumble of memories regarding the Carnival are blurred. I do recall being Wee Willie Winkie with a candle holder, a white nightshirt and night cap and getting on the float outside my uncle Brian's up Addycombe, meeting cousin Claire who was dressed as Looby Lou, I think, with loops of yellow hair under a hat. The theme of our float was obviously characters from childhood rhymes. I may have also been on a float from Thropton nursery at one point. The images I seem to remember and have seen in old photos include the white shirts at the football club stalls as they displayed their trophies, being freaked out by a life size Rupert Bear, and the atmosphere that felt something like *It's A Knockout*, with the football shooting game with holes in wooden boards.

The new carnival Queen in 1977 was Deborah Harrison of Two Trees on the Hillside and the 1978 event was captured in glorious colour by the Upper Coquetdale Film Group. You can see clips on YouTube. Many people's memories include their parents helping out by driving the wagons or knocking in posts on the riverside, of seeing men dressing up as women and the sheer delight of being up on a float; many remember who were the Carnival Queens and can still debate it – Steph Carlyle, Angie Mackenzie, surely Tracy Shadwell...no?

The Carnival was back to a one-day event by 1981, held only on the Bank

Holiday Monday, and it opened at on the Haugh at 1pm with a Dance at 10pm. In 1982 crowds were down to 5,000 despite the baking sunshine with the highlight being a fancy dress and tableaux procession. The then 4-year-old Sean Jobson of Alnwick was dressed up as a punk rocker to win the children's competition.

The following year the Carnival was moved off the Haugh and onto the High Street. Thousands still came into Rothbury and Alnwick District Council helped out the Round Table by lending market stalls free of charge. The entertainment included pageantry and the usual parade of floats was led by the pipe band, but it had all fell a little flat compared to the heydays and 1984 saw the final Carnival, which has now evolved to become the annual Rothbury street fair.

A float from the Railway Hotel

'The Cleopatras' Cottage Hospital winning Carnival Float 1983. Pic courtesy Susan Aynsley.

Carnival Queen Marjorie Jackson with the 5 1/2 pint pot in '72

FOR A PURSE OF GOLD: THE ROTHBURY RACES

The Duke of Northumberland weighed in with a letter to *The Journal* condemning the actions of the Betting Levy Board and the Stewards of the National Hunt Committee when they announced that they would pull finances and stop allocating fixtures to the over 200-year-old Rothbury horse races in July 1964.

The annual one-day event generally and traditionally took place around the second week of April and had so done for as long as people could remember. But when the meetings of 1962 and 1963 were abandoned due to heavy rain and the Coquet bursting its banks and flooding the course, which is now the Golf course, the future of the meeting had been put in serious doubt.

The Duke, who owned the land on which the course was situated, led the two-year fight and campaign to try and save horse racing in Rothbury. The Sport of Kings certainly attracted the tweed-set and Barbour jackets of Northumbrian gentry and farming fraternity and they were bitterly disappointed at the shock decision.

It was the Horserace Betting Levy Board that first plunged the dagger into Rothbury, deciding that the meeting did not reach a high enough standard to warrant further financial support. The Levy Board was a statutory body responsible to the Home Secretary and Government. That then put the National Hunt Committee, three stewards elected from the committee itself, in a difficult position as they could not benefit from any betting revenue raised by the board, but by holding a meeting were contributing to that revenue. So the Hunt Committee withdrew their support for the country meeting, run over what was essentially three fields with a small red brick grandstand, a few sheds and white railings down near the Coquet that lay idle for 364 days a year.

The Duke was incandescent and accused the Rothbury Races of being killed to 'feed the greedy' as he laid into both the Betting Levy Board and the Stewards of the National Hunt Committee. The Levy Board grant to Rothbury was £1,000 and that wasn't really the problem – it was the fact that the Hunt Committee had flatly refused the course any one day fixtures that killed it.

"This has been decided by a body of men who live hundreds of miles away, who know nothing of the recreational requirements of the county, who consult no-one but their officials and who cannot be bothered to attend a meeting or even look at the course. What a farce," fumed the Duke after the Home Secretary announced that no fixtures would be given to Rothbury after 1966.

"The little man as usual can go to the wall, but let us remember that he takes with him all that is best in British life and character. The announcement will cause consternation to many thousands of sporting men and women in the North along both sides of the Border. These people are entitled to know the manner in which the two authorities concerned. i.e. the Betting Levy Board and the Stewards of the National Hunt Committee, have behaved. They are entitled to know of the evasive un-cooperative treatment accorded by them to the committee responsible for the running of Rothbury Races too," fumed the then Duke, Hugh Algernon Percy, who did not attach any blame to the Home Secretary, who he said had acted 'with great courtesy.'

Despite meetings that the Duke and Major Carr-Ellison had with top officials from both bodies, the Duke was convinced that the stewards were determined to finish Rothbury 'because the next communication I received from the Home Secretary…after considering the cost of maintenance of the course and making all of the necessary security arrangements, they remained firmly of the opinion that this small course should be closed down.' He accused the Levy Board of 'from their London offices, destroying a day's sport in Northumberland which has been enjoyed for more than 100 years by thousands – not only of farmers, shepherds and countrymen, but miners from the Northumbrian coalfield and of sportsmen of every description who still think of racing as a sport, and not solely as an industry.'

A last-ditch bid to save Rothbury Races had been launched at the Hedgley Hall, Powburn, home of the vice-chairman of the racecourse committee, Major Carr-Ellison earlier that month. A unanimous decision was made to ask the National Hunt Committee to reverse their decision and chairman Captain L. Scott Briggs was to write to them.

"There is no reason why we cannot run the races without Levy board support if we can get fixtures," said Major Carr-Ellison. "There is plenty of local support, financial and otherwise. But without the fixture there is no hope at all of racing continuing at Rothbury." As well as Carr-Ellison and Scott Briggs, the meeting was attended by Viscount Lambton, Majors Browne and Sample, J. Marshall and J.C. Straker.

The Rothbury Races had been abandoned in 1962 due to a waterlogged course and torrential rain. The course was waterlogged and the meeting called off at the last minute again in 1963 when it was flooded by the Coquet. The course officials had been confident that they would get it on in the run up and Captain Scott Briggs, chairman of Rothbury Race Committee, told the press that: "We have a very good entry indeed and a record attendance. Last year the races were cancelled at the last minute because of torrential rains overnight but the floods have done no harm this year. The course is in excellent condition at the moment."

Scott Briggs had ridden the winner of the Rothbury Cup in 1920, the first year that the trophy had been put up. The tradesmen of Rothbury were canvassed for subscriptions to pay for the purse money in those days, but the practise had stopped and Scott Briggs continued: "It has been tough financially to keep the meeting up all these years but it is like no other meeting—it one of the great sporting events of the North."

The course had a reputation for its beauty but also its toughness for horses and riders – the famous jockey Gerry Scott said Rothbury was his least favourite racecourse because of the downhill section with a sharp left turn into the straight which ran alongside the river - and the Rothbury meeting was believed to be one of the oldest meetings in the racing calendar in England, so when the races were again washed out, there was understandable disappointment.

The going was again wet but the course had dried out enough in places to get the racing on in 1964, but there was a mood of bitterness in Rothbury when they were informed that the meeting was all but finished. Newcastle House landlord Dick Blain said: "Everything is going. We lost our railway, and now we've lost the racecourse."

The local secretary of the racecourse committee, Jack Soulsby, told the press that: "We could make a show of it even without the levy board's money. The owners have been good with their entries. They have not worried about the prize-money for this one day of the year. They have entered for the fun of it – and it is always a successful day's racing."

The 'unjust and uncalled for action' had the race course officials and the people of Rothbury up in arms. Captain Scott Briggs said: "The Government have agreed to back up the Levy Board and the National Hunt Committee and do away with racing at Rothbury, in the face of a petition given to the Home Secretary only this week by Viscount Lambton. This has been a bitter blow, felt throughout Northumberland and the Borders." What made it even harder to stomach was that reprieves were given to the courses at Sedgefield, Stockton, Edinburgh, Folkestone, Pontefract and West Norfolk, which had also been recommended for closing by the Betting Levy Board. 1965 saw the last race at Rothbury, and a crowd of 4,000 who turned out despite rain and a bitterly cold wind watched the final Rothbury Cup fittingly won by 'a comical horse with a mind of his own,' the chestnut gelding Mar Letch.

It was all over by the January of 1966 when the fight to continue racing at Rothbury was lost. Major R. H. Carr-Ellison, the chairman of the Rothbury Steeplechase Committee, told the media that 'the standards and conditions insisted upon by the National Hunt Committee and the Horse Race Betting Levy Board had made it impossible for them to carry on.' The conditions had included a stipulation that Rothbury should have four days racing a year instead of one, while the proximity of the river Coquet was cited as one of the hazards. The main event had been the hunter steeplechase The Rothbury Cup, which included a trophy presented by the residents of Rothbury and district.

Horse racing had occurred in Rothbury from at least 1739, when races were run from the market cross following a show of cattle in the village. In 1761 the Newcastle Courant was reporting that the Rothbury Races would be held in the middle of April as usual so the origins of organised racing on the Haugh certainly predated then.

However, it was claimed that Walter Selby of Biddlestone had started horse racing at Alwinton before the meetings had come down the valley to Rothbury, and a Walter Selby (most probably his son) was certainly one of the course stewards, along with Lord Binnin and Ralph Dodds, at Rothbury by 1861. At the annual hirings and races at Alwinton in 1899 it was said that the games (mostly Cumberland & Westmorland wresting, quoiting, hop-skip-and jump and a running race) were still called the races long after the horses 'had been held there for generations but had been removed to Rothbury and carried on there on a more extended scale.'

The Alwinton steeple chase of 1847 started at Clennell Haugh and crossed the Alwin, ran along Alwinton North Field to a heavy fence at Keb House across the Holstein Burn, west of Barron Mill, along the Barron Haugh and into the winning Chair at Alwinton Haugh, so that must have been the route the course took, but whether they had started earlier than the Rothbury steeplechase is dubious as records for the Upper Coquetdale races only seem to begin around the mid-1840s. There were other races around Northumberland and that at Hexham – 'the heart of Northumberland' – had hit a lull around that time but had been revived, and those at Crook and Wark were similar affairs to Rothbury.

The annual steeplechase meeting at Alwinton in 1853 had only three starters on the three and a half mile course with 13 leaps, one over a brook said to be 15 yards wide. A description of the Rothbury course that year said that it started from the Haugh, skirting the river for around half a mile westerly towards the steward's stand (a substantial wooden erection), round it to run south-west 'along the banks of the Carter, towards the Simonside hills' then along a brow of a hill directly to the east before sweeping to the north to join the part at which the race had commenced. It contained 20 leaps, all but two being artificial, and a water leap of 14 feet faced with a brushed hurdle that stood 4 feet tall. The stewards of the Rothbury course at that time were John Aynsley, Charles Rae, and Thomas Storey. John Gray of Newcastle was the judge and Robert Nevins was clerk of the course. A horse called Glorious Jack was leading in the Coquet Steeple Chase when he jumped a drop fence and tumbled into a double summersault. His rider, Mr. Harper, was thrown but was unhurt and ran to get back on the horse and continued. There was also a race for the Rothbury Plate, Scramble Stakes with five runners and a hound trail with seven entries.

A newspaper reported in 1869 stated that the Rothbury Steeplechases 'were a development of the steeplechases which, originated many years ago by the late Mr. Selby, of Biddlestone, were at first held at Alwinton, a hamlet ten miles further up the Coquet than their present site. It was in the spring of 1853 that, under the secretaryship of Mr James Ronaldson, the meeting was first fixed for Rothbury, and rendered more easily accessible to the urban populations of the county.' So the racing that had preceded that years' meeting at Rothbury must have been on the flat.

The fine weather drew a large attendance at Rothbury Races in 1861 where the Northumberland Steeplechase Handicap was won by Mr. MacAdam's Mauchline. The Ladies Plate, a flat race, was won by Mr. Stewart's Stocton and the Coquetdale Hunt Cup was lifted by Mr. Selby as his horse Prairie Bird took the honours on the course of about 3 miles. Richard Johnson, of York, was the handicapper.

By 1862 the race-day at Rothbury was a huge event in the social calendar and pulled in crowds of many thousands for what was known then as a 'Lady's Day' as it featured the Ladies Plate on the card, and the slopes of Beggars Rigg (named after the Beggartick plants that grew there) were packed with well-dressed ladies enjoy picnics and unparalleled free views over the river and course.

The busy throng also saw episodes of drunkenness and petty thieving as cases often featured at the local petty sessions after a race day, and the Alnwick Blacksmith George Young fell in the Coquet and drowned that year. But it was generally an exciting and fun event with the pubs being packed out and the whisky flowing; in 1862 it was reputed to have been busier than ever with people flocking in from Newcastle, Alnwick, Morpeth and throughout the North in 'all description of vehicles.' There were amusement stalls down the main street of Rothbury on race day until around 1954 as people made their way down to the picturesque course beneath the Simonside hills.

When the saddling bell was rung, the jockeys took their places on the weigh-scales, watched over that year by a 'worthy well-known of the Northern turf' Mr. Benson of Newcastle. As the horses were mounted by the jockeys a low murmur of chatter and anticipation came from the packed Grand Stand, where they made their preliminary canters, coats glistening in the afternoon sun. Flighty, muscled horses whinnying and snorting, pulling on the reigns as they trotted to the starting line while gamblers shouted the odds and cash was passed over in the ring. Old 'Peggy Taft' was racing again that year, and she had long been a favourite of the Coquetdale betting fraternity. She was going off at 3 to 1 and had earned many a 'small fortune and herself an honoured name.' The stewards were Hunter Allgood, Matthew Culley and Anthony Nichol, while the handicapper was R. Johnson and the Secretary and Clerk of the Course was Emphraim Temple. As the hooves thundered across the grass tearing up turf there were wild cries of encouragement, the throng on Beggars Rigg rising to get a better view as the distant horses came up and around the track. The buzz of picking a winner or the tearing up of bet slips as their nag failed to place. 'Montague' won the Northumberland Steeplechase Handicap that year while 'Moderate' took the Ladies Plate. 'Lady Albert' was the winner in the Coquetdale Cup.

The horses being led into the trucks after and people filing away over the bridge and up the hill at the end, the chaos of cars in the village with litter strewn on the grass and bottles dropping out of overflowing bins. Race day was over for another year.

By 1866 there were 15 runners in The Northumberland Hunt Cup and 18 in the Coquetdale Hunt Cup while there was also a pony flat race and a pony steeplechase. The stewards that year were the High Sheriff of Northumberland, Lord Binning, Henry Parker and William Forster, junior.

The races had been run as open handicaps with such notable winners in the past as Ingomar, Prodigal, Star of the West, and Little Jessie, but by the late 1860s at the suggestion of Mr. Selby and others were changed into the 'Hunter's stakes' with stringent conditions. In 1868 the former champion Prodigal dropped dead while leaping the fence at Carterside and was buried right there in on the course. The horses belonging to a family of Forsters won every race at the meeting in 1866. Rothbury had a variety of fences and obstacles making it an interesting course to ride and it is reputed in later days that trainers used to send their horses to Rothbury to see what chances they stood in the Grand National.

In 1871 an objection to Monarch for winning the Northumberland Hunt Cup at Rothbury was over-ruled and there must have been no meeting in 1873 as the following year it was being reported by the Newcastle Courant that the popular meeting had every chance of being revived and 'probably on a larger scale than before.' The Rothbury Race committee met in the Blue Bell Inn in 1875 with Mr. T.G. Donkin of Summerville presiding in the chair. They were congratulated on their succeses and hoped to 'have a still more successful meeting than hitherto held' the following April as 'the amount of added money was to be considerably increased and there was to be a Hunters' Race, open to the United Kingdom.'

The members of the County of Northumberland (Rothbury) Steeplechase meeting elected to the management in 1891 were the chairman Mr. Selby (Biddlestone), Mr. Forster (Middlestone), Mr. Hawthorn (Wreighburn), Mr. Bulmer, Major Browne, Mr. J. W. B. Riddell, Captain Browne, Mr. Tate, Mr. Pawson, Mr. H. Davison, Mr. Alex. Browne, Mr. Bryan Proctor, Leiut. Col. Marshall, Mr. Browell (Snitter), and Mr. John Gallon, the secretary. Mr. Edward Cummings, Mr. Forster of Burradon, Mr. E. Donkin, jun., and Mr. Hedley Davison of Scrainwood were also members present at the meeting

Outside the regulations of the official April meeting, a number of private races were also run for money in the area. A private race on the Rothbury Haugh course, given for free by the Thompsons who farmed Newtown, for

£20, was run between Mr. Wood of the Blue Bell's 'Pickles' and a horse called 'Silvertail' belonging to a Mr. Thompson of Alnwick in 1885. William Crisp was riding Pickles and won easily. George Turnbull of Great Tosson was the judge in front of a sizable crowd. Mr. Turnbull was the owner of a horse called 'Primrose' that had beaten 'Flora Yarra' for a bumper £80 also on the course.

The racing was so popular that almost 500 people turned up to another private horse race for £20 between a horse belonging to Mr. Storer of Healey and Robert Carr's 'Simonside Lass' on Thompson's farm on the Brinkburn estate in the summer of 1903. The race was held over a mile and won by Simonside Lass, who was ridden by H. Taylor of Windy Edge. Mr. Straughan of Healey rode Storey's horse in what was described as an 'exciting contest.' The following year the Rothbury Urban District Council had to issue a notice around the Rothbury Races that gave notice to travelling showmen and others that caravans or other vehicles could not be used for sleeping accommodation on the village green. However, standage for caravans was available on the Recreation ground. Although there was no horse racing at Rothbury during the War Years, the final meet before WWI on a Wednesday in April 1914 proved a tremendous success with the weather being fine and the racing good. The distinctive light blue jacket of the owner and jockey Adam Scott of Whittingham, which had 'so often been shouted home in the north,' was a popular winner in four of the Rothbury races that day, riding three of them himself. Frank Crisp won the Farmer's Race on Peacock II which was another crowd-pleasing success.

In 1925 the Scottish jockey Mr. F. Elliot of Middlestotts, Duns, riding 'Castle Rock' won the Rothbury Cup. There was some controversy the following year when Brig-General Cheap's horse 'Longlands' won the Rothbury Cup but was disqualified for missing the water jump and the race was awarded to 'Castle Rock' and Elliot for a second year running. The Fife Countess of Lindsay's horse 'Pickwell' won at Rothbury in 1927, with 'excitement running high in the Kilconquhar and district over the event.'

By 1931 the steeple chase meeting being held at Rothbury, under the auspices of the County of Northumberland Hunt, was being ranked as the most successful re-union amongst members of the various Hunts in the Border country in the post- First World War years. Playhouse won the Simonside Hurdle Race, while Stripanatit romped home in the Cragside Hurdle Handicap. The Ladies' Cup, which was presented by Lady Lindsay, was won- by Col. R. Milvain's Silver Lad, and Lord Haddington gained popular victory on Merriment IV in the Rothbury Cup Steeple Chase. Free Forester won the Coquetdale Steeple Chase by a length and a half from Ayot. Grantshouse, being ridden by R. Tweedie, lifted the Rothbury Cup in 1934 with Clanchy taking the honours in the Ladies' Cup race.

Rothbury was allocated a National Hunt Plate (steeplechase) of 100 sovs. by the stewards of the National Hunt Committee in 1936. It was reckoned that the event would prove a popular feature at forthcoming Coquetdale meetings, and the local committee of the Rothbury Races held a meeting at the Newcastle House where they stated that the residents of Rothbury would give a cup valued at £40 and a purse of £60 for a 2 ½ mile maiden steeplechase. The Second World War again put a stop to the sport but when racing returned to Rothbury it was as popular as ever, and by the 1950s was booming. The 1954 meeting attracted one of the biggest crowds for many years as the fine weather pulled them in, as well as an increased entry of horses with up to 180 attending, the secretary of the race committee, Jack Soulsby, told the press. The course was said to be in excellent condition and a new grandstand had been erected to go alongside the new one erected the year before, giving a grandstand capacity of 1,000. Some of the jumps had also been rebuilt and trainer J.S. Wright of Grantshouse landed a double with the 6/4 joint favourite Laidsford in the Simonside Cup and the 4/5 favourite Persian Hunt in the Coquet Novices' Steeplechase.

Hispaniola fell and broke its neck in the Carside Novices' Hurdle, which was won by Canny Lad, while the 11/2 Curransport won the Ladies' Cup race and the Rothbury Cup was taken by Yifford who beat the hotly fancied favourite ridden by R. Brewis.

Two years later a great local favourite won the Rothbury Cup. The striking big grey horse is still talked about in revered tones; just mention the Callant and you'll put a smile on the face of an older Rothbury resident. The Callant's great duels with its rival De Combat, known as the best hunters in the North, got everyone up cheering as they galloped around the three-mile steeplechase course. The Callant jumped perfectly to take the honours by half-a-length in a thrilling finish with the jockey R. Scott Aiton, of Legerwood, riding him to victory. The cheers could be heard echoing right down the valley.

 I still enjoy watching the horses being shown around the parade ring as the PA announcer's voice in blow away on the wind and girls pull at their hats to prevent them tumbling across the track. I like to see the bookies in their stalls taking bets and the busy throng at the bar and making their way up onto the terraces, the smell of boiling onions in the air. It would have nice to have seen it at Rothbury. That's why I'm gutted when I hear that Thomas Rogerson has been manning the Tote and I've missed him, or I feel that happy recognition when I spot Frankie Walton studying the form in a programme in the stand on the bitterly cold hill at the Carlisle race track now. Not just because they're a great fellas and I'm pleased to see them, but because they connect me to home

BILBAO, the winner, well over and in the lead at the water jump in the last race at Rothbury on Wednesday.

FOR A PURSE OF GOLD: THE ROTHBURY RACES

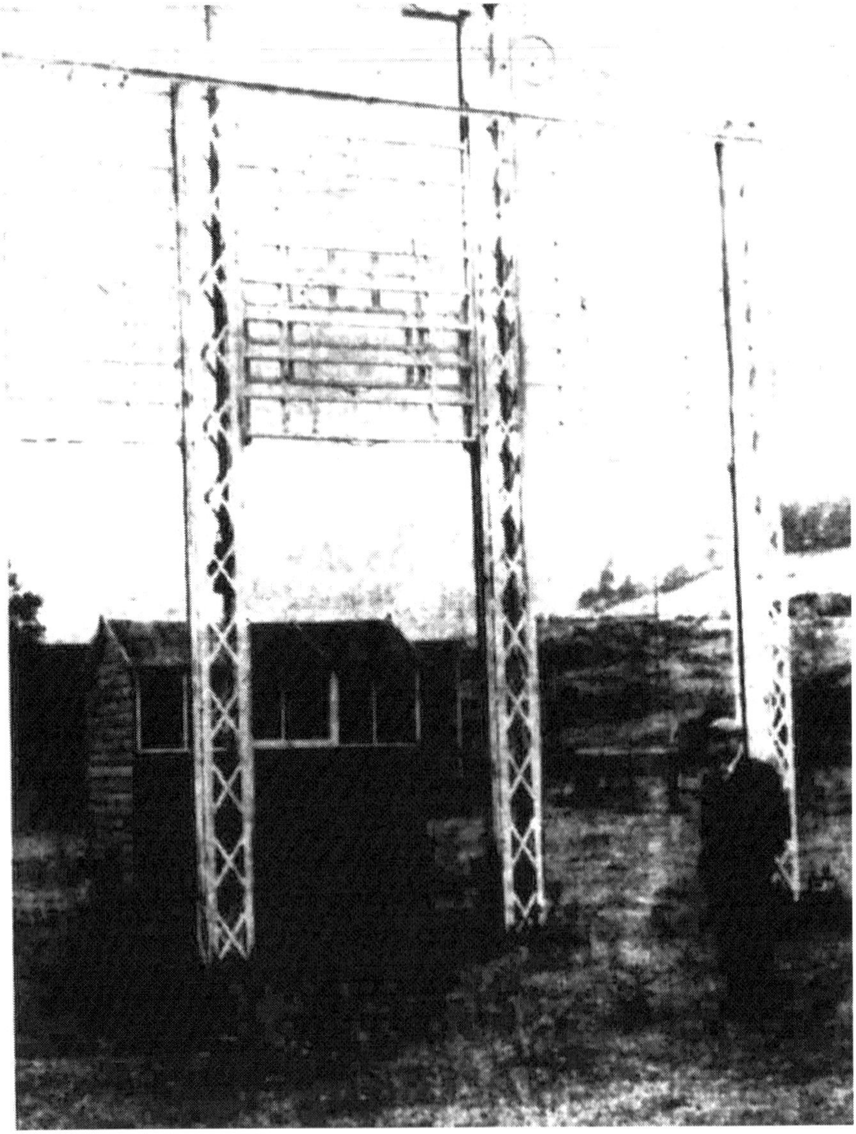

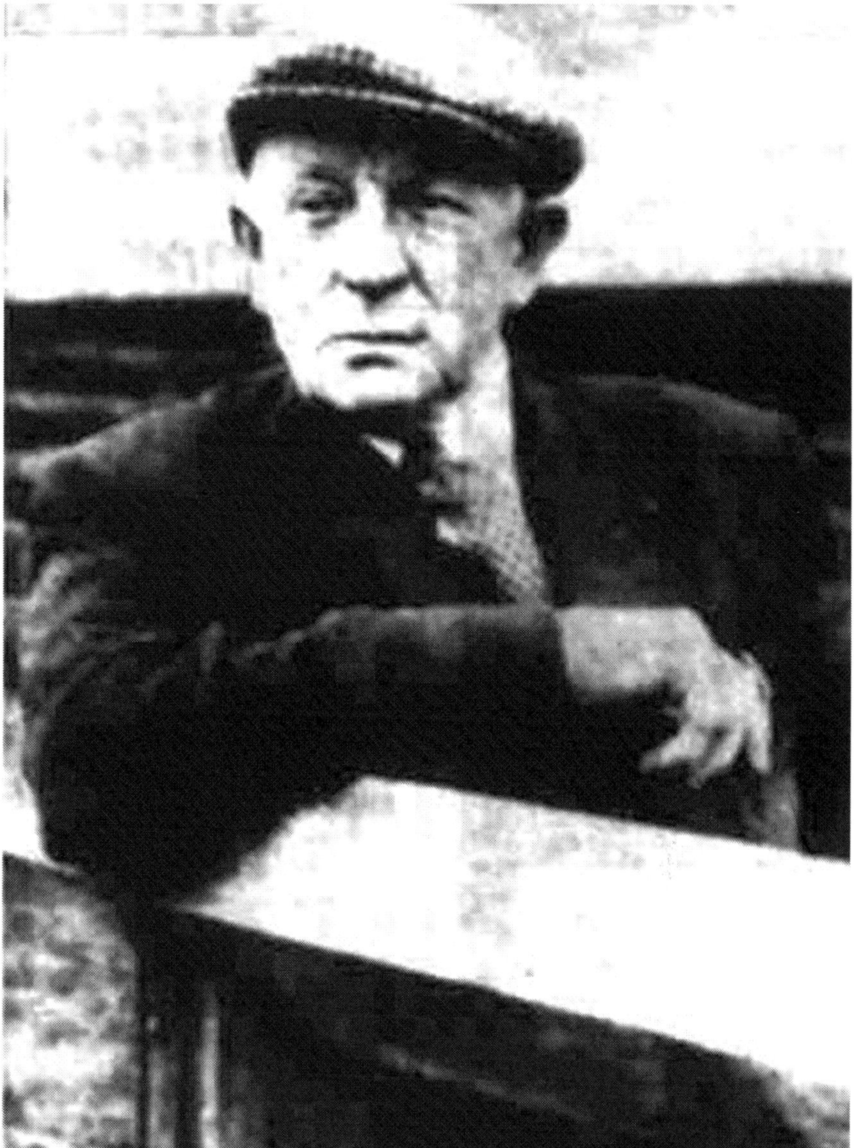

About the Author

Jon Tait is the author of the bestselling walks book 'Northumberland: 40 coast and country walks' from Pocket Mountains. He has also written and published a number of local history books including *Dick the Devil's Bairns: Breaking the Border Mafia*, *Hillmen*: A History of Rothbury FC, *Shielfield is our Wembley*: Celebrating 120 years of the North Northumberland Football League and *Turn up the Bass*, the story of Techno music in the North East during the 1990s. He currently lives in Cumbria with his wife and son and works as a clerk for a trade union.

Also by Jon Tait

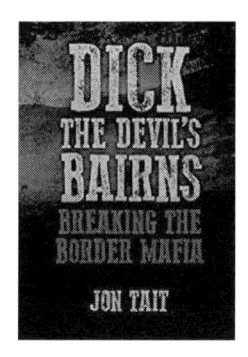

Dick the Devil's Bairns

The English and Scottish authorities took a huge step towards brokering some sort of peace in the area in 1597 when, following a Treaty signed at Carlisle, 54 men, representing the wildest reiver clans, were demanded as 'pledges,' or hostages.

The plan was for them to be locked up as a means to prevent - or at least try and dissuade - their clans and families from committing further violent crime.

Dick the Devil's Bairns is their story; the worst of the worst. The book follows the fate of those selected by the respective nations as doing the most damage by raiding, while examining the historic criminal activities carried out by those families, and others, in earning their outlaw reputations and status.

The story also explores the criminal gang's roles within the context of the wider Reiver society and the part played by their 'Godfathers' in creating the first Mafia-style organisations - and their eventual downfall. Dick the Devil's Bairns is historic true crime at its rawest.

Printed in Great Britain
by Amazon